WITHOUT MARX
OR JESUS

Other books in English by Jean-François Revel

FRENCH

AS FOR ITALY

WITHOUT MARX OR JESUS

The New American Revolution Has Begun

by JEAN-FRANÇOIS REVEL

With an Afterword by Mary McCarthy

Translated by J. F. Bernard

Doubleday & Company, Inc., Garden City, New York

NI MARX, NI JÉSUS by Jean-François Revel
© Editions Robert Laffont, S.A. 1970

Library of Congress Catalog Card Number 72–157576
All Rights Reserved
Printed in the United States of America

Translation Copyright © 1971
by Doubleday & Company, Inc.
Afterword Copyright © 1971 by
Mary McCarthy

To "Tito" Cohen, Moroccan Jew,
Corneille expert, American citizen

CONTENTS

xii   *Contents*

WITHOUT MARX
OR JESUS

Chapter 1

THE NEW AMERICAN REVOLUTION

THE REVOLUTION of the twentieth century will take place in the United States. It is only there that it can happen. And it has already begun. Whether or not that revolution spreads to the rest of the world depends on whether or not it succeeds first in America.

I am not unaware of the shock and incredulity such statements may cause at every level of the European Left and among the nations of the Third World. I know it is difficult to believe that America—the fatherland of imperialism, the power responsible for the war in Vietnam, the nation of Joe McCarthy's witch hunts, the exploiter of the world's natural resources—is, or could become, the cradle of revolution. We are accustomed to thinking of the United States as the logical target of revolution, and of computing revolutionary progress by the rate of American withdrawal. Now, we are being asked to admit that

our revolutionary slide-rule was inaccurate, and to face
the future without that comfortable tool.

Since the beginning of the cold war, leftists and revolutionaries have enjoyed a simple political image of the
world. One placed one's hope in China. Or in Yugoslavia.
Or in Cuba. Or in an explosion in western Europe, such as
the one that occurred in France in May 1968. Or in the
guerrillas of Latin America. Or in a vast uprising of underdeveloped peoples who, as the first order of business,
would slaughter those who were allowing them to die of
hunger in the midst of plenty. One considered every possibility—except the possibility that revolution might break
out in that shameful land, that nest of anti-revolution,
America.

According to this simplistic view, the world is divided
into two camps. On the one hand, there is America, the
citadel of reaction; and, on the other, there is the rest of
the world—the revolutionary camp, composed of everyone
who resists America. The states that are more or less
accomplices of America are sometimes included in the
latter group, for their complicity—as manifested, for instance, in the concept of "atlanticism"—varies in degree.
Sometimes, it is total, as in the case of West Germany
and Great Britain; and sometimes, as with France and
Italy, it is partial. If a country's degree of anti-Americanism or pro-Americanism is the sole indication of whether
it is revolutionary ("Left") or counterrevolutionary
("Right"), it follows that France and Italy are further
to the Left than Britain and Germany. And, at this
point, all other considerations regarding a particular
country's political situation are either disregarded, or rele-
gated to a place of secondary importance. It is a country's
relationship to America that matters.

The basis for such a division of the world, obviously,

is the opposition between capitalism and socialism. Revolution signifies socialistic progress; therefore, it is logical to conclude that the most powerful of the capitalistic countries will be the last to succumb to the onslaught of socialism—that is, to revolution. And, since imperialism is a necessary concomitant of capitalism, it is clear that the United States will move toward socialism only if it is forced to do so from without. Meanwhile, the other nations of the world can console themselves with the thought that, while they may be less accomplished economically and technologically than the Americans—because they are less rapacious—they have at least a monopoly on revolution. Thus, the spirit of revolution and anti-Americanism become synonymous; and American influence is regarded as the invariable consequence of imperialism. This is a belief which serves admirably as a vantage point from which to view, and to judge, any situation anywhere in the world. But for the sake of consistency, this outlook requires the certitude that no revolution can take place within the United States. Or, more accurately, one must be certain that, in America, the only change possible is for reactionary sentiment to increase. The logical conclusion to be drawn from all this is that America is a police state. The liberties enjoyed by the people are allowed because they do not threaten the *status quo*, and because public opinion can always be manipulated by the mass media—a process which is facilitated by the notorious conformity of Americans.

My purpose here in not merely to review this thesis. I have stated it in order to ask how it can possibly continue to be accepted as the basis for political judgments. It is difficult to understand how its conclusions can be regarded as true, when the premises have so often been refuted and criticized, or at least called into doubt, by the very people who accept these conclusions. How is it possible for a theory, which is false in its component parts, to be true as a whole?

The fact is that the Soviet Union, in the last twenty years, has stopped functioning as the heart of the world-wide revolutionary movement. It has stopped putting forward revolutionary propositions, even though this about-face has necessitated the most elaborate interpretative gymnastics in order to explain the Kremlin's continuing military and police regime. Similarly, Mao's China serves as a revolutionary model only for a few occidental leftists, and then only for rhetorical purposes; for there seems to be little relationship between the maxims of the "Little Red Book" and actual conditions in the industrial nations, or even in the underdeveloped countries of Latin America, Africa, and the Middle East. Red China, in other words, while it may be a source of revolutionary impulse, is confined to the realm of emotional abstraction. Its message has neither theoretical content nor practical application.

So far as the self-styled socialist nations of the Third World are concerned—Algeria, Egypt, Nigeria, Congo-Brazzaville, Syria, and so forth—they have only the name, and not the reality, of socialism. Even if we take into account the magnitude of the problems these countries face, we must often conclude that their governments are oligarchies—that is, dictatorships, based upon the necessity of concealing failures, and obtaining the acquiescence of their peoples in an ever-declining standard of living, rather than upon the imperatives of "the construction of socialism" and of "the fight against imperialism." Are these nations really taking their first steps on the socialist road? Or are they merely being exploited by latter-day feudal lords, and manipulated by the Soviet Union and China in the name of socialism? Whatever the answer, one thing is certain: such questions must be asked. And the fact that they must be asked prevents us from stating categorically that the young "socialist" nations of the Third World, and the nations who are in the process of imitating them, are the true children of revolution.

The problem here is that the concept of socialism is terribly confused. It has been subjected to doctrinal or polemical interpretations, and it has been pawed over by politicians and theoreticians who, although they call themselves socialists, do not agree about the true content of socialism. The resulting confusion is so bad that it is difficult to choose, if one must, between the alternatives of capitalism and socialism. It is not as though each of those terms corresponded to a well-defined reality. On the contrary, the intricate and furious ideological storm raging with respect to "Swedish socialism," as well as other conflicts of this kind, serve to illustrate the complexity of an argument which is sometimes almost academic in nature. One gathers that Swedish socialism has not the moral right to make Swedes more prosperous, or better informed, or more "equal" than Czechs or Poles, because it is not "pure socialism" but merely capitalism under a socialist government. Such arguments demonstrate that it is impossible, in any case, to accept at face value the opposition established between capitalism and socialism—according to which one is lily-white and the other coal-black —and to declare that revolutionary activity consists simply in supporting, by any means available, the socialist camp against the capitalist.

A rigid analysis of what is happening within the two groups reveals quite clearly, not the existence of the compact and homogeneous "substantial forms" manufactured by a propaganda machine and perpetuated by laziness, but a multiplicity of forces. Moreover, these forces are often in conflict within a single sociopolitical system, and simultaneously in harmony with certain forces of the opposing system. Thus, for some years now we have described as "revolutionary" the periodic uprisings of the populations of the "peoples' democracies" against their Moscow-directed governments. And we say that the Russians use "fascist" methods to suppress those uprisings. One Soviet observer, Andrei Amalrik, has even devoted a book to the proposition that there will be a "revolution" in the U.S.S.R. in the foreseeable future.*

On the other hand, one of the most striking features of the past decade is that the only new revolutionary stirrings in the world have had their origin in the United States. From America has come the sole revolutionary invention which can be described as truly original. I mean the complex of new oppositional phenomena designated by the term "dissent." Similar movements have agitated western—and eastern—Europe, but these are imitations of the American prototype, or extensions of it, and subsequent to it. In 1964–65, at Berkeley, occurred the first of those student revolts which are a wholly new phenomenon, and which spread rapidly over the country, and then to Europe and the Third World. Even before that, in 1960, there were student strikes, and the first sit-ins in Southern universities protesting racial discrimination and supporting the nonviolent action of Martin Luther King. Dissent, whether it spread by contagion or sprang up simultaneously in different parts of the world, was nonetheless conceived and perfected in the United States. This unprecedented exercise in revolutionary activity, this ubiquitous radicalism, this all-encompassing sedition, has left governments virtually helpless, for the usual methods of repression

* *Will the Soviet Union Survive Until 1984?* Harper & Row, New York, 1970.

are practically useless against it. And European dissenters, who represent the only force which has been able to rouse both the Left and the Right, the East and the West, from their academic torpor, are the disciples of the American movement.

Student dissenters are not, of course, the only group who refuse to compromise in their attitude of rejection and of attack. There are also the black revolutionary movement, and the women's liberation movement, among others. In addition, the traditional forms of social warfare are being used with increasing vigor. During the winter of 1969–70, some 133,000 employees of General Electric went out on strike, and stayed out for more than three months. The result was a new forty-month contract granting a wage-increase of 8 percent per year. In March 1970, a general strike of postal workers broke out simultaneously over the whole United States. The General Electric strike was considered one of the most significant social movements in America since 1930. And the postal strike was without precedent in American history; never before had the postal system, as a whole, been put completely out of commission.

It is difficult to say whether or not dissent will succeed or fail; whether it will persevere until it results in the building of a new society, or serve only to facilitate the triumph of an authoritarian reaction. It is possible, too, that the movement of dissent will become bogged down in intellectual mediocrity and, instead of leading to a real transformation of society, will wander off onto the path of persecutor-persecuted narcissism, and degenerate into a marginal movement so ineffectual that it will come to be tolerated in the industrial states of the world. In other words, it can become either the fulcrum of a new social contract—or a refuge for social deviants. Which of

8   *Without Marx or Jesus*

these things it becomes will determine, to a large extent, the answer to the question of whether the second American Revolution will be the beginning of a second world revolution. It will also decide whether or not, even in America, dissent will attain its positive goal.

At its present stage, we can say that dissent has created one of those states of tension without which no revolution is possible. Eldridge Cleaver—now living in Algeria—has put it succinctly: "It is no exaggeration to say that the destiny of the whole human race depends on the way in which America solves the problems that confront her today. The number-one question of the contemporary world is: will she go to the Right, or to the Left."*

* Quoted by F. and C. Masnata, *Pouvoir, société et politique aux États-Unis*. Paris, 1970 (Payot), p. 5.

Chapter 2

REVOLUTION: The Five Conditions

IT IS HIGHLY significant that the movement of dissent—the only original contribution to the technique of sedition to appear in the past decade, and perhaps since World War II—has originated in the United States. Still, taken by itself, that fact is not enough to warrant our speaking of a New American Revolution, let alone of a subsequent world revolution. But there are other signs. In the midst of dissent in America, certain of the fundamental conditions for revolution have either been fulfilled, or are well on the way to being fulfilled.

Revolution, anthropologically speaking, is a "total social fact." That is, it affects every facet of a culture. By definition, therefore, a "revolutionary situation" exists when, in every cultural area of a society, old values are in the process of being rejected, and new values have been prepared, or are being prepared, to replace them. In order for this revolutionary process to exist in reality, five basic conditions must be met; that is, critical work must have been done in five distinct, but complementary and convergent areas. And I should emphasize that by "critical work" I am referring both to theory and to practice; for criticism is, under one aspect, intellectual, and serves to refute and to reduce to absurdity the established order, to denounce its ineffectiveness, and to propose reforms. Under another aspect, it is active; that is, it serves the purpose of opposing the *status quo* and of formulating methods of resistance and of attack. The list of such methods employed throughout human history is a long one, ranging from the utilization of the existing judicial system (the abolition of an assembly, the forcible convocation of the States-General, as in 1788, in the beginnings of the French Revolution), to armed insurrection. Between those two extremes lie a thousand other procedures: strikes, boycotts, the gathering of petitions and the organization of banquets,* refusal to pay taxes, parades, days of protest, barricading of streets, kidnapping of political figures, hijacking of airplanes, and so forth. Such tactics, however, have no revolutionary efficacy except as part of an over-all strategy. The taking of the Bastille on July 14, 1789, would not have signaled the beginning of a revolution in, say, Sofia. For these means to be effective, it is not enough that the established order be susceptible to sub-

---

* The reference is to the prelude to the July Revolution in France (1848), by which the Orléans, in the person of Louis-Philippe, were finally deposed from the French throne. A campaign of petitions, political banquets, and other manifestations was organized in order to pressure the King to allow liberal reforms. The revolution which followed was almost accidental: during a parade, a shot was fired, and the royal troops responded by firing into the demonstrators, killing sixteen men. The latter were declared to be "martyrs of freedom," and their bodies were paraded around Paris. Immediately barricades were thrown up in the streets, and, when Louis-Philippe's troops refused to move against the populace, the King abdicated and fled to England.

version; it is necessary that a new order be ready to take its place. That is to say, the five conditions prerequisite for revolution must have been realized, and solutions must must have been sufficiently elaborated in five key areas. Those conditions and areas are as follows:

1. There must be a critique of the *injustice* existing in economic, social, and racial relationships.

2. There must be a critique of *management*, directed against the waste of material and human resources. This is related to the preceding critique, since it demonstrates that injustice results in inefficiency, and thus in counter-productivity and in the ruin of a nation's resources. It also calls into question the orientation of technological progress toward goals that are either useless or harmful to man.

3. There must be a critique of *political power*, directed against its source and principles as well as against its exercise, the conditions in which it is exercised, distributed, or monopolized, the localization of decision-making powers, the relationship between the consequences of these decisions for the people, and the difficulty (or the impossibility) for the people of participating in these decisions.

4. There must be a critique of *culture*: of morality, religion, accepted beliefs, customs, philosophy, literature, art; of the ideological attitudes which underlie these things; of the *function* of culture and of intellectuals in society; and of the distribution of that culture (education, communication, information).

5. There must be a critique of the old *civilization-as-sanction*, or a vindication of individual freedom. This critique is aimed at the relations between society and the individual. In it, the individual is considered as a sensitive and original being, rather than as a citizen; and

society is regarded as a means either of developing or distorting the proper worth of each individual. Such a critique measures, for example, the failure of a society to deal with poverty and the sterility of the human relations it establishes (brotherhood *versus* aggressiveness); with the uniformity of the human types it engenders (conformity); in general, with the restraints with which it burdens its people, and the obstacles which it places in the way of the development of individual potential and self-identity. In this context, revolution is seen as the liberation of the creative personality and the awakening of personal initiative, as opposed to the "closed horizons," the climate of frustration and despair, which prevail in repressive societies.

If we examine the period preceding the French Revolution, we find that these five conditions were all present and that, during the previous three quarters of a century, proper solutions on all points had been formulated. In the fields of constitutional studies, economics, scholarship, and education, in the relations between the state and religion, divorce, in the roles of art and the theater in society, in penal law, in the military and civil services, in the press, in trade and the organization of the universities, research had resulted in the advancement of knowledge. At times, new disciplines—such as political economy—had been created. Data had been compiled with a view toward the remolding of society and of its political direction—often down to the smallest detail. By drawing upon these sources, the Constituent Assembly was able to legislate with amazing rapidity—so that that Assembly, and the one which followed it, was able, in the space of two years, to organize a whole new state in all its administrative details, and to formulate that mass of institutions and concepts which successive French regimes, despite occasional setbacks, would continue to exploit until the end of the nineteenth century.

Revolutions, therefore, are not improvised; and they are not accomplished through doctrinal inflexibility. In the first case, a would-be revolutionary imagines that he will "play it by ear" and proceed by means of dialogue with the people. In the second, a dogmatic revolutionary is concerned only with knowing whether his revolution is like earlier revolutions, whether it is proceeding according to the rules. The true revolutionary, however, follows the path of prepared extemporization, as it were; that is, he excludes· no possible expedient, but, once a means is adopted, it is applied rigorously and with technical competence and exactitude. In this case, all that is left to collective inspiration are the basic concepts of historic evolution. So far as the means of execution are concerned, they are evaluated realistically, in the cold light of reason. If revolutions fail, it is because their general concepts are too rigid, precise, and cold, and because the application of those concepts, being ill-defined, does not succeed in changing reality. Unsuccessful revolutions, in other words, are intellectually bureaucratic, and practically amateurish.

The second "fundamental condition" of revolution is of particular importance. Every revolution must formulate economic and technological solutions—solutions more effective than those of the system which the revolution destroys. For the economists of the eighteenth century, the nobiliary system of ownership of the land was both unjust and unproductive. A revolution which is not more technically proficient and more effective than the regime which it supplants, is lost. It will either remain in, or fall rapidly into, underdevelopment; and in such circumstances, it will be unable to accomplish what it has promised. Then, it must make a choice: it must either relinquish power, or it must resolve the problem of maintaining itself in power—by means of a dictatorship.

The five prerevolutionary conditions are inseparable from each other. They are five aspects of a single reality. If even one of them fails to be realized, we may conclude that a revolutionary movement never really existed—or, at best, that the movement must either fall far short of its goals, or collapse.

Regarding the fourth and fifth points, it must be kept in mind that critiques of the moral and cultural orders are relevant only if they are, for the most part, expressed by the governing class itself. All revolutionary trends—whether they are destined to come to fruition imminently or remotely—have this in common, that a group of those who benefit from the *status quo* detach themselves from their class and betray it from within. This was true of a part of the French aristocracy in the eighteenth century; and it was true of the bourgeoisie of the nineteenth century. One must be an aristocrat to denounce the degradation implicit in life at the court of the Bourbon kings; and one had to be a bourgeois to describe accurately the moral world of the middle class. This criticism from above, which is directed against the most subtle cultural manifestations of a system, and which points out that system's shortcomings from the standpoint even of those who benefit from it, is indispensable. It was the aristocrats and the bourgeoisie of the eighteenth century, not the peasants, who were in a position to criticize the religious system; and, without that critique, the revolution would never have taken place. Only the aristocrats and the bourgeoisie, not the peasants, were aware of the need to contest the indissolubility of marriage; and yet, divorce formed a necessary part of the over-all goals of the revolution. Today, dissenters are often accused of being "middle class." And so they are. They cannot be otherwise. For their function, in contemporary revolutionary activity, is to become aware, by experience, of the internal failure of a system of life in the very *milieu* in which it is thought to be successful, and to point out that the system has failed to provide the happiness it was supposed to create.

Finally, there can be no revolution capable of being a model of world revolution except in a society where debate between opposing parties takes place at the highest level; that is, at a level which involves the greatest forces in economics, politics, science, administration, in technology and culture, in industry and communications, in morals and in literature. This debate must necessarily involve a confrontation between the most intelligent of the revolutionaries and the most intelligent of the reactionaries. Only in these circumstances will this debate become "dialectical" and engender a revolution; that is, not merely a local *coup d'état*, even a popular one, but a revolution which can serve as a new prototype of society.

My thesis is that, if a second world revolution is to take place, it can have its beginning only in the United States. And I base that thesis on the following conclusions:

(a) This revolution has not taken place in the communist countries, nor can it take place there, either in the U.S.S.R. or in China.

(b) It cannot take place in western Europe; or, at least, not unless the American Revolution takes place first—or, more accurately, continues to take place. (The same holds true for Japan, which will be discussed separately.)

(c) It cannot take place in the so-called developing countries, or in the Third World. On the contrary, the revolution must occur in the United States before it can happen elsewhere.

These three negative conclusions remain to be demonstrated. But even if they turn out to be valid, it still does not necessarily follow that the revolution of which we are speaking will take place in the United States. For that reason, we must also discuss the question of *why* a revolution, in the full meaning of that term, can take place only in America.*

* This does not mean, of course, that there must *inevitably* be a successful revolution in America. The New American Revolution, like most revolutions, may fail. A successful revolution is a great rarity in human history.

Chapter 3

AN IMPOSSIBLE REVOLUTION:

The Communist Nations

No ONE TODAY, even within the communist parties of the western world, seriously contends that the Soviet Union is a revolutionary model for other countries. Hopes for a form of "socialism with a human face," and expectations of a spontaneous liberalization of the Soviet regime, have been periodically, and invariably, disappointed. At the same time, the Soviet Union's lack of success in the economic field has made its totalitarian regime less and less acceptable. It is no longer possible to justify the suppression of liberty by the imperatives of industrial discipline—especially since it has become obvious that Soviet industry is characterized by waste and inefficiency. The China of Mao Tse-tung offers no more promise than does the U.S.S.R. China has repudiated "economism"; but, for all of that, her people have not regained their freedom. The so-called cultural revolution—which seems

to have been essentially a purge, reinforced, in some instances, by an ominous explosion of collective sadism—
has left intact, or even strengthened, China's dictatorial
political regime and her all-powerful political propaganda
machine. It is hard to see the sense in declaring economic
productivity to be of secondary importance in an underdeveloped country; and that is particularly true if, as in
the case of China, the ideal of austerity which is offered
to the people is not offset by the right to individual
development, and if it is accompanied instead by an ever
more oppressive climate of moral, intellectual, and physical
terrorism.

This refers particularly to austerity in the communist
countries, which is not the kind of austerity that one
can interpret as an investment in the future; it is not
planned, coherent, or due (as we are expected to believe)
to "primitive socialist accumulation." Rather, it is a
state of anarchic poverty, resulting from the underpro-
ductivity of a badly managed industrial machine. Thus,
we are treated today to the spectacle of the Soviets
borrowing capital from Japanese (that is, American) banks,
and asking Ford to build, at its expense, an automobile
factory in Russia. In other words, they are soliciting the
honor of being included among the victims of neocolonial-
ism.

These indications of failure are more or less accepted
as such, depending upon the bias of the individual. Even
on the European Left, which is traditionally well disposed
toward China and the U.S.S.R., it is difficult to find anyone still willing to declare that every instance of Soviet
expansion represents a step forward for world socialism,
or that the Chinese system is a freely exportable model
of "socialism with liberty." (It is true that some students
regard themselves as "Maoists" because they reject all

authority and demand complete individual freedom; but these individuals are simply badly informed on the state of present-day Chinese society.) On the whole, most militant socialists-communists and their sympathizers, or at least those who are open-minded and have access even to a minimum of information, have gradually been forced to recognize, either openly or in their own minds, that the Marxist-Leninist states represent a revolutionary failure. It is no longer possible to maintain that there can be progress in socialism without equal progress in human freedom, and particularly in freedom of expression. We have already seen where that road leads, in the case of National Socialism in Germany and Fascism in Italy. Yet, once we abandon this thesis, we must also abandon all hope in "democratic centralism"—that is, in the Soviet system and the Chinese system. We must even question whether the system of economic management practiced in Russia, China, Yugoslavia, and Cuba deserves the name of socialism—that is, whether it is possible to have a socialist economy without a political democracy. Can we say that the total or partial collectivization of the means of production is "socialist" if, at the same time, the people are not allowed to exercise individual initiative and control, or to share in decision-making and in the exercise of power? Can we say that a system is "socialist" if the great options (often a synonym for great errors) that determine the destiny of a people for generations are determined by an authoritarian minority? Can a repressive totalitarianism which generates underdevelopment be called socialism, even at a purely material level? It is high time to preach what we have learned at high cost: economic socialism cannot exist in an atmosphere of political dictatorship. Any attempt to establish one alongside the other must lead either to caricature, or to tragedy.

Yugoslavia, in which non-Stalinist Marxists have placed such great hope, has confirmed this principle by remaining both ineffectual and repressive. And Cuba, ten years after Castro's triumph, is still bogged down in the morass of authoritarian nonproductivity.* In the most conservative terms, this situation may be expressed by a formula: "Socialism has not yet been realized anywhere in the world." As a corollary, we might add: "The U.S.S.R. is, in any case, the last place where it may be realized; and it is likely that, henceforth, the same prognosis applies to China." To put it brutally: the events of October 1917 in Russia were not the beginning, and cannot become the model, of world-wide socialist revolution.

If socialism, with or without its "human face," has not been realized anywhere, then it is foolish to continue referring automatically to the "socialist camp" and the "imperialist camp," as though revolutionary action were merely a problem of mechanics or of transportation, by virtue of which a maximum number of territories or political regimes would enter into one camp to the detriment of the other. Moreover, this attitude presupposes that only capitalistic expansion is "imperialistic," and that socialistic expansion is not; that is, that only capitalistic nations are capable of seeking to increase their influence in international affairs so as to strengthen themselves as geographic realities. The truth, if we are impartial in our judgment, is that the communist nations and the capitalist nations have been endowed with the spirit of imperialism in approximately equal portions. It is hardly worth mentioning such obvious examples as the invasion of Tibet by China, or of Czechoslovakia by the U.S.S.R.; for those were old-fashioned, almost Hitlerian enterprises, unworthy of the more subtle methods of mod-

---

* See especially *Cuba est-il socialiste?* by René Dumont (Paris, 1970), and *Guerillas in Action* by K. S. Karol (New York, 1970).

ern imperialism which seek to avoid outright military conquest. More representative of imperialism at a refined level is the Soviet presence in the Arab nations of the Middle East, which utilizes the very real problems of these states to aid them in their war—or rather, to push them toward war—while satisfying Russia's own ancient expansionist ambitions in this region. Similarly, the hatred which exists between the Chinese and the Soviets is of the kind that can flourish only when two imperialistic powers have conflicting designs on the same sphere of influence—on black Africa, for example. It means nothing to say that these penetrations into other states are not manifestations of imperialism simply because they are accompanied by an ideological message. Let us recall that it was in the name of an ideology—Christianity—that Latin America was conquered in the sixteenth century, and that Christian principles were as little applied in those countries then as socialist principles are applied in Africa now. It was also in the name of an ideology, which was to remain wholly academic—that of "republicanism" and "progress"—that France built her colonial empire between 1880 and 1914. Ironically, France's ideological pretexts were not far removed from those of communism. Marx deplored the cruel methods of the European powers (particularly those of Great Britain in India) in their seizure of territory and commercial rights in Asia; but he considered that, in the final analysis, this eruption of colonialism represented a progress in civilization, for it would rouse the Asiatic peoples from their torpor and plunge them "into the mainstream of historical development."*

It is clearly a mistake to believe that only capitalism is imperialistic, or that the U.S.S.R. and China are con-

* Wolfe, B. D., *Marxism: One Hundred Years in the Life of a Doctrine.* New York, 1965, p. 36.

genitally incapable of using their systems of alliances to further their own economic, political, and military interests at the expense of weaker nations. We may conclude, then, that there has been no more a revolution in the foreign policies of the communist countries than there has been internal revolution in those same countries.

For the past fifty years, every road seems to have led to increased socialism. Every road, that is, except the socialist road. And the reason is obvious. The purpose of the second world revolution is to create real equality among men, and to give to men the political means to decide for themselves on the great matters affecting their destiny. Therefore, the concentration of all power—political, economic, military, technological, judicial, constitutional, cultural, and informational—in the hands of an oligarchy, or even, in certain cases (Stalin, Tito, Castro), of an autocracy must be the method least likely to lead to such a revolution. And, in fact, what happens under these oligarchies and autocracies is that the oligarchs and autocrats become more and more entrenched in their positions of power, and the solutions that society expects from them are more and more rarely forthcoming. For, unfortunately, the qualities necessary to acquire power (even heroically) and to exercise power (even ineffectually) are not the same as the qualities necessary to resolve the problems of modern society. The result is that, as authority increases, competence decreases. And since no amount of criticism seems able to halt either the increase of the former or the decrease of the latter, society is becoming more and more dominated and less and less governed. In such a predicament, the question of whether one social system is better or worse than another becomes a matter of purely academic interest.

Chapter 4

AN IMPOSSIBLE REVOLUTION: Western Europe

IT DOES NOT seem that western Europe is in any
position to become the center of world revolution, given
the importance and complexity of the goals to be attained, the subtlety of the means necessary, and the
extent of the resources required (resources which run the
gamut from economic prosperity to the individual cultural
level of each citizen). Europe, of course, enjoys an enviable
standard of living, and excellent prospects for continued
prosperity. But it is a prosperity contingent upon fundamental research, the key to which is found in the
United States. Except for Great Britain, no European
country is capable of sustaining a meaningful technological initiative on a world-wide basis. Western Europe,
therefore, cannot contribute to the formulation of the
basic solutions required by the second world revolution—
or, at least, not to such an extent that its contribution

will be perceived by its own people as the matrix of a future civilization. And this perception is essential. Revolution is not purely a matter of technology; but, without technology, revolution cannot put its solutions into practice.

In the last comedy which Carlo Goldoni produced in Venice before emigrating to France in 1762, the protagonist, a designer of fabrics, declares his intention of moving to the French capital because, he says, "It is there that things are happening." It was an inspiration on Goldoni's part to depict an artist, even a purely decorative one, as terrified by the thought that he was not where "things" were happening. This feeling is of the utmost importance. There are societies pervaded by the idea that "nothing can happen here" because, as soon as there is an attempt at innovation, a brake is sure to be applied automatically. And there are other societies in which that feeling is not even perceptible. Governments rarely take note of this sentiment. It is not mentioned in official addresses; it plays no part in statistical tables; it is not written into plans; and historians ignore it, because it is one of those impalpable social phenomena which smack of Sunday-supplement journalism rather than of scholarship. The casual observer, however, easily sees the difference in the behavior of individuals of different societies—just as easily as he sees that leaves look white or green according to the direction of the wind. In one instance, the individuals in a society regard themselves as being in the mainstream of upward-mobility; they are convinced that they can better themselves by bettering their circumstances. In another case, individuals regard themselves as trapped in a gigantic pot of glue, and they believe that they can better themselves only by slipping around obstacles. This attitude is at first a result of

administrative decay, economic privilege, and political dis-
honesty; and then it becomes itself a cause of those things
which caused it in the first place.

This latter feeling is by no means so predominant in
western Europe as in the countries of eastern Europe,
or in certain of the underdeveloped countries, because it
does not correspond to the reality of western Europe.
Europe has changed so much in the past twenty years,
and it is still changing so much, that this extreme form
of individual helplessness, of what-good-would-it-do-ism,
is hardly warranted. Resistance to change has diminished
considerably; but so has the confidence of Europeans in
their *ability to formulate cultural prototypes* and prototypes
of political societies. Western Europeans pride themselves on being able to follow and to adapt, more or less
painstakingly, revolutionary progress; but they do not believe that they can create it or develop it. They are
"involved"; but, whether they are partisans of capitalism
or of Marxism, their fondest hope is to be able to discover
a little personal variant in the application of a model
the basic concept of which escapes them.

Europeans, whether they be revolutionaries or conservatives, and whether they recognize it or not, no longer feel
at ease as anythng but disciples. Not long ago, an anony-
mous hand wrote a striking phrase on a wall of the
Sorbonne: "Imagination has come to power." And what
has happened since then? Nothing. There is only the
past, and nothing but the past. The past has become an
obsession. Everyone is concerned with returning to the
past and reassessing it. Everywhere we witness the automatic invocation of doctrines and events which have been
devoured, aborted, and then classified by history. Imagination, then, seems to be nothing but repetition. The more
one listens, the more one feels that it is. It seems that

one must always go back to something: to Bakunin, to Marx, to Mao, to Castro, to Guevara, to Lenin, to Trotsky, to God, to Buddha, to pre-industrial civilization. And one must always revive something: the Chinese cultural revolution, the Paris Commune of 1870, the Revolution of 1917, the student revolt of May 1968, or the spirit of de Gaulle's appeal to the French on June 18, 1940.

Roger Garaudy, a communist intellectual, was expelled from the French Communist Party because he declared that the world of labor did not have the same sociological composition that it did a century ago; and we regarded it as evidence of "progress" that Garaudy had been able to express this opinion before a communist congress before being expelled. Perhaps we forget that, in the sixteenth century, a man could express his opinion before the judges of the Inquisition before being condemned. The spirit of imitation has replaced that of revolution, not only in the French Communist Party but also in the parties of the Left. Everyone, unfortunately—the young people as much as their elders—seems to ask nothing more of revolution than that it be a pale imitation of an earlier fiasco. And, since there is a multitude of historic failures from which to choose, it should come as no surprise that there are a correspondingly large number of "revolutionary" movements.

American dissent is distinguished from European dissent by the fact that the former is involved in problems which are part of reality. Since the dissenters are certain that they will be able to solve those problems, they do not ignore them. They fight against military service in Vietnam, against racial discrimination, against the destruction of the environment, against the relations of the universities with the military-industrial complex, against governmental indifference toward the American Indian, against the lack of funds necessary to save the cities. For American youth, dissent does not mean the imaginary transference into its society of irrelevant political scenarios, such as Maoism or Castroism; or, if it does introduce such elements, it does so only in small measure, and without using them as an excuse for ignoring real situations. (Some current idols, such as Che Guevara or Castro, are much less remote from the United States, which has interests in Latin America, than they are from Europe; and it is less gratuitous for American youth to revere them than it is for European youth to do so.)

Such examples serve to emphasize that the revolutionary value of dissent is proportionate to its involvement with the concrete problems of the society in which it exists. Dissent should shed new light on such problems, and the opposition which it engenders is more fundamental than, and goes beyond, mere realistic demands. In that sense, European dissenters were correct in maintaining that their ideals went far beyond simple matters of distributive justice (especially increases in wages). But they should have specifically included those matters in their ideals; for, in making themselves appear to be bigots, rather than revolutionaries against the "consumer society," European dissenters have managed to alienate the workers—including the lower middle class, or the *petite bourgeoisie*, who also work for a living.* In America, too, the

* There exists, among European intellectuals, a certain aristocratic disdain for the lower middle class, and for the small-businessman in particular. It is the disdain of the clerk for the tradesman, and of the socialist for the small "proprietor"—even if the latter is actually nothing more than a hired manager. After the referendum of April 27, 1969, in which a large number of intellectuals' votes had contributed to the downfall of Gaullism, a certain number of leftist spokesmen expressed contempt for this victory (which had put an end to eleven years of autocracy) on the grounds that it represented "the triumph of the shopkeepers." This phrase of itself is sufficient indication of how the French Left, particularly among its intellectuals, is devoid of democratic sentiment. When a uni-

best-off of the workers, the "blue collars," feel hostility
toward the young; but this is for reasons peculiar to
America—mainly because of the fear in the workers' minds
of cooperation between the young dissenters and the blacks.
But it would never have occurred to American dissenters to tell the blacks, or the Puerto Ricans, or even the
white workers, that they—the blacks, etc.—were alienated
because they were overconsumers.

Since western Europe is in a position only to follow
the economic movement and not to initiate it, to play an
honorable role but a passive one, what of her situation
with respect to the cultural movement? Hardly better. Expenditure on education, proportionate to the gross national
product, is insufficient in every European country except
Sweden and Great Britain. Only one Frenchman in ten,
for instance, finds it possible, economically, to advance
beyond the equivalent of a grade-school education; which
is to say that, intellectually, France functions as though
it had a population of only five million people. Paradoxically, the administrators of public education in France
react very badly to any criticism of the educational system, particularly at the primary and secondary levels. Their
view seems to be that teachers should overcome material
difficulties and perform their duties despite all obstacles
of a practical nature. This theory of the spiritual value of

---

versity professor, or a Parisian journalist, makes a neighborhood grocer
the target of his attacks on the grounds that the latter is representative
of the capitalist class, he is not only being odious on the moral level; he
is also making a political blunder—a blunder which will assure that the
petite bourgeoisie will swing permanently to the Right in times of economic difficulty. It is obvious that reality is being sacrificed to ideological
considerations when, in countries in which the middle classes constitute
the largest part of the social scale and are often a decisive factor in
cultural evolution, the middle classes are excluded from the revolutionary
table of organization. Ideology requires that the revolutionary class be
composed exclusively of industrial workers—and ignores the fact that
these workers are themselves part of the middle class.

poverty has few serious adherents today. It is hard to believe that among them are the State Inspectors of Schools, even though that agency has the duty of representing the Ministry of Education to school personnel and not of passing along the complaints of that personnel to the central administration. (Indeed, no adequate procedure exists for the latter purpose.)

In reality, the computation of the cost of education in a given society, in relation to the over-all means available and to the goals of that society, has become the subject of a special discipline within the framework of economics and sociology. There is abundant literature on the subject —but literature which is accessible only to specialists in education. The truth is, it is impossible to measure exactly the nature of an investment in education to which the people, as a whole, have consented. All that can be said is that there exists an ideal: the full utilization of a society's human resources, of the abilities of every citizen. This ideal, to be sure, has a sort of negative impact in the economic domain, to the extent that the further a society is from it, the closer that society is to underdevelopment; and the closer it is to the ideal, the greater is its growth in production. But there are also qualitative effects; the increased adaptation of individual talents to the professions because of better educational orientation, and a greater amount of leisure time or of freely chosen activities—that is, on the whole, a happier and more harmonious life for a larger number of human beings. Not only does work become more efficient, which in itself is not enough, but misuse of personnel is reduced. Without that moral and personal effect of cultural advancement, the technological impact of the price paid for education leads to that disequilibrium and to those crises with which contemporary society is afflicted. In every

respect, as Edgar Faure points out, "education Malthusian-
ism is very expensive."*

What part of its income should a country devote to
education if it is to maintain its cultural growth and
avoid regression? France, for one, still follows the rule-of-
thumb established by Jules Ferry: one sixth of a nation's
budgetary funds should be earmarked for public education.
It seems, however, that that percentage is no longer sufficient. Recent studies in the economics of education have
shown that it is not the general budget alone which
should be considered in public education. To it must be
added the expenses of local school systems, the educational
expenses of governmental departments other than those
directly concerned with education, those of private schools,
and above all, perhaps, the direct expenses of families.
As unbelievable as it may seem, in a country where education is theoretically free, direct expenditures by households for education (that is, for the purchase of books
and other necessary materials, for private lessons, for
support of students, etc.) amounted, in 1967, to 8,500,-
000,000 francs ($1,700,000,000)—a sum about equal
to the operating expenses of the public education system
(i.e., to the budget of the Department of National Education, less expenses for equipment).

This spontaneous family assistance to children and
youth, since it must vary according to family income,
contributes to the strengthening of social inequalities and
to increasing the chances for success of some students
and lessening the chances of others. In 1964, for example,
upper-class households spent an average of 1489 francs

* Edgar Faure, Minister of National Education since May, 1968, is the
author of France's basic reform program for education (*Loi d'Orientation
pour la Réforme de l'enseignement en France*). According to this program, French universities would enjoy an autonomy comparable to that
enjoyed by their American counterparts. Unfortunately, however, M.
Faure's *Loi* has yet to be applied in all its amplitude.

($297) per child for education; white-collar employees spent 931 francs ($186); and blue-collar workers spent 675 francs ($135), while the national average expenditure was 1180 francs ($236) per child. All these figures must be taken into account in figuring the cost of education. The best way of arriving at the proper figure is to add up all these costs and to evaluate the result in percentages in relation to the gross national product. It is also the only way—because of the varying methods of financing in different countries—of arriving at fair comparisons. Thus, in 1964, the United States devoted 5.8 percent of its G.N.P. to education; the Netherlands, 5.8 percent; Sweden, 5.7 percent; Italy, 5.03 percent; the United Kingdom, 4.9 percent; and France, 4.35 percent.* The differences among these figures may, at first glance, seem insignificant. Let us remember, however, that a difference of 1 percent in G.N.P. is, in fact, an enormous difference. We can get an idea of the sums involved by noting that the *total* aid of the industrialized countries to the underdeveloped countries amounts to *less* than 1 percent of the G.N.P. of the industrialized countries. In comparing the percentages for, say, Italy and the United Kingdom (both around 5 percent), a very important consideration is the fact that Italy attained that figure only in 1964, while the U.K. had reached it several years before. The efforts of France and Italy, beginning in 1960, are doing no more than closing the cultural gap between themselves and the countries of northern Europe. And, in any case, European cultural development is no more homogenous than European political life, and it cannot possibly enable Europe to overtake, much less surpass, the United States in basic research and scientific creativity.

The situation of education in France is therefore very

* These figures are taken from *Le Prix de l'enseignement en France*, by Pierre Daumard. Paris, 1969.

serious with respect to the needs of the country, and national education has not really been accorded the priority it deserves. Such reforms as exist have been more or less haphazard, and the result of overwhelming crises rather than of methodical planning. In 1968, by stretching here and there, France was able to devote 5 percent of its gross national product to education; but, in the same year, both Sweden and the United States were using more than 7 percent of their G.N.P for that purpose.

It would be illusory to believe that we are now "out of the woods" simply because the peak of the postwar birthrate has been passed. Beyond demographic considerations, we find that we are confronted by a new factor, a demand for education which expresses a social and psychological need. This demand results from the process of democratization, and it requires still more democratization if it is to be satisfied. The growth of educational expenses will therefore continue; and it is irreversible.

In 1969, at the very moment when France was rejecting de Gaulle, she was embracing Napoleon, looking more toward the year 1800 than toward 2000, succumbing to the fascination of the past, spending half of her time commemorating what had been, and dreaming retroactively of giving the world a good thrashing. The occasion was the bicentennial celebration of Napoleon's birth, and there were countless ceremonies, newspaper articles, television programs, and speeches by various politicians, including President Pompidou—all of which occupied France's attention for several months. And, as we were enjoying our visions of past glories, the present was pressing inexorably upon us, and our statistical tables were filling with the grim evidence of reality. In the scales of history, unfortunately, our decade of "grandeur" will turn out to have been a period of mediocrity.

Among the multifarious ambitions of Gaullism, that of cultural progress was one of the most fervently proclaimed, and one of the most cruelly disappointed. Once again, words took the place of ideas, phrases were substituted for action, and results were submerged in a flood of oratory. One of the most striking areas of neglect was in the world of books. Every preparation for revolution must create tools for the popularization of culture—that is, it must make it possible for the greatest number of people to be able to reach the stage of independent critical reflection. In the United States the public library system is the best in the world. In Europe it is a hodgepodge. The statistics given in UNESCO's *Statistical Yearbook*—of which the 1965 edition is the latest—and summarized below, will serve to illustrate that fact.

Regarding the domestic market for books, we find that the most effective of all official methods of subsidizing books is by subsidizing public libraries. Direct subsidies, of course, cannot be given objectively except for the purpose of acquiring scientific or scholarly works. Library purchases are part of the normal market, and they allow the everyday reader to keep abreast of literary and documentary events without having to buy every book that appears —which would be impossible. One often hears Great Britain cited as an example. In that country, libraries systematically absorb between two and three thousand copies of every book published. The publisher therefore is not reduced to choosing between having a best-seller on his list and showing a deficit. In book publishing, average minimal sales are what assure the continuity and the quality of books.

Now, in UNESCO's *Yearbook*, we see that, in the Federal Republic of Germany, 10,988 public libraries make some 22,000,000 books available to the reading public. In Great Britain, there are 40,000 libraries, and 77,000,000 books. But when we look for the statistics on France, we find no figures; instead, there are the three little dots which mean "figures not available." Those three dots are a symbol that one is accustomed to find after the names of such places as the Ryukyu Islands, and Portuguese Guinea. Is it possible that, in a country as strongly bureaucratized and as firmly administered as France, there are too many libraries and too many books to count? Hardly. It seems rather that UNESCO, in an act of commendable delicacy (and in accord with the French government), refrained from publishing figures which would have been too embarrassing for France. Instead of statistics, there is a note commenting on the absence of statistics: "There is, in France, a great variety of public libraries, and there are, moreover, numerous private libraries"—the latter being wholly irrelevant to the question—without counting "the libraries of the Feminine League of French Catholic Action" and "innumerable [sic] lending libraries in the parishes, those of the youth movements [?], etc." The true explanation, however, is to be found only in the annual budget of the French Republic: France spends less in buying books for the public than Spain; although it must be admitted that she spends more than Turkey.

In the external—that is, the foreign—market, the situation of French books has deteriorated so badly that the Economic Council (using statistics furnished by UNESCO) took special note of it in a report on the development of the rest of French commercial services (published in the *Journal officiel* of January 28, 1969). We find in this report, under the heading of "author's rights," that the French economy, beginning in 1961, has ceased to profit from book exports; that is, France is now paying out more money to foreign publishers—either for translation rights, or for the importation of books—than she is taking in. It is not that France produces fewer books than in the years prior to 1961, but that other countries are producing, and exporting, more than they were before that year.

Production figures for French books have remained static. In fact, the figures have been the same since 1860. For more than a century, the number of titles published every year has varied between 12,000 and 14,000. In 1964, for instance, 13,479 books were published in France; in West Germany, 30,798; in the United Kingdom, 26,-123; in Spain, 15,540—and these figures exclude textbooks. Of France's 13,000 titles, if we subtract translations and reprints, we find that there were only 5000 or 6000 new titles in 1964.

In foreign countries such as Italy, Greece, Spain, and even Switzerland, English books (as distinct from "English-language books"), which are protected in the American market, have maintained their position better than French books, even though, in those countries, the French language enjoys a position at least equal, if not superior, to that of English. In an article in the *Times Literary Supplement* of July 24, 1969, the president of the Book Development Council (an agency which has no equivalent on the Continent) writes that book exports are surpassed only by exports of whisky, agricultural equipment, and luxury textiles. The reason for this is that, because there is a strong domestic market for books in Great Britain, the English edition of a book can take care of varied sectors and increasingly satisfy all requirements—including foreign requirements.

These figures are intended to suggest the fallacy of believing that Europeans—or at least Latin Europeans—

are, on the whole, more cultivated than Americans. Actually, the reverse is true. Hardly any American town that is more than a village cannot boast of a respectable public library of its own; and even the smallest of these libraries, since it belongs to a state-wide library system, can obtain practically any book requested, within a few days. And we should never forget that the United States is the birthplace, and the home, of the inexpensive paperback book and of mass culture. It is obvious that cultural growth and the democratization of knowledge go hand in hand with the extension of fundamental and applied research, and with the spirit of inventiveness and of the *avant-garde* in the arts. Contrary to what is generally believed, these phenomena are mutually complementary rather than mutually exclusive. What is happening in the United States today is what happened in nineteenth-century Europe: the ever-increasing popularization of culture is being accompanied by a growth in the creative power of the *avant-garde*.

As in the case of culture, the level of political information—which is an indispensable component of any modern revolution—is very uneven in Europe, and varies from country to country according to the degree of liberty allowed to television, the medium which has become the chief means of political culture for the masses.* The over-

* One often hears it said that the official enslavement of French television is of no great importance, or at least that one regime derives no more advantage from it than another, since the Fourth Republic controlled television just as stringently as did de Gaulle's Fifth Republic. That is true, so far as it goes. It is worth noting, however, that, on the eve of de Gaulle's return to power, there were approximately 600,000 television sets in France; ten years later, there were some 12,000,000. This rate of increase corresponds to that of newspaper readership in the period from 1830 to 1880. Morally speaking, if censorship of the press at the end of the Restoration had been as criminal as it was to be fifty years later, and, politically, if the laws of 1881, establishing freedom of the press, had not been voted, the consequences would have been quite different from those which obtained during the Restoration. We have not yet finished paying the price of the television censorship of the past

all consequence is that revolution in Europe is caught in the bottleneck of political strangulation and overwhelmed by the institutional cacophony of the Continent.

Non-communist Europe includes three *de facto* dictatorships: Greece, Spain, and Portugal. At the other extreme, there is a group of democratic nations with socialist tendencies: the Scandinavian countries, West Germany, Holland, and Great Britain. In this second group, the various freedoms are more or less wholly secure, and information is free of direct censorship. Between these two extremes are France and Italy, countries in which the existence of strong communist parties guarantee power to the Right (which is either conservative or vaguely reformist, according to the circumstances of the moment, but which is uniformly free of any tendency toward creative use of the imagination).* There can be no revolution in France or Italy because, in theory, the opposition party wants to create a revolution while, in practice, it does not want to create a revolution. This situation serves to obviate the possibility of any revolutionary thrust; and, at the same time, it prevents the formation of an effective opposition party—and by "effective" I mean a party which might eventually come to power—by making it seem that such a party would necessarily be reformist, centrist, etc. Thus, opposition in those countries remains purely academic, for most of the people care little about an opposition which has not the slightest chance of ever coming to power.

---

decade—a period during which, elsewhere, the medium was transformed into the paramount means of public debate. The primitive state of French political consciousness which resulted from that censorship will very likely be a durable phenomenon, and one which will prove to be a surprisingly effective obstacle to all revolutionary propaganda.

* I emphasize "*creative* use of the imagination." Imagination can be either operative, and transform reality, or illusory, and become a means of fleeing reality. The so-called grand design (*grand dessein*) of General de Gaulle is an example of the latter.

Chapter 5

THE IMPOSSIBLE REVOLUTION: France

The french left in 1970 is the perfect example of an impossible revolution. The vehicle of change, as soon as it starts up, is immediately braked—by the Left. Meanwhile, the Right, in the seat of power, is making concessions; or rather, it is having concessions torn from its grasp in the streets. These concessions are granted only when the breaking point has been reached—a ploy which confers a double advantage on the Right: first, it can wait until the last possible moment before yielding; and then it can reap the harvest of a progressive image which these concessions entail. Thus, the Left is condemned to the role of eternal opposition, without ever assuming that of the future party in power. No other distribution of power seems possible, either through the electoral process or through violence.

It is difficult, even for a Leftist, to explain exactly

what the French Left is. The Communist Party? No; because it does not practice internal democracy, and because the communists have not, up to now, respected the liberty of any of the states in which they have risen to power. In that respect, the myth of "Italian communism," on which the French Left has survived for fifteen years, seems lately to have followed "Yugoslav communism" to the grave of liberal illusions. The non-communist Left? Again, no; because the non-communist Left is composed of both social democrats, who adhere to socialist doctrine, and of liberals, who will have none of socialism. Moreover, the social democrats, if we ask them whether, on coming to power, they would abolish capitalism, are visibly embarrassed. If by abolishing capitalism is meant large-scale nationalization, then their fellow leftists would accuse them of reformism, while the Right would accuse them of attempting to abolish private property in favor of collectivism. There is also a Left which defines itself as both non-communist and non-socialist, and which is very difficult to pin down. When the political wind is blowing in the direction of a popular front of the Left, that is, toward union with other parties of the Left— or at least toward that comparatively chaste form of union which consists in refraining from opposing one another in elections—this party ebbs toward the Right Center as soon as tempers have begun to cool. The leftists? Among present-day leftists, two currents are discernible. There is an old current, which includes the small extremist groups: dissident communists, Trotskyites, anarchists, P.S.A., U.F.D., P.S.U.,* etc. And there is a new current, comprising dis-

* These acronyms designate, respectively, the Independent Socialist Party, the Union of Democratic Forces, and the United Socialist Party. It is an indication of the effectiveness and of the policies of these transitory splinter groups of the Left that, today, even Frenchmen do not know what all these initials stand for.

senters and the movement of dissent The first group has
never carried much political weight. The second, however,
which has lately come to the rescue of the minorities of
the Left, has great psychological importance. It has demonstrated its effectiveness as the nemesis of moral passivity.
At the present time, however, it is difficult to think of the
leftists in terms of political power—except as factors in the
strengthening of the power of the Right.

Given the situation described, it is easy to conclude,
and it is often concluded, that the Left is incapable of
exercising power because it is incapable of agreeing on a
platform and therefore of forming a governmental majority. This assertion is worth examining. Is it true that
the Left cannot come to power because it has no common
minimal platform? No, it is not true—and the truth is
perhaps harder to bear. Contrary to what is so often heard
on this subject, the various groups which compose the Left
have several times, between 1965 and 1969, reached a fairly
general state of agreement on a platform. The P.S.U.
(Parti socialiste unifié, or United Socialist Party) candidate in the presidential elections of 1969, for example, put
forth a program which was, on the whole, a page from
Mendès-France, rewritten in mildly leftist style. The fact
is that platform differences on the Left are neither more
nor less pronounced than those which occur in the Gaullist conglomerate.* The difference is that the latter is held
together by the possession of power, while the Left, at first
glance, is fragmented not by the inability to *define* its
policies, but by its reaction to the possibility of attaining
power as such. I mean that, as soon as the Left is faced
with the eventuality of a victory, it falls apart. And it is

* See the analysis of these programs in: Marc Paillet, *Table rase*, Paris,
1968; François Mitterrand, *Ma part de vérité*, Paris, 1969; J.-J. Servan-
Schrieber and Michel Albert, *Ciel et Terre, manifeste radical*, Paris, 1970.
The latter book is discussed elsewhere in the present work.

this nihilistic reaction which dictates the choreography of that elaborate ballet of coalitions and ruptures witnessed in the political arena.

In the French Left, unity exists only when it serves no purpose; as soon as it begins to be useful, it falls apart. The proof of this principle was given in the election of October, 1969, at Yvelines, when Rocard, the candidate of the United Socialist Party, defeated General de Gaulle's former Premier, Couve de Murville, thanks to a coalition of communists, socialists, radicals, and centrists. (And thanks, too, one should say, to Couve himself, who predictably failed to inspire the electorate when he offered a diet of platitudes leavened by skepticism.) It was a clear victory, and it was celebrated by the Left as a demonstration of its ability to "face up to Gaullism" in certain circumstances. The key words, of course, are "in certain circumstances." In my opinion, this victory, instead of giving joy to the Left, should have provoked sadness; for it is likely that the success of the coalition was possible only because of its patent uselessness. Such victories count for nothing. Only victories which *confer power* have meaning. The anti-Gaullist forces which, in the preceding spring, had been incapable not only of supporting, but even of proposing, a candidate for the presidency, seemed able to act only when it was a question of an operation without practical significance.

An example of the fear of power which characterizes the Left in France is given by the polemics which surrounded the question of whether or not the Left would support Alain Poher during the presidential elections of 1969. Most of the intellectuals with whom I discussed this problem evidenced great revulsion at the idea of supporting a candidate who was not an avowed socialist. (I will not discuss the motives which inspired the Communist

Party in its bitter campaign against Alain Poher—motives which, though less admissible than those of the non-communist Left, were nonetheless considerably more rational.) The non-communist Left was the only political force which, if it had rallied around Poher, could have assured his success and, at the same time, ousted General de Gaulle's supporters. It was a question of deciding whether or not the latter objective should be given priority. Certainly the question was debatable; but what actually happened was that the question was not debated at any time during the election campaign. Instead, what France heard was an argument substantially as follows: "We would vote for Poher, since the main thing is to beat Pompidou; but we hesitate to do so, or we will even abstain from doing so, because he is neither a socialist nor in agreement with the Communist Party." In other words, Poher was being blamed for not doing exactly what François Mitterrand had done in March 1967 during the legislative elections, or in December 1965 during the presidential elections. Nonetheless, during those two campaigns of Mitterrand's, these same people, representing the same factions of the Left, had announced that they were not satisfied by those very same principles, programs, and alliances which they were now saying were indispensable and to which they swore they would rally—but only as soon as it had become obvious that such principles, programs, and alliances would not be realized, or were not even realizable.

It is a matter of continuing astonishment that most of the spokesmen of the Left are unable to distinguish between solutions which have a chance of being realized, and those which have no chance. During the presidential elections of 1969, it quickly became clear that, given the absence of a common candidate from the Left, only two candidates were really in the running: Poher and Pompidou. The other candidates could talk to their hearts' content about their aims and goals; but in no case could they seriously propose being elected and winning power. Voters were free to deplore the political situation by virtue of which their choice was limited to Poher and Pompidou; but no one imagined for a minute that there was really any other choice. Moreover, that choice probably reflected the reality of French politics; for it would be naïve to imagine that the intrigues of any politicians could cause a change in the Left at the moment when post-Gaullism was falling into disgrace. Nor would abstention have provided an alternative, for it is universally understood that, in elections, abstention is never neutral but always benefits one or the other candidate; the candidate being, in this case, Pompidou. Therefore, no matter what one's beliefs were, and no matter what one's regrets, once it became clear that the Left could not unite to present a candidate, the campaign boiled down to a contest between Pompidou and Poher.

The function of politics is to react to real situations, and not to line up realistic situations, side by side and on a footing of equality, with pipe dreams. If a waiter asks you to choose between spaghetti and potatoes, explaining that there is nothing else on the menu, there is no point in saying that you prefer caviar. The question is, spaghetti or potatoes; and nothing else. In politics as in the kitchen, one may dream of circumstances in which the fare offered would be more palatable; but to dream is not the same as to act in accordance with a given reality. To act is to make a decision in conformity with reality, and not according to nonexistent alternatives. Reality, no doubt, is often only imperfectly satisfying; but, at a given moment, we must sometimes learn to accept and live with such imperfection. Later, we may be able to evoke the vision of a different alternative; that is, we can convert a preferred alternative into a concrete choice. But the prospect of a valid course of action for the future does not relieve us of the responsibility of making a choice with respect to reality as it exists at present. If we are faced with two hypotheses both of which may be realized in practice, and if we refrain from comparing them to hypotheses which have no chance of being verified in the immediate future, we automatically limit ourselves to considering the respective advantages and disadvantages of the concrete solutions which really exist. For, politically speaking, to make a decision because of, or in favor of, something which will never happen, is the same as making no decision at all. In other words, a realistic political solution always has concomitant disadvantages. Therefore, if we reject every solution which has disadvantages, we are soon left with no solutions.

An analysis of the diverse motivations which dictate the preferences of the French Left reveals that many decisions are made less on the basis of what it is possible to accomplish than of what it is fashionable to believe. In other words, the Left does not make decisions in terms of power but of programmatic elegance. The indispensable prerequisite of a goal then becomes not that goal's attainability, but its laudability—and the esteem which it will procure for those who propose it. The man who might have proposed the abolition of slavery in the year 200 B.C. surely would have deserved all the praise he got; but it is safe to say that no politician would have made such a proposal. It was certainly necessary that there be men who, at the moral level, condemned slavery even at a time when there was no chance of its being abolished, so that, eventually, it might in fact be abolished. But if these same men, at election time or in some other moment of political crisis, had refused to choose between a despot and a democratic candidate, on the grounds that neither one of them was against slavery, they would have succeeded only in delaying the eventual liberation of the slaves. If politics is to be the art of the possible, it must first become the art of the actual.

Finally, I should say that to belong to the Left in France seems to be, above all, to affirm that one is more purely Left than other men of the Left, to prove that one's fellows on the Left are hardly more than rightists. What saves the Right, in the final analysis, is the paralyzing fear of the Left that it may be suspected of being reactionary. In moments of crisis, when there is a possibility that power might change hands, the Left seems suddenly obsessed with the necessity of announcing that most of its allies are indistinguishable from the party in power. Thus, in 1968, it was declared that there was no difference between Mitterrand and de Gaulle; and, in 1969, that Pompidou and Poher were the same man. What the Left was really saying was that all political action was useless, since the two candidates in each case represented between 70 and 80 percent of the electorate, and that consequently it was impossible for the Left to take control of the state. In the light of that event, it is more difficult than ever to explain the cries of joy with which revolutionaries seem to greet such lugubrious compatibility between candidates.

Nearly as shocking is the attitude of contempt which French socialists (France is surely the country where one finds the least real socialism in proportion to the number of intractable socialists) apparently feel obliged to adopt with respect to British Laborites, German Social Democrats, and Swedish socialism, the latter now being the *bête noire* of our revolutionaries; that is, of those who have forgotten that, in the phrase "to make a revolution," the operative term is "to make." What right, one wonders, does the most backward group of the whole European Left have to take such an attitude? The same may be said of the Left's contemptuous condemnation of every form of progressive capitalism, of the industrial revolution and of technological progress, in the name of a sort of Sunday socialism. This particular attitude amounts to the choice of underdevelopment so as to save oneself the trouble of having to revise one's dogmas.

By a diversity of roads we are led to the same conclusion: the French Left is concerned about everything—everything except that which is within its reach. Every nonconservative force in France splits down the middle and becomes ineffectual as soon as a point of political impact is approached. The communists of the C.G.T.,* for example, take very strong stands when the party in power is firmly established and when there is no immediate danger of change, through elections or otherwise; but as soon as change comes within reach, they do an about-face. This situation cannot be explained solely by the *de facto* connivance of the communists and the Gaullists in preventing the unity of western Europe. It betrays a psychological attitude: a basic respect for established authority, a fear of change, and an attachment to an all-pervasive routine. The two parties each have their role to play: the Gaullists can, with virtual impunity, condemn the communist conspiracy, while the communists are helping the Gaullists to rid themselves of Leftists and recalcitrant centrists. In exchange, the communists have been granted a monopoly of opposition which is to be exercised in periods of calm, by means of which the party is strengthened as an organization the chief goal of which is to perpetuate itself as it is. It is essential to both the Gaullists

* The C.G.T. (*Confédération Générale du Travail*, or General Labor Federation) is France's most powerful union. It is communist-controlled.

and the communists that the two parties be able to fight each other, but without ever destroying one another; for each is the goose which lays the golden eggs of the other.

In view of this situation, it is not hard to understand the triumph of conservatism in French politics. On the one hand, the Communist Party itself is conservative, in that it preserves itself intact despite Budapest, Prague, de Gaulle's return to power in 1958 and the student revolt of May 1968. On the other hand, the non-communist Left, as soon as opportunity knocks, either becomes intensely occupied with internecine fighting over details, or increases its demands to the point where it is assured that it will be able to reject in advance anything that may actually be offered.

For the French Left, politics is anything that one may wish to call it, except action. The Holy Grail of socialism has attained a state of such ineffable purity that there is no place for it anywhere in the present social situation. The practical result is that no one moves for fear of moving in the wrong direction. Words have become more important than action; and the idea that, in politics, action is an element which may have greater importance than words, is one that does not occur to many people.

The Right does not do much better, for that matter, and it has become accustomed to ignoring what happens in the country. Typically, we see such regions as Brittany, which exists in a state of perennial semi-rebellion against the government, turn out religiously to vote for the government in every election. In April and May 1969 the whole country began suddenly and openly to declare, as a national truth, that the policies of Gaullism had failed utterly. People who, for ten years, had been unable to listen to a word of criticism of the government without becoming angry, now out of the blue were willing to accept as a basic premise (now promoted to the rank of a self-evident truth) that de Gaulle had left France in a miserable condition. The people were convinced of that truth —and then, in a bizarre exercise of logic, they turned around and voted into the highest positions of power the former collaborators of the fallen general. And the men they elected were those gentlemen of whom it might be thought that they had collaborated with de Gaulle either out of conviction, in which case they were intellectually unfitted for office, or against their convictions, in which case they were morally unsuited. Almost everyone agreed, for example, that the Stabilization Plan of 1963 had been an unqualified economic disaster; but, in 1969, the Ministry of Economics was given once more to the author of that Plan. All this, of course, is perfectly logical; and this Minister, along with his colleagues and his masters, after a few months of mourning, can throw himself once more into the joys of self-congratulation—and forget to mention that the true savior of the franc,* at the end of 1969, was Mr. Willy Brandt, who was the best Finance Minister that France has had in a long time. It must be said, however, that the slight improvement in our balance-of-payments position, and the slowing of monetary depreciation, by no means constitutes a cure for the backwardness of France in a variety of domains. People are aware of this backwardness and say that it is inexcusable; that is, that it could have been avoided. The French missed the opportunities offered by the sixties; and they failed to take advantage both of capitalism and of socialism. The Gaullists failed to keep faith with their supporters; but those supporters, just like the opposition, are incapable of learning the po-

---

* By devaluating the mark. In this respect, it should be noted that the various monetary victories claimed by Gaullism ended, in fact, in a disaster: between 1958 and 1969, the franc's worth decreased 40 percent in comparison to the German mark.

litical lessons implicit in that failure. Elections, it seems, have nothing to do with what one thinks, experiences, says and sees every day. And it always seems to happen that certain independent journalists (who are more or less critical of the Gaullists, as are those of *Le Monde*) wait until after the elections to bring out the most damning evidence in their files. Such was the case with their files on the telephone situation, which were opened only after the legislative elections of June 1968; and with information on the Ministry of Cultural Affairs, which was only published after the presidential elections of 1969. The reason given is that prudence requires journalists to refrain from "putting pressure on the voters." One wonders what the publication of news (not to mention editorials) is, if not pressure. It seems that voters may be guided only when they are unable to translate that guidance into political action; that is to say—and here we return to the point from which we started—when guidance serves no purpose.

By the same token, every criticism of the economic situation is interpreted, even on the Left, as evidence of "consumerism" and of technological alienation. Nonetheless, it was a widely accepted belief (even by the Left) in the period 1960–1965, that one of the "dialectical" virtues of Gaullism was that it would be able to renovate the industrial and administrative structures of the country. Without a particle of evidence to that effect, everyone attributed to Gaullism the ability to create a new society— as though an authoritarian regime could exist only for the sake of a vision of the future. It is hardly axiomatic that the neutralization of the parliamentary system, and increased governmental control, are the price which a modern nation must necessarily pay for a state of constantly changing economic and technological complexity. Such an assumption ignores the fact that authoritarianism can also

be the instrument of outdated concepts, that General de
Gaulle's political philosophy was, in many respects, wholly
archaic—so much so that the general was willing to jeopard-
ize the future of the nation in order to attempt to reconquer for France a place in the diplomatic and military
sun. To make matters worse, even the game which the
general thought he was playing was out of date; for power
no longer comes from military might or diplomatic victories, but from those very investments in the future which
de Gaulle neglected. Our mistake, in other words, was that
we did not perceive that, behind the flood of progressivist
terminology, it was the aim of the de Gaulle regime to
re-establish the traditional value-system of the Right with
which Gaullism was impregnated. This error of interpretation was not peculiar to Frenchmen, but was shared by
many expert foreign observers as well, such as Stanley
Hoffman,* who were convinced *a priori* of the renovative
power of Gaullism, and who did not see the discrepancies
which existed between official statements and the reality
of everyday life in France—discrepancies which are characteristic of every country held back by conservatism and
stupefied by propaganda.

Such backwardness is all the more shameful because of
the length of the term of office allowed under the Fifth
Republic, which is almost twice as long as those granted,
for instance, in the United States. It is easy to forget that
the stability thus afforded to the executive branch (a
stability which renders that branch as immune to criticism
as to pressure) has a somewhat ominous aspect: it enables
a regime to make mistakes for a longer period than would
otherwise be possible. And the practical inability of Frenchmen to recognize such mistakes when they see them is a
national catastrophe. French citizens are perfectly willing

* See *The New York Times*, Book Review Section, April 10, 1966.

to accept the fact that the French nuclear policy of the past decade has been a fiasco and ruined the country into the bargain; that the battle against the American dollar has destroyed the value of the franc; that French atomic submarines are outdated the day they are launched, etc. But they are willing to admit these things only when it is clear that one can no longer do anything about them. Even worse, such facts are transformed into reasons why the new government should be given *carte blanche*—the new government being composed of more or less the same men as the old government. Every criticism, every demand that we stop for a minute and take stock of ourselves, is branded as impractical; and the stock answer is, "Wait six months, and you'll understand." Those who believed, in 1962, that de Gaulle would make France the dominant industrial power of Europe, would reform public education, the budget, administration, and so forth, realize in retrospect that such hopes were vain; but now they expect the same things from de Gaulle's successors, and they are willing to give as much power to the latter as they ever gave to the General. The projects of the supporters of M. Pompidou and M. Chaban have the same basic characteristic as those of the former supporters of de Gaulle: they make no distinction between plans for the future and the concrete accomplishments of the President and the government. For purposes of political argumentation, there seems to be no difference between the two. The only exception occurs in the event of a conspicuous failure—in which case the whole thing is ignored, and a new leaf is turned over—so that one may begin writing precisely the same thing on the other side.

On both the Right and the Left, therefore, political action seems to be wholly independent of day-to-day experience. Voters of the Right and the Center admit, and see evidence every day, that Gaullists are inefficient managers, and that, over a period of ten years, they failed to make of France what she had the potential to become. At the same time, they seem incapable of finding replacements for the Gaullists and of insisting on the application of clearly defined solutions. For the voter, it is not a question of changing the basic orientation of society or of challenging the capitalist system, but of being enabled to rise above the mediocrity into which the nation as a whole has fallen. For France does not even possess the technical advantages of social inequality—so much so that, in December 1969, President Pompidou was able to rejoice in the fact that France had, by the narrowest margin, avoided bankruptcy.

The theoretical programs of the Left today are as divorced from reality as those of the Right, and they deserve to be examined to see whether or not they are workable. According to the possibilities upon which they are based, they may be stated as follows:

First hypothesis: The establishment of a "people's democracy" upon the heels of a Soviet invasion of France. Given the actual state of international affairs, this is an unlikely eventuality, and one which corresponds to the wishes of only a tiny minority of Frenchmen—and even of French communists.

Second hypothesis: The establishment of a "people's democracy" as the consequence of an internal revolution. This is an impossibility because of the present state of public opinion and because of the existing relationship among the powers-that-be in France.

Third hypothesis: The establishment of a socialist regime "with a human face"; that is, a regime which would respect fundamental human liberties. We should note, first of all, that we are talking about a kind of socialist regime which has never existed in any country—a consideration of some importance when one is talking about realistic political solutions. Moreover, it may be doubted that the communists themselves can have much faith in this solution, given the fact that they are unable to practice democracy within their own party structures. There is little reason to think that they could be any better at it on a nation-wide scale. But even supposing that the communists would be willing to guarantee these liberties without reservation, the fact still remains that those who advocate the abolition of private ownership of the means of production constitute (including the communists) no more than 15 to 20 percent of the French electorate; and that is a liberal estimate. It is difficult to admit that, of the 45 percent of the electorate who belong to the Left, less than half really want to see the means of production collectivized. So far as the partisans of revolutionary socialism, other than communists, are concerned, they are a very small minority; moreover, many of them are anti-communist—a situation which renders their program impossible to realize, at least in the immediate future.

Since none of the three hypotheses given above, which represent the three fundamental options of the Left, is workable, and since any other option raises the abhorrent specter of reformism, what remains to the French Left? Nothing. Nothing, that is, unless the Left changes drastically. In other words, the situation is one of an "impossible revolution." Its chief characteristic is that everything that is workable is considered to be nonrevolutionary, and everything that is revolutionary is nonworkable. The only way to break out of this vicious circle would be to formulate concepts which correspond to the real situation of

France, and of Europe generally, and to abandon those formulated in a completely different context. One cannot be both a legitimist and a revolutionary at the same time.

The only new sound heard from the French opposition in a long time has been Jean-Jacques Servan-Schreiber's *Radical Manifesto.** He quite literally struck dumb both the Left and the Right by the audacity of his theses—and then was rewarded by a storm of reaction: a resurrection of Centrism was proposed by some; by others, the whole-hearted pursuit of a consumer-society; a few were in favor of a socialistic abolition of private property, and others proposed a post-Kennedy Kennedy-ism, while still others suggested dressing up the reformist monster so that it would seem less repellent. In other words, everyone began rummaging around in the closets of history and dragging out the solutions of the past. In the midst of all the legalistic quibbling about inheritances, the budget, and kindergartens, which followed the publication of the *Manifesto*, it seems to have escaped the notice of many people that this book was the only recent political work which, both emotionally and analytically, faced resolutely toward the future rather than toward the past; that it was not a sort of verbal jigsaw puzzle, like most of the Left's programs, which one had to assemble out of ready-made pieces, but a real effort to look toward the future.

The central idea, in fact, of the *Radical Manifesto*, is that no society existing today is able to serve as the literal model for a future revolution, but that, to the contrary, every revolution—as the word itself implies—is an invention. Certainly, the act of invention does not require that one ignore all considerations of the past; but what is happening today is that the Left is succumbing to a sort of pseudo-leftist rigidity, which consists of being mesmerized

* Paris, 1970.

and immobilized by the past to such an extent that one is unable to derive any profit from it. It is really a political neurosis—in the strictest clinical meaning of the term— by virtue of which one is imprisoned by stereotypes created in one's childhood and unable to benefit from later experience. To create a revolution means to create new patterns of behavior—or at least new interpretations of behavioral patterns. And this is the cause of many of the misunderstandings concerning both the *Radical Manifesto* and *The American Challenge.** One hears such things as, "Servan-Schreiber says that society has but one goal: profit." This is certainly false, of course; Servan-Schreiber says that society's goal must be, not profit, but growth— which is something entirely different. "Profit" means gain from private enterprise, while "growth" refers to the whole economy. It is almost axiomatic that the central fact of human history since neolithic times is that, in the last two centuries, national economies have ceased to be static economies and have become growth economies. Thus, every economic system which is incapable of assuring growth is doomed by the verdict of history. And that, as hard as it may be to admit, is the situation of the socialist countries.

This does not mean, however, that growth alone is a panacea, or that it is, of itself, a solution. That would be like saying, "My boy is growing X inches a year; so that is the end of all my troubles." Growth is a necessary condition; but it is not a sufficient condition. Growth is that which is absolutely necessary in order for us to be able to accomplish anything; but what we can accomplish on the basis of growth can be either for the better or for the worse. And this point is another element of controversy (this one rather curious, except when one remembers that people seldom read the books that they talk about) re-

* New York, 1968.

garding Servan-Schreiber's thought. It is said that "Servan-Schreiber is on the side of management. For him, the main thing is to manage businesses efficiently, in such a way that they show a profit; and the rest will follow automatically." It must be particularly disconcerting for Servan-Schreiber to hear such things, for what he set out to prove was precisely the opposite. For him, the crises and unrest that afflict industrial societies today are the result of their total and anarchic subjection to the laws of economics. The *Radical Manifesto* contains several examples demonstrating that it is precisely when a business is managed most efficiently, according to its own point of view, that it often causes the most harm to the community and even to the whole of humanity. The thesis is wholly Marxist: the subordination of politics to economics is the great sin of the past century.

Revolution, therefore, must bring about, in the present state of affairs, the separation of political power and economic power—a separation which, if we think about it, exists hardly anywhere in the world today. In some places, as in the capitalist countries, politics is subordinate to the interests of those who run the economy; in others, as in the communist countries, the economy can be scuttled with impunity, and the people plunged into misery, by the political governing class. Generally speaking, and unfortunately, the qualities necessary to attain power and retain it are not the same as those required to exercise power competently and impartially. The discrepancy between politics and economics—the archaic state of political power in the midst of ever-progressing technological power—is, I have believed for several years, the true crucible of revolution.*

The real question about the *Radical Manifesto* does not

* Cf. my *Lettre ouverte à la droite*, published in 1968.

concern its direct approach, or its lucid and concrete demonstrations which contrast so happily with the insipid political literature to which we have become accustomed. The real question is whether or not the *Radical Manifesto* has the strength to break the chains by which French politics is held prisoner. But where is the majority capable of handing power over to Servan-Schreiber's partisans? The *Radical Manifesto* is attacked from all sides; by the Right, because of the too-revolutionary nature of some of the measures it recommends (limited inheritance, separation of economic management and capital), and from the Left because the book is "reformist," endorses the principle of private enterprise, and does not respect the inviolable sanctity of socialism. Taking such things into consideration, could Servan-Schreiber's success at Nancy, in the elections of June 1970, be repeated on a national scale? It is possible that it might, in presidential elections. So far as legislative elections are concerned, however, it would be much more difficult—at least, until something can be done to break loose the communist bloc of voters, which represents 20 percent of the electorate and which, given the present situation of political parties, could never contribute either to the formation of a legally elected government or to a revolutionary uprising.

In Italy, there are certain characteristics not unlike those which obtain in France. As in France, there is a sufficient number of revolutionaries to put a halt to reformism, but not enough of them to make a revolution.

Europeans, therefore—and especially the two principal Mediterranean groups—can be saved from their internal diseases only by the realization of political unity. For the past decade, we have witnessed instead the rebirth of the nation-state. And, here again, there has been a convergence of Right and Left—that is, on the one hand, of nationalism, and, on the other, a fear of a capitalist Europe, or a "Europe of monopolies." In fact, however, a system of European capitalism would surely have offered less opposition to the workers' battle for a new economy than has a capitalism fragmented into national dwarfs. The probable result of this persistence of the nation-state is that northern Europe, Britain, and West Germany will, despite electoral vicissitudes, evolve more and more toward "revolutionary reformism"; while the other countries of Europe will remain bogged down in a static antagonism engendered by the opposition of the two principal and irreconcilable blocs representing domestic public opinion. Despite their superior flexibility and dynamism, the northern countries will be too weak to avoid dependence on American creativity, or at least too weak to give a world-wide impetus to solutions which they may devise.

The authors of the *Radical Manifesto* admit, for that matter, that it is not possible to start a revolution in a politically fragmented Europe; even more, they maintain that only a *world* government will be able someday to undertake real revolutionary action. If this is indeed the case, can we hope that Europe—however retarded, divided, and clumsy it may be—will be able to play a revolutionary role by becoming, or becoming again, the cradle of a new "spearhead culture?" I mean, not so much in the areas of science and technology, in respect to which Europe has already emasculated itself, but in the area of new ideologies, of new sensitivity, of new morals, of new arts corresponding to the new means of communication. Unfortunately, given the relationships between situations, in this domain also Europe is divided into almost irreconcilable groups. There is the southern group, with its two clerical dictatorships, its one confessional republic, and its one crypto-confessional republic. And there is the Anglo-Germanic-Nordic group, ruled by a liberal individualism which is guided in turn by socialistic reformism.* With these geographic entities, we find also, and above all, two groups of intellectuals, one of which confines itself to implementing the American ideology of twenty years ago: efficiency, output, organization, identification of technological progress and moral progress—an ideology which has now been revised, even in the United States. The second group rejects that ideology *in toto*, including growth, technology, and science itself. These intellectuals have great prestige and influence; and they are dominated by an obsession with the past and a hostility to science. They spend most of their time devising, with inexhaustible ingenuity, updated and often clever rebuttals according to doctrinal paradigms originally articulated in keeping with the standards, and the license, of a prescientific culture; and they are moreover permeated with an anachronistic sense of their own cultural superiority. For them, as for the medieval cleric, culture is a means of separating themselves from the rest of mankind, and of feeling superior to the crowd; and this is the source of their contempt for all forms of expression addressed to that crowd (except when such forms have publicity value to themselves), and their frequent reconstruction of more and more esoteric cultural terminologies. This kind of culture—even though it is itself permeated by trends of revolutionary origin, such as Marxism, psychoanalysis, and surrealism—has ended up by creating an identification of leftist feelings with antiscientific and antitechnological feelings. Science equals capitalism; that is the slogan to which it is all leading. A culture of this kind is therefore unable to lay down the guidelines appropriate to the problems con-

* Inequality of income is much greater in France than in Britain or Germany. (See the figures in *Le Monde*, June 12, 1970.)

fronting the modern world; and, in this area also we may say that the revolution, when it comes, will not take place in western Europe.

Certainly, western Europe will undergo changes in mentality; but these changes will be dictated not from within, but from abroad, because the elements capable of rejoining the mainstream are undoubtedly too small, and too far removed from the seats of power. We should keep in mind that most European intellectuals belong simultaneously to "the establishment," in the most official, bureaucratic, and administrative sense of that term, and to the opposition. They are at once the rulers and the revolutionaries. They therefore function simultaneously as a class critical of the political oligarchy, and as a cultural oligarchy opposed to all criticism directed against themselves.*

* A tragicomic demonstration of this situation is furnished by the University of Vincennes, which was established in 1968 as an experimental model of French higher education of the future. The concept of managerial autonomy was soon replaced by one of a self-perpetuating oligarchy. Little *cliques* of friends, and even of families, reassembled in the twinkling of an eye at the new university even more shamelessly than they had at the old one.

Chapter 6

AN IMPOSSIBLE REVOLUTION: The Third World

A THEORY WAS developed in the past ten years to the effect that no revolution can ever again emanate from the industrialized nations of the world. The liberal or semi-liberal regimes of those nations, it is said, have handily anticipated the goals of the revolutionaries, and through the relative prosperity which reigns in those countries, have lessened the need for revolution by satisfying the workers' material needs. And, finally, the ubiquitous hydra of propaganda, whose perfidy is often proportionate to the degree of freedom of information, has perverted the conscience of the people and led them so far astray that they prefer immediate and partial satisfaction to future and total freedom.*

* It is easy to recognize here the reformist-revolution dichotomy—fatal to any action—which marked the Constituent Assembly of 1789. The Assembly was reformist, since it had united itself to the transformation of absolute monarchy into constitutional monarchy; and it should therefore have been prevented from exercising a legislative function.

A consequence of that belief has been the tendency to seek the sources of revolution in the nations of the Third World, among the people who live in real misery. There were Frenchmen, around 1960, who seriously believed that, if there were to be a revolution in France, it would necessarily have to begin among the *maquis* of Algeria. Today, these same Frenchmen have transferred their hopes to the guerrillas of Latin America or to the Arabs of Palestine. When that same line of reasoning is applied to our own societies, we hear it said even that open and complete fascism would have more potential than an amorphous and semi-repressive liberalism; for then at least the opposing camps would be distinct and the order of battle clearly defined.

Such attitudes reveal, first of all, a fear of complexity; and, next, a bad memory—we forget that the industrial societies of the world are already the products of a first revolution, which began in the eighteenth century and increased in momentum throughout the nineteenth. The problems which arise with respect to the future should be dealt with as such, even if it happens that they do not always correspond to difficulties that have already been resolved. The myth of a revolutionary Third World—by that, I mean a Third World which is intrinsically and automatically revolutionary—is evidence of a nostalgia for the past, or, once more, of an obsession with the past. Obviously, one cannot start a revolution in a politically liberal industrial society by copying the tactics of a peasant uprising in feudal times, or by emulating those of a war of national liberation waged by a colonized people. Nor can it reasonably be believed that a revolution, even one which is initially successful, can spread from a less complex society to a more complex one—that Castroism, say, can infect West Germany or Britain. It is hardly likely, therefore, that the underdeveloped countries can become a revolutionary model for the industrial powers.

Is it possible, however, for them to act as such a model for themselves? We can, in fact, conceive of an archetypical Third World revolution the effect of which would be threefold: to free the Third World from the imperialism of the wealthy nations, to develop it economically, and to organize it politically. Unfortunately, one of the consequences of living in an underdeveloped society is that one's revolutions are also underdeveloped. When we discuss imperialism and its responsibility for underdevelopment, we will investigate which is the cause and which is the effect. But, for the moment, let us observe simply that the countries of the Third World have no choice other than between two imperialisms—excluding, of course, the imperialism which they direct against each other, which is not always negligible. The question that concerns us is that of knowing whether, within whichever of the imperialist systems, a revolution can occur in the Third World. My answer is in the negative, and my reasons for that answer are those which follow.

First of all, a necessary condition to a revolution in Third World nations is that there be available an immediate solution to the problem of economic underdevelopment, and that that solution be capable of application by the Third World nations themselves. But even those countries of the Third World which have sufficient resources for this undertaking would not be able to utilize them effectively, because they lack administrative efficiency and sufficient leadership and management personnel. The second reason is that most countries of the Third World are without democratic traditions and are governed by authoritarian regimes—which leads us into the vicious circle of incompetence-dictatorship-corruption-*coup d'état-*

purge-reinforced dictatorship-greater incompetence-greater underdevelopment. My third reason is that the countries of the Third World are almost all buried in the past, from a cultural standpoint; moreover, in the grips of a passion to "find their roots," they have a tendency to sink deeper and deeper into the past, and thus to apply the most effective possible brake to any progress: the Islamic religion, the tribal organization of black Africa, the caste system of India, and so forth. The traditional concept of the family, masculine pride in the number of children produced, the reluctance of the poor to make use of contraception, religious beliefs, and, finally, ignorance, all serve as a sort of cultural braking mechanism, and increase considerably the difficulty of holding down the birth rate. In consequence, the rate of demographic growth remains greater than the rate of economic growth. This cultural braking action increases considerably the difficulty of holding down the birth rate—as a consequence of which, the rate of demographic growth remains greater than the rate of economic growth. My fourth point is this: the spirit of nationalism in the Third World eliminates any tendency toward self-criticism and inclines the people to attribute their underdevelopment to conspiracies. Every war of national liberation increases nationalism a hundredfold—and quite rightly; but once independence has been attained, nationalism leads to xenophobia and to racism, becomes an obstacle to development, and eventually leads to attempts to compensate for economic failures by military successes. And, of course, these attempts lead to more economic failure. The maneuvers of a revolutionary leader in a country of the Third World are delicately balanced; for a leader, if he is to stir up the peoples of the Third World, must appeal to nationalism and revive traditional values. The Bolivian diaries of Che Guevara make it clear to what extent, in areas characterized by illiteracy and poverty, the peasants are indifferent to purely political and social appeals. But subsequently to convert nationalism into an authentic revolution is a feat which has, up to now, rarely succeeded—and, in any case, has never succeeded permanently. To take nationalism and rebaptize it as "socialism" does not suffice to make it constructive.

To sum up, we may say that there can be no revolution in the Third World unless there is an economic breakthrough; and an economic break-through is impossible without the help of a truly revolutionary industrial nation. A revolution is also impossible because, since these countries lack political and administrative know-how, revolutions lead to oligarchies and dictatorships which belong neither to the Right nor to the Left. They are then neutralized by cultural and traditional recidivism—whereas every revolution must necessarily be the invention of a new culture. And, finally, the revolution is neutralized by nationalism, or folklore.

These observations will most likely be branded as reactionary. After all, one of the essential objectives of decolonization was to allow the oppressed peoples to rediscover their cultural personalities. And Frantz Fanon, in *The Wretched of the Earth,** has loudly proclaimed that every revolution in the Third World must operate within the framework of nationalities, and that internationalism would be inoperative in those regions unless there were a profound reawakening of the identities of the various peoples. If we admit that liberation, for colonized nations, consists first of all in the rejection of another nation— in "disalienation"—and that this rejection entails running a full circle until the point of alienation from oneself is reached, then the bizarre concept of a revolutionary in

* New York, 1965.

love with the past, is in no way contradictory. Even in Europe, the revolutionary movements of 1848 coincided with the reawakening of nationalism. The Italian *Risorgimento* was a process of decolonization, with respect to Spain, Austria, France, and the Papacy. Today we still talk about Europe in terms of regions. The historically dominated groups—the Catalans, Bretons, Welsh, Flemish, Basques—all address their appeals against the dominant nations to Europe at large—or, rather, they address them to the true nations of Europe, as opposed to the states of Europe.*

Even the diversity of examples demonstrates the fuzziness of the concepts employed. Some of the human groups mentioned are, or have been, oppressed or suppressed—culturally, in any case—within an economically developed area. Others inhabit areas most prominently affected by the phenomenon of underdevelopment—Africa, especially—and not by a relative underdevelopment (as that of Brittany in comparison to Paris, which is a case merely of being less developed), but with a very real, basic underdevelopment, the main characteristic of which is that the rate of economic growth is less than that of demographic growth. In the case of the first groups—

* De Gaulle never spoke of a Europe of nations, but only of a Europe of states. The proposed law of referendums, which was rejected on April 27, 1969, was dictated by preoccupation, not with the decolonization of the French provinces with respect to Paris, but, to the contrary, with the imposition of fragmentation, so that the regions thus affected would never be able to be integrated into any future European region and would therefore remain "altogether French." It was a project directed less against the provinces than against Europe. So far as the state was concerned, de Gaulle described it, in February 1953, as "a political, economic, financial, and, above all, a moral entity, which is sufficiently alive, established, and recognized to win the sympathetic confidence of its citizens, to have its own policies, and, if necessary, to receive the sacrifice of their lives from millions of its people." It goes without saying, I might add, that the "sympathetic confidence" required has less chance of disappearing within the framework of centralized absolutism than within that of regional federalism.

those within economically developed areas—some of the groups in the process of "decolonizing" themselves are economically more dynamic and wealthy than their former "colonizers"—the Flemish with respect to their Walloon colonizers, for example—and, politically, more reactionary.

The fact is that disalienation does not necessarily coincide with revolution. The Irish disalienated themselves heroically regarding the English—and then turned their country into one of the most backward and most obscurationist states of Europe; so much so that today there is more revolutionary potential among the English than among their former victims. A nation has the right, certainly, to reclaim its past; but there is no guarantee that the exercise of that right will automatically engender revolutionary dynamism. Such dynamism requires that cultural liberation be creative, and that it be accompanied by political reform and economic progress.

In *A Wreath for Udomo*, a *roman à clef* inspired, in part, by the career of Nkrumah, Peter Abrahams* puts the following propositions into the mouth of his protagonist, an African leader:

"Our country has, or rather had, three enemies. Of one of these, I have made an ally. But let us say that there are three. The first of these is the white man. And then, there is poverty; and, finally, the past. These are our three enemies. When I came here, I thought that I would have to face only one enemy, the white man. But, as soon as I had gotten rid of him, the other two enemies appeared; and they are even more powerful and dangerous than the white man. Next to them, the white man seems almost an ally; and so, I have converted him into an ally who fights at our side against poverty. Now, he works for us, so that those who come after us will have bread and a place to

---

* A black novelist, born at Johannesburg.

live. There are now schools and hospitals in our land. Our young men and young women are beginning to awaken from their torpor. Why do you think I have spent so much money to send them to foreign lands? Because I need them to fight at my side against our third enemy, our worst enemy: the past . . . For the sake of appearances, I have performed the rites of juju; I have participated in blood ceremonies; and I have prostrated myself before the altars of our ancestors. But now, I will do so no longer. Now, there are enough young people who have put aside these outdated superstitions for me to be able to undertake the extirpation of everything that is ugly in our past. And you, Selina, and you Adhebhory, whom I once loved as a brother, *you are of the past*. I shall destroy you, because it is you who are the obstacle to the evolution of a greater Africa. Go, fight me in the party conference, and you will see who will win. You come too late, my friends. Too late . . ."*

The most counterrevolutionary alliance that can possibly exist in the Third World is that of socialism with the past. Taken together, they have the effect of perpetuating economic stagnation while justifying political dictatorships. The question of socialism of the world of 1970 is not that of how to go about establishing socialism so that a revolution may take place, but of how to establish socialism and nonetheless have a revolution. The astonishing variety of African socialism—Padmorian socialism, the black socialism of Senghor, the spiritualist socialism of Kofi Baako, the austerity-socialism of Nyerere—conceals what is in fact a deep conservatism. "African socialism is a reassuring theory; it signifies that nothing will be

---

* Quoted by Yves Bénot in *Idéologies des indépendances africaines*, Maspero, 1969. M. Bénot, who declares himself to be "resolutely on the side of Marxism," considers this passage to be a "concentration of real history" which reveals "the meaning of that history more than all the researches of the sociologists and the economists."

changed. But, in all cases, it offers the comforts of patriotism in place of the concrete problems of development."* We can therefore doubt the perspicacity of Chou En-lai who declared, after a 1964 tour of several African countries, that "revolutionary perspectivies were excellent for the whole of the African continent."** The truth is that, if socialism has not been able to create a revolution in the former empire of the tsars, which has a strong statist and administrative tradition and had already begun the process of industrialization, it seems hardly likely that conditions necessary to make socialism truly revolutionary will be realized in the countries of the Third World. In such countries, socialism is only a borrowed term, sometimes accompanied by ineffective collectivization, which has been thrust upon peoples who are not ready for it. It is an imitation, here too, and not a solution dictated from within by their own problems. It does not furnish the solutions that are needed to enable the people to overcome their poverty and accede to political reality. It is not their revolution—that is, it is not the transformation which is the reverse side of their alienation.

It is a mistake to believe that colonization is the only cause of underdevelopment. In North Africa, for example, Ibn Khaldoun was already able, in the fourteenth century, to describe the "structural blockage"*** of Moorish society. This blockage, or prolonged stagnation, which reportedly began at the end of the Middle Ages, made possible the colonial conquests which were to come in the nineteenth century, and initiated underdevelopment. Underdevelopment is not the same thing as penury; for almost all of mankind had almost always lived in penury until the be-

* Yves Bénot, *Idéologies des indépendances africaines.* Maspero, 1969.
** Quoted by Albert Meister, *L'Afrique peut-elle partir.* Seuil, Paris, 1966, p. 318
*** The expression is that of Yves Lacoste, in *Ibn Khaldoun, naissance de l'histoire passé du tiers monde.* Paris, 1966.

ginning of the phenomenon of growth. Penury itself, in effect, takes care of its own demography. But underdevelopment is a modern phenomenon, and it is due to the "sanitation revolution" which gave an impetus to demography without providing a corresponding economic development. In Europe, demographic growth follows, rather than leads, economic growth, scientific knowledge, the industrial revolution, and the sanitation revolution. There, resources increase as the population increases, and growth in both cases has the same cause: applied science. But that is not the case in the Third World. Underdevelopment, therefore, can be traced equally to two causes: structural blockage and colonization. If Europe had not intervened, the nations of the Third World could have evolved or fallen apart in their own way—though it is hard to imagine what that way would have been. But, once exposed to technological civilization, they were condemned to become either an active and creative participant in it or to disappear. Japan is one of the nations who realized this.

This new departure does not presuppose merely the borrowing of western technology, but also the reconstitution of the social, cultural, and political conditions which made that departure possible in the first place. Many of the rulers of the Third World have not grasped this fact. They seem to believe that massive infusions of credit and technical assistance into traditionalized societies will be enough to bring about economic progress.* Such progress, however, presupposed a political metamorphosis, and not merely an imitation revolution—which is most often a simple *coup d'état* carried out by the military and, for the occasion, referred to as "socialist." Cultural originality

---

* On this subject, see *l'Idéologie arabe contemporaine*, by Abdallah Larroui (Paris, 1967); also, *L'Afrique peut-elle partir* (pp. 221–22, note) by Albert Meister (Paris, 1966).

does not consist in warming over the past. Certainly, the world of tomorrow should not impose a uniformity of life styles. A new kind of diversity should be born, but it must be a diversity that results not from dependency upon a tradition—which, quaint as it may appear when viewed from without, is not nearly as comfortable when lived from within—but from freedom and creativity. It must be a freely chosen diversity, and not one that is set up as a tourist attraction.

I have no intention of denying the right of a people to cultural originality, or their right to a diversity of cultures and life styles. But I must say that the practice of denouncing the uniformity of technical civilization in the name of traditional cultures, or of life styles inherited from ancient systems of production and social organization, seems to me to be erroneous. Uniformity will not be conjured away by evoking the past, but by the growth of individual creativity which has become possible with the advent of technical civilization and of liberal societies —regardless of the opinions of the detractors of the latter. The very existence of those detractors, in fact, constitutes an example of what I am saying. The life styles taken from our pre-industrial past have been, in every respect, corroded, permeated, or repressed by the products and practices of the societies created by the industrial revolution. The only question remaining is that of whether the older societies will be content to subsist on the crumbs from the table of the new societies, or if they will become creative in their own right. In the first hypothesis, they will become more and more dependent on machine societies, but under their most useless aspects, while preserving a past which will become weaker and weaker and more and more nega- tive—so that they will end up as it were, living in an atmos- phere of sorcery lubricated by Coca-Cola. In the second hypothesis, cultural originality will begin to emerge in accordance with the facts of modern life, and the people of these societies will share, not merely in the leavings of the industrial societies, but also in their vital forces.

On the whole, the charge of uniformity in industrial societies may be accurately described as superficial. A superior technique, a superior product, has always replaced all others as soon as its existence became known, because people have preferred it to all others; and the reasons for that preference are so obvious that one cannot pretend to be unaware of them without seeming naïve. Except for a rich man "roughing it" out in the woods somewhere, no one insists any more on cooking over a wood fire rather than with gas. Tools of stone disappeared everywhere as soon as metal tools became available; and they did so without the help of any "deceptive advertising." It is to be hoped that the newest printing techniques, the best construction material, and the most effective means of transportation will also be accepted as quickly as possible, for they conserve human effort while producing a superior result. Uniformity, therefore, in that sense, is a benefit.

The same thing does not hold true, of course, of cultural uniformity—which is often more constraining in older and more traditionalist societies than in those which are more highly evolved. Technological plenty, in fact, opens the door to the formation of unexpected cultural minorities (of which the hippies are one example), to the diversification of life styles and—to choose at random— of artistic creativity and of styles in clothing. Because of technological advances in the United States, American products, American techniques in the use of space, and even American customs, have rapidly invaded countries of related industrial levels, to the extent that we now speak of the "Americanization" of Germany or of northern Italy. It is true that when we are in Germany we can believe that we are in the United States; but when we are in the United States we do not necessarily have the impression that we are in the United States. The multiplicity of life styles in that country is, in a sense, more protective than in Europe, because those styles are differentiated within the framework of an industrial society rather than being remnants of the past. One can live one way in Arizona, and a completely different way in New York, or in California, or in Maine—although everywhere that life style will be equally modern. The choice is not between the Paris subway and a restored monastery in Burgundy. American diversity is not merely defensive in nature. (Anyone who believes that man's sole refuge is in the past, and regards an urban, mechanized civilization as somehow lugubrious, has never had to spend a Sunday afternoon—preferably during the winter—in a village of Brittany or of Emilia.)

Finally, it should be noted that the Americanization of the world does not result only from American technological superiority, but also from the use of the esthetic imagination, which is more pronounced in the United States than anywhere else in the world, in the plastic arts, new musical forms, in the audiovisual arts, in furnishings, in the dance, and in the theater. It can be argued, of course, that the prototypes of contemporary architecture and contemporary furnishings were of Scandinavian or Italian origin. Even so, the fact remains that the Americans, and not the Scandinavians or the Italians, tranformed these prototypes into commonplace realities. They made of them a style of decorating, a standard of comfort and of esthetics, both in private homes and in public places, in kitchens and in offices. They articulated, in effect, an "art of living" that is much more accessible, and much more real, than

its European counterpart, for all the latter's aristocratic
(and mythical) pretensions. The sole support of cultural
diversity will henceforth be technological uniformity; and
it will be a cultural diversity which aims, not at preserving, but at discovering. The minorities of the future will
be constituted on the basis of choice, and not of custom.

In the past, the diversity of cultures was balanced by
the uniformity of individuals within those cultures. That
is, individuals were created by cultures. In the future, cultures will be created by individuals. The cultures of the
past, although they differed among themselves, created
individuals who resembled one another. Henceforth—and
the process has already begun in the United States—individuals, on the basis of their affinities, will regroup to
create cultures which will no longer be wholly conditioned
by a system of production. We tend to forget too quickly
the despotism exercised by our traditional cultures—the
prisons which we called villages, tribes, parishes, corpora-
tions, and families.

It is true, of course, that every civilization, every group—
even the most humble and the most barbarous—has acti-
vated, in one way or another, an aspect of human potential
which, in other societies, has been repressed, or even
allowed to remain dormant. But it has never been possible to change culture without changing society, unless
one was, like Montaigne, one of those rare and privileged
beings who was in a position to observe and compare
various usages. One of the effects of world revolution
must be precisely to free the individual from cultural slavery
within the group in which chance has caused him to be
born. This will lead, in effect, to a planet-wide social
uniformity, and to a cultural polymorphism, governed by
choice and discovery, within that society. Consequently,
the society in which revolution has the best chance of

taking place at present is the one in which that double movement is taking place; that is, tension between socio-economic uniformity and cultural polycentrism—the latter resulting from a multiplicity of initiatives and not from the juxtaposition of traditional beliefs and ancestral customs imposed upon the individual.

It is difficult to see how a revolution capable of transforming the Third World politically and psychologically, culturally and socially, as well as economically, can take place unless there is first a cultural revolution, and unless this is followed by massive global aid (with no strings attached) from the developed countries—which leads us back to our original conclusion, for it presupposes a new kind of revolution in the developed countries themselves.

Chapter 7

FROM THE FIRST WORLD REVOLUTION
TO THE SECOND WORLD REVOLUTION

CURRENTLY, the meaning of the term "revolution" has been stretched to cover all sorts of minor agitations and frustrated intentions. When a people rise up to fight for their independence, against foreign oppression—as in the "Algerian Revolution," or in the "Hungarian Revolution" of 1956—these are not revolutions, in the proper sense of the word, but insurrections. A man is not necessarily a revolutionary when he fights to defend his life, or to escape from a prison. I might even say that external danger has the effect of retarding or hindering the authenticity of revolutionary evolution; for that evolution must have, as its principal motive, the intention of recasting totally the organization of society and the system of human relations. As we have seen, a war of national liberation may coincide with a purely revolutionary program (this was the case of the first American Revolution); but it may also be completely innocent of any revolutionary characteristics so far as the results are concerned, even though it may have made use of the methods and phraseology of revolution in its initial phase. Extremely violent insurrectionary movements—for example, the Paris Commune of 1870—run the risk of being incapable of assimilation by a society as a whole, when that society is not ready to translate such progress into viable institutions. This is often the case when a movement of insurrection coincides with the collapse of a regime, and when that collapse is due primarily to defeat in a foreign war. In such instances, the precarious condition of the state allows the insurgents to seize the centers of power, or at least to occupy government buildings, with deceptive ease; but this in no way implies that the majority of the community is ready to accept radical and definitive changes. In such a situation, one of two things may happen: either the insurrectionary minority will retain the centers of power only so long as these latter are inoperative, and will lose them when national life begins to revive and organize itself (this is what happened to the Paris Commune), or the insurrectionists will retain power, but, when confronted by a society everywhere in retreat and incapable of carrying out the wishes of the government, they will feel themselves justified in establishing a dictatorship. And, of course, once a dictatorship begins, it cannot, by definition, stop being a dictatorship—as witnessed by what happened in Russia after October 1917. When the state becomes no more than a device for preserving the state, then it matters little what its origins were. It is, in any case, totalitarian, and therefore reactionary. It is a mistake to think that Stalinism is a betrayal of Leninism. Neither Lenin, if he had lived, nor Trotsky, if he had remained in power, would have acted any differently from Stalin. All of their writings, all of their actions, and all of their speeches between 1917 and 1924, reflect the practice and the theory of a thoroughly Stalin-style dictatorship. They began in January 1918 by dissolving, with the help of the army, the Constituent Assembly set up by elections—elections in which the Bolsheviks had received only one quarter of the votes. From that moment, as Rosa Luxemburg has pointed out so well in *The Russian Revolution,* Lenin and Trotsky began from the principle that they knew the minds of the people better than did the people themselves. As Lenin remarked at the Tenth Party Congress, held in March 1921, the Party "alone is capable of grouping, educating, and organizing the *avant-garde* of the proletariat and of all the working classes—that *avant-garde* being the only force able to offer opposition to the inevitable oscillations of the petite-bourgeoisie." And Trotsky, on the same occasion, added that "the Party is compelled to maintain the dictatorship, regardless of temporary wavering, and even regardless of the transitory hesitations of the working class."

In one is willing to distinguish between a revolutionary undertaking and a revolution, if one is willing to judge revolution on a basis other than that of fads, if one can believe that the only real results are long-term results, if one is willing to qualify as "revolutionary" only those concerted and permanent transformations which mark the passage from one civilization to another (for the term has no meaning when we apply it to the least little change)—if we are willing to do all those things, then it is possible that history can provide us with an idea of what a world revolution should be. Except for the revolution that we are expecting (or that we can hope has already begun), there has been only one other world revolution in modern history. And that was the revolution

which consisted in the political transformations that were
effected during the second half of the eighteenth century
in England, in the United States, and in France. The
English roots of those changes go back further than that,
to the seventeenth century; and the consequences of it were
opposed in France and on the entire Continent during the
whole of the nineteenth and twentieth centuries. But
even the retrogressions, the restorations, and the coun-
terrevolutions took place within the framework provided
by the new civilization which had been born of that first
revolution. Authority henceforth found its source in those
subject to authority, or rather in those who delegated
authority; the contractual concept replaced that of divine
right, or of the right of the strongest; the power of the
law took the place of personal power; an egalitarian society replaced a hierarchical society; a separation was
effected between state and church; knowledge and, in general, culture were freed from political and ecclesiastical
control. All of these things, however precarious they may
have been, and no matter what the degree of hypocrisy
with which they were put into practice or of brutality
with which they were sometimes suspended, served to re-
model the political life of the world. And that revolution
was, in any case, the only revolution ever to keep more
promises than it broke, and to create a world that more
or less conformed, or at least was comparable, to its original ideals. In other words, it was the only revolution, up
to the present, to succeed.

We must be prepared to be generous when we judge the
success of a revolution, for it is a remarkable accomplishment even when a revolution manages to create a
society that is not diametrically opposed to the one that it
set out to create. In the case of the first world revolution,
and despite all of its failings, we may fairly say that more

of its programs were translated into reality than were not. This is, at the very least, true for those regions which were at the center of that political tranformation. In other regions, it may be noticed that application was more theoretical than practical, for, as has often been observed, juridical and representative democracy seems to be able to function with a minimum of probity only in those cultures in which that democracy has been formulated or with which it is historically associated. Nonetheless, it is striking that the vast majority of societies which had previously acquired or perceived a concept of the state, experienced the first revolution as a new political prototype, and the consequences of that revolution as irreversible. Everyone imitated it, even if only superficially. The totalitarian regimes themselves took refuge behind constitutions and electoral farces, while declaring that the relatively honest elections of other countries were comedies. Open attacks against the principles of the first revolution, as against those in the Nazi, claimed to oppose them on their own ground, by superseding them with a more effective and more meaningful system of representation. The same thing holds true, although in another context and with more honorable intentions, but for analogous reasons (and identical abuses), in the case of the "democratic centralism" of the dictatorship of the proletariat. The complex of events at the end of the eighteenth century, therefore, created a universal frame of reference, even in the eyes of those who wished, and still wish, to be free of it. Everything considered, we can conclude in all prudence, after the lapse of two centuries, that the first revolution *really took place*—which is very rare for a revolution. So far, it has been the only revolution to succeed in that regard.

With respect to the second world revolution, it is clear

that it can have only one goal, on which all other goals, however numerous, must depend. And that single goal is the establishment of a world government. Just as the first world revolution consisted in substituting institutions for the despotism of rulers in the domestic affairs of the state, so, too, the second world revolution must consist in replacing despotism with institutions in the area of international relations; or, more accurately, it must consist in the abolition of international relations. On that, depends all else, including the establishment of economic equality and the abolition of social classes.

Chapter 8

THE BIMILLENNIAL TERROR AND THE END OF FOREIGN RELATIONS

THE EXPRESSION "world revolution" means, simply, revolution; for the revolution of the twentieth century must, of its nature, be world-wide, or it will not be a revolution at all. The meaning of the term "the revolution of the twentieth century" is equally clear: the revolution that will solve the problems of the twentieth century. Such problems are not hard to identify, and I should mention a few of those upon which not merely human progress but human survival itself depends: we must eliminate the threat of atomic suicide; we must enforce disarmament and put an end to war; we must stabilize the birth rate; we must equalize the standard of living; and we must protect and make use of the earth's resources in accordance with a unique plan of conservation and development. Even this preliminary list is sufficient to make clear that the problems involved can be solved only on a planetary scale, and by a world government. World government is the only possible goal of a revolution today, as it is the only goal which can make a revolution feasible. And this government must be constituted in such a way that relations based upon association take the place of those based upon domination, so that the material and intellectual resources of humanity may be placed in a common stockpile accessible to all men.

There is nothing more naïve than the accusations of political naïveté brought against all projects aimed at the establishment of a supranational authority, because nothing is more limited than the substantialist or essentialist concept of nationalities which says that the shapes of nations are eternally inscribed "in the very nature of things." The proponents of that concept forget that the modern state and nation were born of the first world revolution, and that they were built on the ruins of a variety of systems founded on feudal, ecclesiastical, provincial, corporate, familial, and military links, all of which emanated from sources of power, and from a distribution of power, which are not almost unintelligible to us. To the men who existed in that particular "nature of things," however, these systems seemed indestructible. French "foreign policy"—an expression contradictory in itself—is today the last refuge of political archaism, the preferred playground for the narcissistic game enjoyed by outdated statesmen. It is a game in which these men take all their regressive impulses and compulsions and refashion them into fantasy situations: rivalries, competition, tricks, perfidy, shows of force, armed clashes, vainglorious ritual, the wholly useless ceremony of official visits, the sanctioning of humiliations inflicted or received, of insults and homage, and of the losing or the saving of "face." All this rigmarole is irrelevant to the basic decisions which man must make.

Moreover, it tends to distract men from the serious questions that should occupy their minds. It is clear that the nation-state henceforth can serve only to polarize the most regressive tendencies of people and their rulers, and that it favors the selection of rulers from among the most aggressive, cynical, and unscrupulous sort of men—that is to say, from among those who are least capable of understanding the world as it is today and of ameliorating its condition.

If it is true to say—by inverting a formula of Clausewitz's—that foreign policy is war begun by other means, then we can conclude that the abolition of what we call foreign policy will be one of the essential components of the future world revolution. And it will also be the key to all the other changes that constitute that revolution.

Foreign policy is, in effect, war, in the sense that there is no plausible foreign policy that does not imply the threat of war. "Diplomatic relations" are ineffective unless they are one side of a two-part alternative—the other of which is war, or at least a nonmilitary version of war, such as the breaking of alliances, sabotage of international conferences, verbal aggression, radical devaluation of monies, excessive tariffs, expulsion of foreign nationals, prohibition of air travel, and so forth. But now, for the first time in history, it is no longer utopic to say that we must put an end to war; because, for the first time in history, the end of war has become a necessity. As Proust observed, disease is the only doctor who can exact obedience from a patient. Man of the post-1945 period is the first who has been forced to face the possibility that he may, as a species, disappear from the earth. And when man's only choice is between a necessary peace and a collective suicide, then the chances of the former are relatively good. We cannot, of course, ignore the possibility of a racial death-wish. This phenomenon, described by the psychoanalysts, is a device by means of which we transfer our own aggressivity to someone else and then, imagining that we are threatened by him, we begin making threats ourselves in order to provoke him to attack us in the hope that he will kill us. In modern societies, however, the death-wish has been controlled to the extent that it is not a serious obstacle in relations between individuals; and there is no reason to believe that the same thing could not be done regarding relations between societies.

Certainly, we should not ignore the "secondary benefits" of our Proustian disease. The existence of "foreign policy" is a cause of stagnation, or of withdrawal. By strengthening the paranoia of nationalism, and legitimating the most reactionary regimes and the blindest trends in public opinion, foreign policy has always been the principal obstacle to every revolution, or the chief means of neutralizing the results of revolution. Danger from without, or "international conspiracies," furnish governments with the pretext for postponing permanent problems indefinitely, in favor of the will-o'-the-wisp of artificial crises. It also serves to perpetuate conservatism or dictatorship in the name of public safety. Moreover, nothing is easier to conjure up —or really to create—than a foreign menace. Human aggression and the taste for self-destruction which it conceals, the oversimplification of reality made possible by the *idée fixe* that one is being persecuted, the psychological relief provided by that oversimplification, and the intellectual sloth which it encourages, all make it easy to mobilize the masses in support of a mission which is as obsessional as it is evanescent—and all the more so since four fifths of mankind has no source of information other than the state which governs them (or claims to govern them). We should not be surprised, therefore, that, since 1945, there has been an armed conflict on the average of every five months.* Nor should we be surprised to see specialists in the phenomenon of war emphasize, unceasingly, the incredible disproportion which exists between the "objectives" of wars—even when those objectives are attained, which is rare—and the losses which they entail in every area; or even when we see them emphasizing the discrepancies between the importance of the reasons which justify war, and the insignificance of those same reasons, which becomes so sadly evident, after it is all over.** Most, if not all, foreign policy therefore finds its source in political pathology. For there is such a thing as political pathology, even though interpretations of history which are formulated in the light only of economics, or of the imperialism of economic hegemonies, have not taken it into account. Psychology and psychosociology have demonstrated the political "awareness" has had little influence on that pathological causality.*** Only

* The figure has been computed by George Thayer, in *The War Business*, New York, 1969.

** On this subject, see the words of Gaston Bouthoule, especially *Les guerres, La guerre,* and *Avoir la paix.*

*** See Konrad Lorenz, *An Aggression*, New York, 1966. The book was published in German as *Das Sogenannate Böse, Zur naturgeschichte der Agression.* The literal meaning of the German title is "The Pretended Evil: A Natural History of Aggression." The book was translated into French under the debatable title of *L'Agression, une histoire naturelle du mal* (1969), despite the fact that Lorenz's whole point was that there was no such thing as natural "good" or "evil," no such thing as morality or immorality in biological phenomena, and that man, consequently, should never condemn without correcting, but should observe in order to neutralize—just as a man with a heart condition, or a hemophiliac, takes his illness into account in the organization of his life. See also Robert Ardrey, *The Teritorial Imperative* (1966); Gérard Mendel, *La Révolte contre le père* (1968); Alexander Mitscherlich, *Die idee des Friedens und die menschliche Agressivität* (1969).

institutions, therefore, can neutralize it, and make evident its pathological character.

In relations within families, between cities, religions, professions, competing firms, and between the social classes that compose a national group united under one legal system, it has long been recognized that one's beliefs, however reasonable, do not justify taking the law into one's own hands. It is difficult to understand, therefore, how such a subjective principle could have gained the force of law in international relations. This is a paradox, and one which Jean Monnet—a contemporary who has had ample experience with this monstrosity—has denounced with eloquence: "I am astounded by the difference between the principles that we apply within our frontiers and those that we apply beyond them. At home, men discovered long ago how to resolve conflicting interests between divergent interests, and they no longer make use of force to defend themselves. Rules and institutions have created a statutory equality. At the international level, however, nations behave the way individuals would if there were neither laws nor institutions. In the final analysis, every nation is determined to retain its sovereignty; in other words, every nation arrogates to itself the right to be both judge and prosecutor in its own case."* This state of affairs will seem as incredible to men of the future as a father's right of life and death over his children seems to us—a right which, nonetheless, has been perpetuated in the form of modern warfare.

The second world revolution will therefore consist in putting an end to that notion which is the source of all evil: the notion of *national sovereignty*. It is impossible, from a purely practical standpoint, and even abstracting

* Quoted by Anthony Sampson, in *The Anatomy of Europe*, New York, 1969.

from moral considerations, for us to continue to allow the application of a principle according to which a state may, for example, massacre or imprison a part of its population, or reduce it to starvation, without anyone being allowed to intervene, because it is forbidden "to interfere in the internal affairs of another country." This same principle formerly allowed a father to kill his children, without outside interference, for every man was master in his own house. The first consequence of a pseudo principle of internal omnipotence is to allow any oligarchy to torture or to abuse a people as though that people were its property—and then to create a disequilibrium which results in international conflict. Moreover, and directly at the international level, it is equally impossible, from the practical standpoint, to allow any of the historically accidental groupings that we call nations to endanger the entire human race under the pretext of exercising its so-called sovereignty. And this is indeed the case in our age of "domino-theory wars" and atomic or bacteriological warfare.

Only *multilateral* agreement on reciprocal controls, leading to planetary multinational law, will allow us to escape safely from this absurd situation. *Bilateral* accords must be avoided like the plague, for they are only the framework for warlike foreign policies, local hegemony, or imperialistic domination either fantasized or real. General de Gaulle, for example, had a horror of anything multilateral in diplomacy, and it was his desire to substitute bilateral *ententes* for every international contract—*ententes*, it goes without saying, in which France occupied, at least in de Gaulle's mind, the paramount position. It was an archaic concept. Since the dawn of time, man has had ample opportunity to observe that a bilateral international contract is no contract at all, since it confers, by its very nature, the right to a unilateral denunciation of the agreement. It is hardly flattering to our political self-esteem to consider that a man who had never grasped that essential fact could pass himself off as a diplomatic wizard. If anything, it demonstrates how politically primitive we French are at the level of world affairs. If, for instance, a cabinet member said that employees who were injured on the job should go begging in the streets for charity, rather than receive Workman's Compensation, he would be laughed out of office. But when the same thing happens in foreign policy, we see nothing ridiculous about it.

What would be most natural for the world today would not be national sovereignty, but international sovereignty. The most common objection is that international sovereignty would merely disguise a relationship of domination—as does the "equality before the law" of citizens in the nations of today. I would say that that is true. And I would also say that the objection is stupid, since it is premised upon the confusion of several phenomena which are, in reality, quite distinct. Because there are real social injustices in our society, it does not follow that it is wrong for me not to be allowed to murder someone, or to blow up my apartment building and kill everyone in it. Like civil society, world sovereignty alone is not sufficient for security; but it is beyond a doubt necessary for it. For someone to be in good health, he must, first of all, be alive. And that is precisely the case here. Thus, we can say that the notion of a world government is no longer utopic; for the time has come to conclude that either world government must come into being, or nothing else will remain in being.

Beyond guaranteeing survival and security, however,

world government will have an intrinsic revolutionary momentum, for it will oblige mankind finally to focus its attention on qualitative problems rather than on quantitative power relations. Up till now, in effect, every step forward, every improvement, has been interpreted in terms of power. If there is a revolution in a country, everyone says that the country has become *stronger*—and the country in question then feels that it has to prove that it is, in fact, stronger. So primitive is mankind that we are unable to speak of success in other terms.

The criteria of success for the communist countries ceased long ago to be communist. They have become instead those of the most hidebound *Realpolitik*, weighted down with such things as "nuclear capacity," and wholly irrelevant to a new spirit of human freedom. The space flights of the Russians, and the satellite launched in April 1970 by the Chinese, have been hailed as great accomplishments; and so they are. But they are great accomplishments only in the same sense that the first rockets, launched by Hitler in 1944, represented a great accomplishment. The choice offered by Hermann Goering to the German people, of "guns or butter," has been decided by the communist regimes in favor of the guns. And they made that choice not only because of a predilection for guns, but also because they were unable to produce any butter. We have only to remember Mussolini's Italy to recall that the sacrifice of a people's standard of living to the tools of the politics of power, and the offer of the comforts of chauvinism as a drug against hardship and against the temptation to complain, is the classic policy of dictatorships. Domestic fiascoes, and the periodic necessity of putting down revolts in satellite countries, leads to the giving of priority to the military arm of the state. It is easier to become a great nuclear power than to become an affluent society; and the less one is the latter, the more necessary it is to become the former. In the case of the Chinese satellite, the domestic propaganda machine must have had a field day, for the Chinese people are very poorly, if at all, informed on world events. It will be recalled, for example, that their government did not even tell them about the American landing on the moon. Seven hundred million Chinese, having no frame of reference, no doubt exaggerated outrageously the importance of their satellite in the history of the conquest of space. (It is even possible that the younger Chinese, who are unaware of the Soviet satellite launching of 1957, thought that theirs was the very first satellite.) It would certainly be necessary for the communists to build up their military power in order to defend socialism —except that there is no socialism. But, on the other hand, if there were true socialism, its power of contagion would be so great that there would no longer be a need for such great military power. Given the contagion even of the mirages of socialism, we can see how easily and quickly real socialism would spread over the world. But, since real socialism does not exist, we are left with only the reality of military might, which has become a means without an end.

This military might is but another name for foreign policy. It leads only to suicidal wars in which ideological factors are secondary, and has become more than ever the source of human poverty. On the one hand, it absorbs the resources by means of which we could put an end to poverty; and, on the other, it increases poverty. Today, between 7 and 8 percent of world-wide production is consumed by military expenses—the equivalent of a growth rate that would be enough to save the countries of the Third World, and even to give them a growth rate higher than that of most of the developed nations. This percentage, it has been estimated,* is approximately equal to the combined annual income of the peoples of Latin America, the Middle East, and Southeast Asia (including India and Pakistan).

Such expenditures are fatal, not only directly, in the properly economic domain, since the underdeveloped countries allocate to their military budgets an average of twice the amount that they receive in aid from developed countries, but also indirectly, by taking funds away from things as essential as education and public health. The world is full of edifying examples of the freedom of people not to control their own destinies. Egypt, with a population two-thirds illiterate and a per capita annual income of $150, spends 10 percent of its gross national product on arms—to which is added military aid from the Soviet Union. China, with a per capita income of $150—i.e., equal to that of Egypt and Bolivia, though lower than that of the Ivory Coast or of Iran—devotes between 8 and 9 percent of its gross national product to military spending.** Obviously, the populations so gravely compromised by these expenditures, both now and for the future, have no opportunity to participate in these decisions—decisions which are literally killing them—nor even vaguely to suspect what is involved. As the ignorance of the people is systematically preserved, the omnipotence of the oligarchs can only increase.

This ignorance is less pronounced in some of the developed countries in which one can still criticize excessive military spending. But, up to the present, such criticism

* These are the figures for 1967, taken from a report of the U. S. Arms Control and Disarmament Agency, the results of which have been published in "The Cost of World Armaments," by A. S. Alexander, in the October 1969 issue of *Scientific American.* The figures for 1970 would be even higher.

** These figures apply in 1966, and should be revised upward for 1970.

has not been sufficiently strong to have any effect upon
the investments of the principal military powers. Even
so, some nations have understood what is involved. Japan,
where, up to now, every proposal for the creation of a new
army has been blocked by public opinion, spends four
times as much on education as on arms; which explains,
to a large extent, Japan's imminent accession to the rank
of the nation with the world's highest standard of living.
Canada, the Scandinavian countries, Belgium, the Netherlands, Luxembourg, Italy, and Switzerland have had,
though to a less extent, either the wisdom or the good
fortune to spend more on living than on dying. Most of
the industrial and education nations, however, are destroying themselves with their military budgets. Despite
their comparative wealth—an average annual per capita income of $2300—they refuse to alleviate the ills that are
overwhelming them, and they are sacrificing, for the sake
of military equipment, the resources that would enable
them both to cope with their internal tensions and to fulfill their responsibilities with respect to the underdeveloped
nations. The countries with a positive rate of growth, even
though they contain only a third of the world's population,
are not content with figuring into their reserves some 90
percent of the world's funds, which have been earmarked
for that purpose. They have even increased the military
expenditures over a two-year period (1965–1966) by 35
percent for the NATO nations, and by 29 percent for the
nations of the Warsaw Pact. Obviously, mankind, which
already has enough atomic bombs to wipe itself out several
hundred times over, is determined to spend $400 billion
more for arms during the period 1970–1980; that is, an
amount equal to what was spent in the whole world, with
results that are well known, between 1900 and 1970. To

put it another way, they are going to spend the equivalent of the gross *world* product for ten years.*

Only a revolution within the developed countries, who are also the military powers, can put an end to this political madness. Or, to put it more accurately, and in terms free of value judgments, revolution is becoming inevitable because of the growing number of vital problems which have been rendered insoluble by the great waste of resources. This revolution can only take place—which is not the same as saying that it must necessarily succeed—in those countries where the government has not had the prudence, or the means, entirely to abolish freedom.

* Computed on the basis of the gross world product of 1965 and of the value of the dollar in the same year. Cf. the October 1969 issue of *Scientific American*, and also *The Year 2000* by Kahn and Wiener. Since no one seems particularly impressed by the cost in human lives, I will confine myself to mentioning them in a note. It is estimated that, in the course of the last decade, about 700,000 persons were killed during China's internal struggles; 500,000 died as the result of the Indonesian massacres; and 250,000 lost their lives during the civil war between Nigeria and Biafra. In Vietnam, 42,000 Americans have been killed, along with 110,000 South Vietnamese and 650,000 North Vietnamese. To these figures must be added those of the deaths in the Algerian war of 1960–1962 and in the Middle Eastern conflicts. Altogether, the number of people killed in this period of "peace" is roughly equal to the number of dead during the First World War. At the beginning of 1970, about one fourth of the sovereign states of the world were engaged in either an internal or a foreign war. The figures are those of Geoffrey Kemp, of the Massachusetts Institute of Technology, quoted in *The New York Times* of June 1, 1970.

Chapter 9

FROM FREEDOM TO SOCIALISM:
A One-way Street

THE HISTORY of the past century demonstrates
that the capitalist democracies can evolve toward socialism
much more readily than socialist regimes can evolve toward
democracy. In other words, the transition from political
democracy to economic democracy is possible, but the
transition from economic democracy (the latter being, obviously, theoretical and nominal) to political democracy is
impossible. Moreover, the absence of political democracy
destroys the conditions that are necessary to the existence
of economic democracy. To put it in still another way: the
second world revolution can take place only in those
countries where the first world revolution has been translated into reality.

This observation often comes up against post-Stalinist
prejudices, according to which the so-called "formal" freedoms are said to have no revolutionary utility. If these

freedoms are of such little account, however, I wonder why governments are so afraid of them, and why censorship and police states are so commonplace. The fact that all citizens cannot take equal advantage of their legal freedoms is a reason to fight so that everyone may enjoy equality. It is not a reason to fight in order that these freedoms may disappear from the world altogether. Freedom, as imperfect and unjust as it may be in practice, is still the indispensable foothold of all revolutionary action. Experience proves that no internal revolution is possible under a totalitarian regime, and that such a regime will usually collapse only as the result of military disaster in a foreign war. People who say they would like to see a "hard-nosed" government installed, so that they might prove their revolutionary mettle against a worthy foe, remind one of a weight lifter who cannot lift ten pounds and asks for the two-hundred-pound weights. The most striking thing, however, is that those people who say they despise the formal freedoms are among the first to demand them as soon as they suffer the least injustice. And they are the first ones to express loud indignation when, say, a newspaper is closed down, or when there is the least irregularity in judicial or electoral proceedings. I am not saying that they are wrong in doing so. But it should be clearly understood that one cannot protest when the victims of Franco, or of the Greek colonels, or of the Moscow courts are deprived of rights that are customary in British courts, and, at the same time, revile English-style democracy as a form of antiquated liberal corruption.

Criticism of "liberalism" seems to hinge on the confusion of economic liberalism with political democracy. Such misunderstandings indicate the hardening of a society's political arteries, and lead to a choosing up of sides on the basis of paradox rather than reality: liberalism *versus* revolution, reformism *versus* socialism, intelligence *versus* reason, democracy *versus* elections—and other metaphysical flourishes generally more in vogue in drawing rooms than in prisons.

The choice, in fact, has never been between such abstract terms, and the historical process has never taken place in such terms. If it is true that the results of the first world revolution are inadequate, then the second world revolution must complement them, not destroy them. Liberty is not the middle-class luxury described by the false disciples of Marx and by the true disciples of Marcuse. Liberty is, or should be, the life's breath of socialist civilization. It is empirically false to say that "the worker has nothing but contempt for a liberty which allows the intellectual to say whatever he wants in his diary; what he wants is the consolidation of revolutionary gains." Economic liberation will never take place without free criticism; and "revolutionary gains" have been destroyed, not by an enemy from without, but from within, by the absence of democracy. All of the clandestine critical writings that have recently come out of the U.S.S.R. on this problem are based on the fact that the absence of democracy has caused the failure of socialism in the realm of the *practical*—abstracting from all moral considerations. They leave to specialists the question of whether a socialist economy is intrinsically inferior to a capitalist economy. Here, again, speculation on the alleged virtues intrinsic to the two systems is purely metaphysical; which means that we can say nothing certain in that regard, because there is no recorded instance of a socialist economy ever having existed. If there is a practical failure, it is because no economy, of whatever kind, can function when it is regulated by an oligarchy which makes all the decisions, and which reacts violently to attempts at participation on the part of interested parties. In other words, if there the Soviet system has been a failure—and the consensus seems to be that it has been—it failed for political reasons.

A capitalist country is likewise in jeopardy when its leaders wrap themselves in the cloak of authoritarianism and make their decisions secretly, in the dim light of their sovereign incompetence. And, at that point, capitalism, too, is up against a dictatorship. No economy can survive in a technological age unless it is constantly being challenged and renewed by the collective intelligence of its citizens. "There has been a general lowering of creative potential among representatives of all the professions"— such was the verdict spoken by Sakharov, the academician, Medvedev, the historian, and Tourtchine, the mathematician, in a report presented to Messrs. Brezhnev, Kosygin, and Podgorny in 1970.* They emphasized several times "the close relationship between the problem of technical and economic progress and that of freedom of information," and they deplored the fact that "bureaucracy, administrative isolation, unimaginative attitudes toward one's work, and the absence of initiative [in short, the classic symptomatology of decay in any economy] are becoming more and more common in scientific and technical organizations."

Scientific and technological progress itself was born of the right of free inquiry, of the right of free criticism— rights which were aspects of the liberal revolution. There will never be a socialist society unless it allows the pursuit of scientific and technological progress; and therefore, there will never be a socialist society unless it allows cultural freedom. The connection between those two elements is not accidental, but essential. Socialism cannot exist without scientific progress because socialism cannot exist in

* Published in France in *Le Monde*, on April 11, 12, and 13, 1970.

penury. Poverty automatically causes the rebirth of inequality. The only possible form of socialism is that of "scientific socialism"—not in the sense in which Marx and Engels understood that expression, but in the sense that a society in which scientific activity exists can become a socialist society. Moreover, that scientific activity must enjoy complete freedom of research. In the Soviet Union, science is preoccupied with purely military objectives, and with goals that are worth more in prestige than in practical results; in other words, Soviet science is controlled by political and nationalistic aspirations. This is also true, of course, although to a less extent, of the capitalist countries. The situation is particularly shocking in the Soviet Union, however, because of that country's comparatively low standard of living, and because the expenditure of vast sums for military and political objectives means that the Russian people are being deprived of even the basic necessities of life. The most frequent complaint of Soviet scientists is that fundamental research (and not only applied science, which is less susceptible to dogmatic control) is hobbled by the doctrinal imperatives of dialectical materialism—as demonstrated by the Lysenko affair. This situation is a particular handicap to biological research, since biology has more ideological implications than does physics; and it entails almost complete paralysis so far as economics, sociology, history, and psychology are concerned. The second world revolution will therefore consist in large part, and perhaps essentially, in the establishment of intellectual and informational autonomy with respect to political power. That is the key; and, under this aspect also, democracy is the matrix of socialism.

When Andrei Amalrik (*Will the Soviet Union Survive Until 1984?*) attempts to explain the stasis of Soviet society, he, like Sakharov, is almost forced to fall back on

Tocqueville's analysis of democracy as a life style. There is a *homo democraticus*, who is created by civilization at the same time as democratic institutions are elaborated. Without *homo democraticus*, these democratic institutions are as useless as the refrigerators that we sometimes see peasants using as a sort of high-prestige closet, without ever plugging them in. "The ideas of self-rule, of the same law for everyone, of individual freedom, and of individual responsibility—which is inseparable from individual freedom —are almost completely unintelligible to the Russian people," writes Amalrik, "and even the word 'freedom' is understood by the majority of people as being synonymous with 'disorder.'" If the forty-or-so pages of Amalrik's book continue to be read for a long time, it will be because they are the converse and the refutation of *The Prince*, and a demonstration that politics is not a problem of power and of the state. Varga, a Marxist economist, was well aware of the link between social catalepsy and the repression of collective intelligence. In his (posthumously published) indictment of Soviet social management,* he wrote that "official ideological propaganda often causes, in many citizens, a fatal case of indifference to ideological

* *Le Testament de Varga*, Paris, 1970. Varga was People's Commissar for Finance in Hungary in 1919. After the abolition of the communist regime in that country by Bela Kun, Varga was summoned to Russia by Lenin, and he remained there until his death in 1964. He maintained his contacts among Russia's rulers, and his election to the Academy of Sciences in 1939 shows that, at that date, he was not a member of any opposition. Varga's *Testament*, however, evidences disagreement with policies of which, for fifty years, he had openly approved. Such documents as those of Varga and Sakharov and their friends remind one of the secret letters of Fénelon, Vauban, or Saint-Simon to Louis XIV. Moreover, the same stratagem is used to make their criticism palatable: their purpose is to serve the *true* glory of the King, and to return to the *true* Marxism-Leninism—whereas, in fact, the logic of the arguments presented leads, in one case, to the rejection of the monarchic principle, and, in the other, to a rejection of "democratic centralism" and of the whole mythology on which it is founded.

devaluation, of skepticism, and even of cynicism." What Amalrik's essay adds to this is the pervasive presence, throughout his argumentation, of his experience of the Soviet moral universe, and his description—couched in carefully neutral, and almost indifferent, terms, like the composition of a schoolboy—of the great sterile mass of people and of the state, who, like two blind men, stand staring at each other, thinking that they are really seeing each other, as though they were still gifted with sight. This inability to change one's attitudes, both among rulers and among the people, reveals once more the essential, non-accidental nature of the link between political dictatorship and social reaction. When Andrei Amalrik was arrested in May 1970 it was not "accidental," but "essential," and he had foretold his arrest with as much certitude as the astronomer who foresees the appearance of a comet.

It is a mistake to believe that the communist countries will, or can, gradually open up to democracy after they have consolidated the bases of socialism. The truth is that the longer dictatorship continues, the more fragile those bases become; and the more fragile they become, the more necessary is dictatorship. To be sure, there was a certain amount of "liberalism" under the Khrushchev regime, but a liberalism so circumscribed that we must stretch a point to call it liberalism at all. It was under Khrushchev that the Hungarian revolt was put down, that Imre Nagy was executed, that Boris Pasternak was compelled to refuse the Nobel Prize, that experimentation in painting was condemned (by Khrushchev himself), and that dozens of death sentences were handed down against Jews accused of being "parasites" and "corrupt." Under Khrushchevian liberalism, the number of political prisoners and of labor-camp inmates remained the same as under Stalin. People are quick to remind us that Soviet intellectuals, such as

Aleksandr Solzhenitsyn, enjoyed a certain amount of freedom under Khrushchev. That is true, so far as it goes; but
it does not go far enough. The fact is that not a single
work of Solzhenitsyn's was ever published in book form
(that is, in a form available to the general public); and
that the maximum amount of "freedom" accorded this
author was to allow him to publish *One Day in the Life of
Ivan Denisovich* in a magazine (*Novy Mir*). On a comparative basis, I am perfectly willing to admit that there
was more freedom in the U.S.S.R. under Khrushchev than
under Stalin; but hardly enough to warrant our speaking of
"Khrushchevian freedom" in absolute terms. Moreover,
what freedom there was under Khrushchev was quickly
suppressed by the regime that followed him. The concept
of "liberalization" can appear only in political civilizations
already familiar with alternate periods of freedom and dictatorship, with regimes founded on law and regimes
founded on force. In the history of western Europe, people
who lived under despotic regimes preserved the notion of a
democratic society. Sometimes, they had had no direct
experience of democracy themselves, but had only read of
it in histories of Greece and Rome—which had been synopsized into a form of battle between despotism and freedom. Every despotism, therefore, from the Caesars' to the
Nazis', has always been perceived as the *loss* of an earlier
freedom. To this perception was always coupled both a
belief in eventual liberation and the subliminal image of
an earlier, liberal regime—even though the latter might
assume the modest form of a municipal exemption or a
provincial parliament. The ability to believe in the eventual
suppression of the Greek colonels or of Franco, of Pétain
and Mussolini, presupposes the existence of a large group
of citizens who have been influenced by a different political
society, to the extent that they have a clear idea of what

they want to substitute for their present form of government. Thinking along these lines, one is tempted to believe that there exists, in every authoritarian society, a considerable number both of citizens who recognize that society as authoritarian, and of rulers who are ready to grant freedom of expression—but only after, say, the price of meat has reached a reasonably low level, or a particular military-diplomatic offensive has been brought to a successful conclusion. To believe this is to forget that, in these societies, the people have no historical or theoretical frame of reference for criticism, other than authority; and therefore they lack the psychological resources which are a prerequisite of any liberalizing process. These psychological resources are present, however, among the rulers of societies in which dictatorship does not exist for its own sake, but in order to suppress something else. In such cases, the rulers are perfectly willing to let their people speak out on subjects that are of no political importance, and so long as this freedom is not a threat to their own power. Such was the phenomenon of the "liberal Empire" of Napoleon III, in which the government took a strictly empirical and practical view of censorship. At the other extreme are such men as Louis XIV, or Brezhnev, or Mao, whose view is entirely metaphysical. King Louis' suppression of religious freedom (by the revocation of the Edict of Nantes), and Brezhnev's edict forbidding abstract painting, had nothing to do with politics. Their aim was to preserve the integrity of the monarch's and the oligarch's self-image.

It is illusory to believe that liberty can be added to a social system the way madeira can be added to a sauce, at the last minute and just before serving it up. For a twenty-year-old in China, the term "liberalization" can have no meaning, except perhaps as a synonym for "revisionism," which to him signifies critical opposition of any kind. When a Chinese youth hears the term "cultural revolution" (a term coined by Stalin, incidentally, and then taken up by Mao), it means only one thing to him: the destruction of all opposition, and the silencing of all criticism. What makes this system a bad one is not an esthetic or a moral consideration, but a purely practical one: a society that works this way must inevitably fail— if only because it will be rejected as a model by anyone who knows any other way of doing things. The difference between an authoritarian government and a democratic government is that, under the authoritarian one, the facts are the only things that enjoy freedom of speech, and the people must wait for them to speak—that is, they must wait for a catastrophe—before being allowed to ask where they are going. Under a democratic government, however, the people are allowed to foresee disaster, and, if necessary, to adopt new means or a new goal. The trouble with failure, as a sign that we must change our direction, is that it comes too late. There are safer indications. Above all, we must know what is the "threshold of perception" of disaster within a society; we must know the danger signals, and we must know the controls by means of which this information can be translated into political action. There have been some examples of people who were completely deprived of this threshold of perception (the ancient Gauls, for instance), and who paid for it by being annihilated. In most societies of the past, however, the repercussions of failure were felt, not by the government, in the form of political change, but by the people, in a worsening of their condition. And the most notable achievement of the first world revolution was that it reversed that process.

Societies that did not undergo the first world revolution have found it impossible to evolve toward political democracy from their state-controlled economies—economies which are supposedly a sort of antechamber to true socialism. On the other hand, it is hardly debatable that societies affected by the first world revolution have shown a tendency to evolve from political liberalism toward economic socialism. (To accept that, we must be willing to define as "socialist" the process by which the rights of labor are increased, and the arbitrary power of capital is reduced.) The history of the social movement in Europe and in the United States, from the beginning of the nineteenth century, shows a tendency toward socialism within liberal societies. The history of the labor movement is too well known to bear repetition here, but I would like to recall one particularly significant fact: the oldest form of trade unionism is that of Britain. This means that the modern methods of acquiring and defending the rights of labor were first conceived and put into practice in the country where political liberalism had its start. There was a connection between the electoral revolution (the Reform Bill of 1832) and the founding of Robert Owen's Trade Union, in 1833, which was the first workers' cooperative in history. There was a reciprocal link between the Trade Union Congress of 1868 and the formation and growth of the Labor Party in the years following. Even today, British unions are among the most powerful in the world; and Britain is one of the few European countries where the general strike is not illegal. British unions did not consider themselves counterrevolutionary when they formed a political party in order to acquire power and work within the framework of parliamentary institutions. And, for that reason, most of the specific social gains of the modern labor movement were realized in Britain before any other country; and they were usually realized more completely there than elsewhere.

This latter fact is sufficient indication that political freedom is a potent weapon in the battle for economic equality. If further proof is needed, it may be found in the fact that the evolution of the liberal societies during the period 1815–1970 has led, despite some setbacks, to a steady decline in inequality, and to the strengthening of labor's rights. If we take any country which had parliamentary democracy for most of that period, and if we compare that country's situation in 1850 and 1950, or in 1900 and 1970, we find it hard to believe that we are still talking about the same country. There seems hardly any resemblance between the rights of labor at the beginning of that period and at the end of it. And the same thing holds true of women's rights, children's rights, and employees' rights.

It is so widely accepted that political democracy tends toward economic democracy that totalitarian states find it necessary to suppress the former in order to prevent the latter. The strategy of such states, as we know, is to win over the workers by paternalism and populism, and by coming out against bourgeois "corruption." And, at the same time, to revoke the rights of labor: the right to unionize, to assemble, to strike, to petition, and to vote. It is also wrong to affirm, as many leftists and radicals are doing today, that liberalism and fascism are identical; and this holds true even of "repressive" liberalism, in the meaning that Marcuse attaches to that term. According to the intellectuals who preach that politically irresponsible thesis, liberal capitalism is even more dangerous than fascism, because it has the *appearance* of democracy. It is sufficient to note here that, in those countries that have known real fascism, no one subscribes to such a thesis. Italian workers, for example, know only too well that a strike under Mussolini was very different from a strike under de Gasperi.

Revolution consists in transforming reality. The real counterrevolutionaries are therefore those self-styled revolutionary purists who reject all change on the pretext that it is not complete, and that it is taking place "within the system." Under those conditions, there would never have been any social changes at all. When Nero passed a law giving slaves legal recourse against the abuses of their masters, the Romans would have had to reject that reform, one imagines, because it was taking place "within the system," and because it was predicated upon the existence of slavery. And today, if we followed that same reasoning, we would have to reject the concept of profit-sharing, since it gives workers a certain control over real profits and therefore over the direction of the economy, because profit-sharing operates within the system. That profit-sharing can be a factor in changing the whole system never seems to occur to these Platonic revolutionaries. They are too accustomed to thinking of things as pure forms and separate essences, all neatly filed away in separate categories. And, worst of all, they do this in the name of history and of dialectics. A wise man once said, "There is an alphabetical ignorance, which precedes learning; but there is also another kind of ignorance, which we might call doctoral, that is created by learning and replaces the alphabetical ignorance which has been destroyed."*

The vague outlines of the second world revolution have already been sketched out by the first; and the first world revolution is the tool which makes the second one possible and which specifies its content. The goals of the second revolution existed, in embryo, in the political climate created by the first; the establishment of economic and social equality in, and by means of, cultural and personal

* Montaigne, *Essais*, I, 54.

liberty; and the guaranteeing of security by allowing the participation of all citizens in political decisions. The accomplishments of the first world revolution are the *sine qua non* for the second; for, before a brain can be developed, there must first be a nerve cell.

Chapter 10

VIOLENCE AND REVOLUTION

FREEDOM SHOULD not be viewed only as a relationship between the individual and his rulers. Seen under
that aspect, freedom is an abstraction—and an abstraction
that has become a target in the academicians' criticism of
liberalism. The relationship between the governor and the
governed is only the framework for something much larger,
for a complex of elements which includes, above all, participation by the collective intelligence of the people in the
governing (or the subversion) of a society. It may be that
this was the secret of the "break-through" by the countries
involved in the first world revolution; for those countries
allowed their governments to be influenced, in one way or
another, by the creative contributions of a large number of
its citizens; and the governments then made use of those
contributions in the management and modification of
public affairs. Therefore, to speak of freedom only in terms

of "guarantees" between people and government is like describing a great laboratory in terms of its unions and its pension plan. Certainly, unions and fringe benefits are important to the laboratory's researchers as an affirmation of their rights. But in today's societies, every citizen is assuming more and more the role of a researcher; that is, of a seeker after truth; and many people suffer as much because "nobody is listening" to them as they do because they are underpaid. Moreover, they feel that they are being underpaid because nobody is listening to them. A society in which nobody is listening is an oligarchy—and a society ruled by oligarchs will dry up and rot away because, statistically, four or five men can have fewer new ideas than a hundred million men. When a citizen cannot criticize a worthless political or economic policy without being sent to prison, then the whole of that society is in danger—not only because one of its members has been subjected to "an intolerable violation of the rights of the individual," but also because a workable alternate policy may have been lost and buried forever. Revolution, obviously, must include socialization of the imagination.

Freedom must be defined first of all as revolutionary productivity. And it is for that reason that censorship —the withholding of information by the state—is incompatible with revolution. Without productivity by the collective intelligence of the people, there can be no new solutions. We often tend to forget that revolution involves the creation of new cultural models and of a civilization superior to the one in which we live. The first world revolution, it will be recalled, did not stop at distributing land among the peasants.

If we conceive of freedom as an abstract quality, we are led to an equally abstract conception of violence; for freedom and violence can only be defined in relation to each other. Where strikes are legal, for example, to go out on strike is to make use of a weapon from the arsenal of rights and freedoms. Where strikes are not legal, however, to go out on strike is to have recourse to violence. The history of insurrections, upheavals, and civil wars teaches us that some fundamental social transformations have been brought about without violence, or with very little violence —in England, for instance—and that some extremely violent undertakings have resulted in no basic changes at all. There are comic-opera revolutions in which many people are killed; and there are true revolutions without bloodshed.

We often hear the question "Can there be a revolution without violence?" There has always been a great deal of debate over the matter, but never a satisfactory answer. Somehow, when people start discussing the question of violence and revolution, they tend to fall back on the same tired old arguments that everyone has already heard. No one seems willing to stop arguing long enough to allow for the accumulation of documentary evidence and the interpretation of results already obtained. One of the most striking characteristics of European civilization today is that the extreme accessibility of documentation, the ease with which one may acquire classic works and pursue the study of history, had not led us to draw any lessons from the experiences and controversies of the past. And, strangely enough, the intellectuals are bigger failures than anyone else in this respect. The accumulation of knowledge, instead of gaining time for us, seems to have brought on an attack of amnesia, a seizure of Montaigne's "doctoral ignorance," a fatal tendency always to begin from zero— or, worse still, to remain at zero. At the same time, some of the stereotypes of the past, half-images stripped of their context, still weigh upon us: the Paris Commune of 1870, the Revolution of 1917, the Chinese war of revolution. And, of course, that is all we need to complete the paralysis of our imagination. So, we do not learn from the past; instead, we imitate it.*

Our most frequent error is to confuse the means and the end. Both Machiavelli and Montaigne observed that, by diverse means, we come to the same end. We might add that we also come to the diverse ends—opposite ends— by the same means. The first thing that must be said about violence is that, in itself, it is neither revolutionary nor counterrevolutionary. Historically, however, it has been more a weapon of counterrevolution than of revolution. It has served more to oppress than to liberate. The three modern European states of the extreme Right—Mussolini's Italy, Hitler's Germany, and Franco's Spain—all had violent beginnings. Franco came to power by means of a military insurrection against established authority. Hitler and Mussolini made use of terrorism and armed bands of thugs, although they both rose to power within the letter, if not the spirit, of the law, and with popular support. And, to the Left, the upside-down revolution of Stalinism has kept itself in power by means of violence. History contains many more examples of the success of repressive violence than of insurrectional violence. One must be very careful, therefore, in recommending the use of illegal action against established authority; for established authority itself has a pronounced tendency to make use of illegal means to rid itself of its adversaries. And, generally speaking, established authority is in a better position to benefit from such an operation.

Violence has no more revolutionary or counterrevolutionary content than, say, a scalpel has medical content. To believe that the indiscriminate use of violence will

* See Max Gallo, *Gauchisme, réformisme et révolution*, Paris, 1968, and *Tombeau pour la Commune*, Paris, 1971.

advance the cause of revolution is like believing that we can obtain a miraculous cure by plunging a scalpel into any part of the body. Real revolutionary activity consists in transforming reality, in making reality conform more closely to one's ideal, to one's point of view. That transformation can be achieved only through revolutionary *means*. Sometimes, that means is violence; sometimes, it is not. In any case, violence, as a means, does not always signify the same thing. To publish an antigovernmental tract is considered "an act of insurrection," or of violence, in some countries, and it is perfectly legal and commonplace in others. The strike of French customs officials in May and June 1970 was generally regarded as a violent act, even though it consisted merely in the literal interpretation of customs regulations. Its effect was more "violent" than the bombing of a train would have been, or an armed attack against the Élysée Palace by those same customs officials. The strike resulted in the paralysis of international transports at the French frontier, the loss of a great deal of money by French commerce and industry and also by foreign countries whose economy depends in part on trade with France. By hitting the established authority in France where it hurt most, the customs officials were able to obtain a much more satisfactory response to their demands than would have been possible if they had simply gone around breaking windows. Moreover, they achieved something else: they focused attention on the absurdity of customs barriers in western Europe and, thereby, gave Europe a push in the direction of unity under a supranational authority—which I, personally, consider to be one of the goals of revolution.

Within that context, we can easily see that violence does not necessarily consist in illegality. We might even say that the more legality there is in a society (that is, the

more a society is permeated with the results of the first
world revolution), the more violence should be subtle and
directed against well-chosen and meaningful goals. Violence is most effective when it is used within the existing
legal situation, because then it can obtain a maximum
number of concessions while leaving itself open to a
minimum of retribution. The best example of this is the
action of Martin Luther King in the United States; for
King's "nonviolence" was, in fact, a form of violence. To
boycott the public transportation system of an entire city
is much more "violent" action than to beat up a policeman in the Place de la Concorde. There is an apparent
nonviolence which is really more violent than an act of
spectacular brutality; and political violence does not always
boil down to a punch in the mouth or a rifle shot. In an
insurrection, therefore, it is best always to begin legally,
or with a certain number of legal steppingstones—which
are precious possessions, and must be religiously preserved.
Then, if all does not go well and it seems that the enemy
will win after all, these same legalities can serve as a
means of strategic retreat, and prevent the insurrectionists
from being wiped out. Revolutionaries should always choose
strategy over tragedy. But, if that principle is to be applied,
revolutionary leaders must not be actors, but impersonal
interpreters of the men whom they represent, and more
solicitous for the interests of their followers than for their
well-being.

Martin Luther King was the prototype of the kind of
leader, of the charismatic hero: a hero whose authority
derived from popular support and from his sensitivity to
collective needs of his people. But he was a hero in the
most noble sense of that term. He was never a demagogue,
and he was always close to the blacks whose suffering and
energy he was able to channel. And, the more prominent

he became, the more he seemed inclined to self-effacement. He was resolutely opposed to any "personality cult," and he quashed any tendency toward authoritarianism in the movements he directed. In other words, he led an intensely political life, but he never made a political career out of it.

For all of that, King was a man of action. The jury that conferred the Nobel Peace Prize on him in 1964 was not rewarding him for his good intentions. In the ten years preceding the award, King had succeeded in obtaining, or in having enforced, legislation that was of capital importance for the black community of America. But he was not content merely to bring about those moral changes that are a necessary part of revolution. He also proved himself a master tactician in the organization of those demonstrations which are the milestones of racial progress in America, from the bus boycott of 1955, in Montgomery, to the march on Washington in 1957, to the great demonstration in Chicago in 1966.

The man (or his employers, as yet unidentified) who shot Martin Luther King at Memphis, in April 1968, did not assassinate merely a great orator or the soul of the antiracist movement, but a political concept. This concept was based on a coherent analysis of the situation. It was King's belief that the blacks, if they wished to achieve integration and equality, could not begin by destroying the institutions and violating the constitutional principles whose benefit and protection they were claiming. Instead, he proposed that the blacks concentrate on keeping the whites on the horns of a dilemma, a dilemma that would compel them to one of two alternatives: the recognition of racial equality, or the condonation of illegality.

King's order of battle varied according to circumstances, from day to day. Its core, however, remained constant, and centered around conflict at the local level against virulent racism in some parts of the South. It centered, too, around King's church, where his Sunday sermons often turned into political orations. When King rose to national prominence, he began adroitly to play off the federal government and the Supreme Court against the governors of the states and the local mayors. In a characteristically American paradox, it was the F.B.I. that protected King from the local police; and there were episodes that Europeans regarded as absolutely stupefying in their implications. On one occasion, for example, President Kennedy telephoned King, who was in jail in Birmingham, and then called Mrs. King to give her news of her husband.

Kennedy's interest in King and his work was not academic. In 1963 the President prepared, in consultation with King, a new voting law—a law which was passed in 1964, and signed by President Johnson. According to its provisions, blacks who wished to vote were now allowed to register directly with federal officials, and thus bypass the obstructionism of local or state officials. Such achievements provoked counterattacks by the racists and brought things to a crisis; and then, federal agencies were obliged to intervene and to send troops to the South in order to uphold the decisions that they had previously been compelled to make. Thus, for King, nonviolence was not the same as nonactivity. The abolition of segregation and discrimination in public places, in public transportation, in schools and universities, in employment—these are hardly the results of passivity.

Such has been the battle for black rights since 1954; that is, since the decision of the Supreme Court in the case of *Brown v. Topeka Board of Education*, which declared unconstitutional the maintenance of separate school systems for blacks and whites. It has been a winning battle. Today, there are 434,000 black students in American universities, out of a total black population of 22 million—a ratio higher than that of French university students to France's 50 million inhabitants. But this kind of success presupposes two things: there must be a strong constitutional consensus, and there must be freedom of the media. All the freedom marches, all the speeches and meetings, would have done little good if television had not brought them into practically every home in America. To illustrate the power of the mass media: one day Dr. King was sentenced to pay a small fine, which he refused to do since it was his intention to go to jail. At that point, the judge who had sentenced King paid the fine out of his own pocket (with a good deal of grumbling), because he knew that all the television cameras were waiting for King outside the courthouse.

Today, Martin Luther King's methods and goals are being challenged. The methods, because nonviolence itself has died a violent death, since Black Power and the Black Panthers have destroyed the constitutional consensus (without, however, losing the attention of the television networks) and replaced it by subversion. King had foreseen this imminent possibility, and warned that "riots are the language of those to whom no one listens." King's goals have also been attacked, since it is no longer certain that Afro-Americans want integration, and since many of them demand instead "a multiracial state within national unity." To attain economic and political equality while preserving cultural autonomy and emphasizing "ethnic pride," and to demand territorial independence, goes far beyond King's aims. Indeed, it goes in a direction other than that which King had mapped out. Even so, a Black Panther leader, Bobby Seale, recently declared that "the program of the Panthers is not very different from that of Martin Luther King. We have simply progressed to another tactical level."

It remains to be seen if the Panthers' new "tactical level" will end in a victory or a retreat for the black revolution. The transition to wholly illegal action makes sense only if there is a reasonable chance of being able to attain power; otherwise, it must lead to the destruction of the insurgents. But the possibility of seizing power diminishes in proportion to the complexity of society and of the existing political machinery. And, conversely, the more rudimentary the state is, the better the chance of violence to destroy it—and the less the revolutionary value of violence. Between 1946 and 1964 there were approximately 380 *coups d'état* in the world.* And their frequency is increasing: since 1964, there have been between 25 and 30 *coups* every year—but they are usually military *coups* and of questionable revolutionary authenticity, although that is one of the characteristics that the authors of the *coups* always claim most vociferously.

If we examine the effectiveness of that form of violence known as political assassination, we find identically negligible results at both ends of the scale. Kennedy's assassination, for example, brought about no changes, either in American society or in American political institutions, because the American constitutional system is too strongly integrated to be much affected by such events. In a highly developed police-military state, such as the Soviet Union, insurrectional violence would have no chance of overthrowing the regime. In a democratic state, such as Great Britain, it would have no chance either—but for different reasons. In the Soviet Union, an insurrection is technically impractical, at least for the foreseeable future. For it to succeed, it would have to be preceded by a state of greater economic disintegration than presently exists, and by an

---

* The figures are those of Edward Luttwak, in *The Coup d'État: a Practical Handbook*. New York, 1969.

about-face on the part of the military leaders. In the case of Britain, an insurrection would have no chance of winning the support of the majority of the people, because there are already a number of other ways by which the people may bring about the changes they want, and because of the differences between the social subgroups which always exist in complex social systems.*

It is true that violence can be used more easily in a democratic society than elsewhere; but it is also true that violence in a democratic society loses much of its revolutionary impact. When the law foresees the necessity of, and authorizes, various forms of opposition, then the politicial return on illegal violence is low. The best return is obtained by the maximum utilization of legal means, in conjunction with the prudent use of violence; that is, violence must cease before the reaction that it provokes becomes greater than the action that it produces. The proper mixture of legality and violence is most difficult to determine in democratic societies; but it is also in democratic societies that, once the proper formula has been found, the results have the best chance of becoming permanent. (I do not mean to imply that revolutionary changes can be brought about solely by parliamentary means in the broad meaning of that term; that is, by negotiations and agreements in which there is a winner and a loser. This idyllic concept is too easy a target for the critics of "reformism" and "liberalism," if, by those terms, we mean that the people should wait patiently until the privileged classes decide to abandon their privileges. It is a concept as clumsy as its antithesis: the abolition of capitalism in a single stroke. Capitalism has

---

* We saw an example of the way this differentiation works in the fall of 1969, when striking French electrical workers were forced to return to their jobs by pressure from workers in other industries, who had become unemployed because of the lack of electricity.

never been abolished in a single stroke, except in those
countries in which it never existed.)

The existence of social classes is based upon conflicts of
interest; and such conflicts have never yet been resolved
exclusively by the application of understanding and good
will. It is a fact, therefore, that relations between social
classes—relations that are conditioned by those conflicts
—are relations of violence, either potentially or actually.
This violence exists both on the part of those who dominate
(in which case it is directed against those who are dominated) and on the part of those who are dominated (and
who struggle against that domination). It does not follow,
however, that when the dominated classes accept a partial
victory, they are in fact acquiescing in the *principle* of
domination. If that were so, we would still have slavery.
And this mistake is committed on both sides of the
political fence. The extreme Right and the Ultraconserva-
tives think that every concession implies the immediate
collapse of the dominant system. On the Left, there is no
distinction made between Blum and a Nazi; and, from
the viewpoint of Charles Maurras' "national revolution,"
there would be no difference between Blum and Trotsky.
To a Nazi, Roosevelt was a communist; and to a communist, Roosevelt was Hitler with a smile.

It is equally untrue to say that terrorism, riots, and
guerrilla warfare are the only possible forms of violence. In
many cases, these particular forms have more negative
than positive effects. What is true, however, is that domination will not recede until it is *forced* to do so. But the
forms which that force may assume are innumerable, and
vary according to circumstances. For instance, several
industries were nationalized in France because of the insurrectional impetus which followed the Liberation, and
because the proprietary class, compromised as they were

by their collaboration with the Germans, did not dare protest too much. There was a similar wave of nationalization in Britain at the same time, in the wake of the Labor Party's electoral victory; and it went off very smoothly, despite the fact that the head of the defeated Conservative Party was the embodiment of triumphant patriotism. There has therefore been a shift in British public opinion in favor of this kind of force; but the same thing does not hold true in France, where the Right always manages to circumvent force, or to neutralize its effects— unless (as happened in 1936) fear prevents them from doing so.

There is a great deal to talk today about a new kind of violence, "urban guerrilla warfare." In France, we have heard the spokesmen for the leftist movement known as the Proletarian Left compare the attitude of France's ruling class *vis à vis* the other classes to that of the Nazi toward the French during the Occupation. That is obviously an overly pessimistic view. The truth is that Frenchmen got along much better with the Germans in 1940–1944 than they get along among themselves right now. I am not attempting to justify guerrilla warfare by saying this. On the contrary, my purpose is to point out to the theoreticians of the Proletarian Left that Resistance terrorism and the *maquis* were not strong enough even to drive out the Germans, without the help of foreign armies.

Relations between dominators and the dominated have not yet reached the breaking point—i.e., the point where insurrection and its variations would be the only possible solution. Consequently, there are still many ways in liberal societies by which coercion may be used to the benefit of the dominated. (Such situations are as numerous as there are degrees of oppression, because in liberal societies, no one is *totally* excluded from the exercise of power.) The use of pure force, by definition, tends to benefit the strong rather than the weak, for people are classified as "strong" or "weak" in proportion to the amount of force that they are able to apply. It is true that, in societies where the people are not protected by law, the oppressed man's only means of attack are terrorism and armed violence; but that does not mean that terrorism and armed violence are necessarily successful, even in those circumstances. The degree to which such undertakings are dangerous is clear from the fact that the police always accuse dissenters of "terrorism" and "armed violence"—unless the dissenters beat the police to the punch and accuse them of the same thing. The validity of a revolutionary method cannot be judged only by the degree of injustice that is protested, but also by the attainability of the goal that is sought.

Finally, and above all, revolution is only partly the accomplishment of militant minorities; it is, and must be—if its results are to endure—the occasion for multiple changes at every social level. The story that revolutions are made by a handful of conspirators is based upon the precedent of the Russian Revolution, and it proves nothing. Its only reason for existence is to flatter the egos of revolutionaries who regard themselves as specialists, and who believe that revolution is a monopoly within which there is a Hollywood star system. These revolutionary "leaders" talk a lot about the spontaneity of the masses, but they are quick to condemn that spontaneity if it does not harmonize with their own ambitions. They are outraged when the people demand reforms that do not have their approval; and they say that a worker is "alienated" when he goes beyond the guidelines that they have set up. This reintroduction of a power elite into a revolutionary framework is one of the principal reasons why revolutionary activity in Europe lags so far behind that of the United

States. It had engendered intellectual dogmatism, encouraged people to take refuge in the past, and produced both theatrical strategies and tactical flops. European culture is a censorship culture, both on the Right and the Left. An event must be repeated, or denied, or interpreted, until it conforms to an approved model of events. (By a curious coincidence, it was de Gaulle's aim also to remake France to the point where it would resemble Richelieu's France; and the most intransigent of his opponents shared this aim, except that the France they proposed was that of the Paris Commune.)

The purpose of revolution, however, is neither to titillate doctors of the law, nor to fulfill prophecies. By definition, revolution signifies an event such as has never taken place before; an event that comes to fruition by ways that were hitherto unknown in history. When we use the word "revolution," we must necessarily speak of something that cannot be conceived or understood within the context of old ideas. The stuff of revolution, and its first success, must be the ability to innovate. It must be mobility with respect to the past, and speed with respect to creation. In that sense, there is more revolutionary spirit in the United States today, even on the Right, than there is on the Left anywhere else.

Chapter 11

ANTI-AMERICANISM AND THE AMERICAN REVOLUTION

ANTI-AMERICANISM is one of the great psychological phenomena of our time. Moreover, it is a phenomenon that must be taken into account in that mixture of fact and hypothesis which allows us to conclude that America faces a future of revolution, and that the American Revolution will be the one most likely to bring about the changes that the modern world needs.

It is difficult to determine the causes of anti-Americanism without describing its symptoms. The two factors are inseparable, even though the symptoms are amenable to analysis, while the causes are only a matter of conjecture. In analyzing the symptoms, we must distinguish two basic kinds of anti-Americanism. There is one kind, which is founded on reasonable criticism and on precise data, and which is justifiable in relation to political goals and clear value judgments. And there is another kind of anti-Americanism, characterized by a quality of obsession, and by the rejection of any attempt at rational appraisal—or even irrational, but intelligible, appraisal. By an "irrational, but intelligible, appraisal" I mean a point of view which, even though it may be partisan and subjective, may still be modifed by a presentation of facts. For there are partisan positions that have a form; and there are partisan positions that have no form. In the first case, whether we are talking about arguments or about sympathies and antipathies, there are clearly distinguishable pros and cons. In the second case, the pros and cons frequently exchange places, because they are based only on emotion, which itself is changeable; and so, with arguments for and against something being used interchangeably, the only consistent element is the person's determination to preserve his grievances intact.

Let me give an example of what I mean. Early in 1970, I visited the United States for a few weeks. (That was not a long time—but it was long enough to make me forget, or at least to make me less conscious, of some of the absurd themes so familiar in Europe.) Upon my return to France, I was astonished by some of the responses to my comments on America. I said, for instance, that the United States seemed to be in the process of change; that protest, dissent, and opposition to authority and to the past seemed more pronounced there than anywhere else. The answer I got was: "The assassination of Martin Luther King, and the trial of James Earl Ray, prove, beyond the slightest doubt, that America is a fascist power."

This kind of answer has several causes. First of all, it did not contradict what I had just said (even though it was intended to do so) because political assassinations and dubious trials are hardly incompatible with a revolutionary situation. Quite the contrary. It springs, I think, from an unwillingness to use facts as the basis of opinions, or to regard certain kinds of facts even as remotely possible. It also reflects a determination to regard, as specifically American, certain situations that, in fact, are less serious in America than elsewhere. There is something wrong when we hear the whole of America condemned on the basis of a single questionable trial—especially when that condemnation takes place in the country of the Ben Barka affair; or when we hear America condemned for violence, in a country where the O.A.S. flourished. One wonders what a French leftist would say if we put Pompidou's words into his mouth, and then criticized him for it? What would be the reaction of an Italian communist if we tried to prove that Italy is fascist by citing the position of a socialist leader? The Frenchman would answer that the May uprisings and M. Pompidou are two different things. And the Italian would answer that, after all, not all Italians belong to the Socialist Party. Yet, in the case of America, we are unwilling to make the same distinctions. The European Left refuses to admit even that there is an American Left—let alone that it is more powerful than the European Left. We seem to be incapable of recognizing anything but Rightist tendencies. And that inability makes it possible for one of France's most intelligent and sophisticated political commentators to say: "In the United States, Mr. Nixon's only serious rival, for the moment, is the racist Wallace."*

Even if we are willing to make allowance for a sort of long-distance alarmism—in Europe generally, but especially in France—which consists in boiling Britain down to Enoch Powell, and Germany to von Thadden, and in overestimating the Right in other countries so that we can swallow our own Right, we must still admit that

* André Fontaine, in *Le Monde*, June 21–22, 1970.

this view of American history has been expurgated or censored. When we invoke the name of Joseph McCarthy and say that he was the only representative of the real America, we are ignoring the fact that McCarthyism was finally beaten—just as Barry Goldwater was overwhelmingly defeated in 1964. The truth of the matter is that the extreme Right has never been successful in America. (Even McCarthyism was a sort of garden-variety Nazism of which the Germans would easily have been able to rid themselves in 1931.) We should ask why and by what means Americans have been able to apply the brakes to Rightist trends. And by "we," I mean the liberal democracies of Europe, which have never been conspicuously successful in preventing the rise of fascism. But, instead of looking for reasons, we continue to dig out examples of Rightist phenomena in America, and then to juggle conclusions and to ignore the final outcome of events. Let us imagine, for example, that a book about the Dreyfus affair was published in America, and that the book ended with Dreyfus' first trial and his discharge from the army, so that the reader was never told the whole dramatic story of the man's eventual exoneration. That is not very different from what Europeans do when they pretend that there is no American Left—whereas, in fact, the American Left is probably the world's only hope for a revolution that will save it from destruction.

In America, when discussing the manifestations of dissent—refusal to serve in the armed forces, refusal of research centers to work on military projects, the solidarity of many young people with the blacks, with the Indians, and the Puerto Ricans, and so forth—I often heard this question: "Yes, but is this all leading *to organized activity?*" (Up to that point, the only organized activity that I had seen was the "underground railroad" to Canada, for the benefit of men escaping from the draft.) It was obvious what was meant by "leading to organized activity." The young men who asked that question were really saying that they would like to qualify for the semifinals of revolution by organizing their own socialist party, with conventions, committees, election of officers, theoretical guidelines, and coalitions with other parties. What I found most surprising in all this was that the most conspicuous merit of the French movement of May 1969 had been that it was a nonorganized and nondirected explosion of revolutionary sentiment, which had somehow managed to shake up the bureaucrats and disturb the ideological routine. Why should unorganized activity be a virtue in Europe, and a vice in America—especially when this new type of revolt was not born in Europe, but in America, where it has not been smothered under the weight of pseudo-Maoist rhetoric and where it is continuing to get results? The movement of dissent in America has disconcerted the powers-that-be in politics, in economics, and in culture. Nonetheless, it is not precisely an economic upheaval by an oppressed class, or a political movement by an opposing party, or a cultural rebellion by a subversive school of thought. Certainly, dissent includes these three aspects. For example, students supported the California grape workers' strike by not allowing grapes in campus dining rooms—a move which severely affected the grape growers, since university dining rooms feed about six million students, professors, and staff members. Politically, they transformed Senator Eugene McCarthy, then the most outspoken opponent of the Vietnam war, into a national and an international figure during the 1968 presidential primaries. Culturally, they have abandoned traditional American moral values, rejected the idea of intellectual coercion in education, begun a sexual revolution, and invented a life style (in dress, the use of drugs, music, contempt for material possessions, and sexual attitudes) which runs directly counter to the middle-class ideal of respectability. When dikes break, it is impossible to keep the water from spreading. In the same way, dissent always affects more than one area. Thus, the California grape workers were not merely exploited workmen; they were Mexican-Americans, and their economic struggle was identified as that of an oppressed minority. The students, in support of the strikers, agitated not only for higher wages, but also for Spanish-language classes in public schools, and for Spanish-language intelligence tests for Mexican-American children. The Chicanos, as Americans of Mexican descent are called, are English-speaking American citizens, but they wish to preserve their own culture, their "ethnic identity." They refuse to be domestic colonials, as several regional minority groups have become in France. This idea of a national community is not so much a part of the dissent movement as it is part of America itself; for Americans have always regarded their country not as a "unit," but as a community, where the cultures of minority groups are preserved and assimilated rather than destroyed.

On the whole, American dissent has had much better luck than the European counterpart in attaining well-defined goals. Once again (because it is important), I cite, as an example, the research centers that have refused to undertake, or to continue, projects of military value. On the other hand, university dissent in America did not succeed, as it did in Europe, in completely closing down the schools. But then, American higher education has not been weakened either by change or by its inability to change. The approximately twenty thousand students at Berkeley continue to receive an education that is regarded as the finest available in America—and probably in the world; and this in spite of the fact that the Sorbonne-like immensity of the institution and of the plant causes problems similar to those of European universities. In other words, American dissent has been able to avoid one of the great dangers of change: the destruction of the object of change before change can be affected, in which case the revolution leads to underdevelopment and, thereby, destroys itself.

American dissent therefore fulfills (despite some of its negative aspects) one of the necessary conditions for revolution: it is contesting moral values, modifying alternatives, and, in general, criticizing cultural standards. Moreover—and this is very important—dissent is doing all this within the context of the American situation as a whole. And, in any event, its effectiveness is undeniable, and superior to that of dissent in France.

One day, I told a Frenchman about American student participation in the California grape strike. For a second, it looked as though he were going to be deprived of his image of America as reactionary. But then he came up with an answer. "Nonsense," he said, "they're probably eating grapes from Israel." The utter absurdity of exporting grapes from Israel to California never occurred to him, let alone the fact that having Israeli grapes available in California would have put the California grape growers in a worse predicament than ever. What he was concerned about was identifying his two pet hates: Yankee capitalism, and Zionist imperialism—the latter being a disguise of the former. Following that line of thought, it became clear that the students were supporting the Chicanos in order (somehow) to enslave the Palestinian Arabs. And the logical circle was complete. I should point out one thing: the man I was talking to was not some drunk I met in a bar, or an uniformed Maoist crank, but a well-known political journalist—a man who is thought of as a "great reporter."

According to this man's thinking, the imperialistic pro-Zionism of the United States does not prevent Americans from being rabidly anti-Semitic at home. And this anti-Semitism is but one aspect of the over-all racism which is, as every good European knows, the chief characteristic of Americans. In fact, shortly after leaving my great-reporter friend, I ran into a lady novelist of the extreme Left, who asked me, in a tone that implied she already knew the answer, whether there was "still as much anti-Semitism in America." I answered that I had always heard that there was a certain amount of anti-Semitic discrimination in America, in certain clubs and restaurants, but that I had never seen any during my visits there. She counterattacked vigorously, offering to show me a list of some twenty or thirty New York restaurants where people with Jewish names were automatically refused reservations. To avoid a fight, I answered that her information might be correct, but that it did not coincide with my own impressions of America. And I added: "Moreover, there is a law in New York against discrimination in public places. If anyone does discriminate, he can be taken to court." And there the discussion ended. It was not until I had a chance to think about what the lady said that I reached the boiling point. There are presently six million Jews in America. Why are they there? Because they, or their parents or grandparents, were chased out of Europe by persecutions, or by pogroms at the beginning of the century in Russia, and in Hungary, Romania, and Poland. They are in America because in Europe we had Hitler, and the racial laws of Vichy France, and roundups of Jews in France. In fact, at the very moment that that woman was lecturing me on anti-Semitism in America, there were signs of a strange public delirium in France, in the form of rumors: a "rumor from Orléans," a "rumor from Amiens." The content of these rumors was that women in those two cities had gone into Jewish stores— and had never been heard from again.

Barbarous, bloody, fanatic, narrow, repressive Europe. Europe, which has always practiced anti-Semitism in all its forms, from subtle harassment to planned genocide; Europe, which climbed to the pinnacle of anti-Semitism in our own time, and, during the Second World War, killed almost twice as many Jews as are presently living in the United States.* And I had listened politely to a European, a Frenchwoman, as she condemned American anti-Semitism in the allocation of reservations in a restaurant.

Now long after that encounter, I went to see a documentary film of Frédéric Rossif's, entitled *Pourquoi l'Amérique?* (Why America?). If one can take the film at face value, the whole history of the United States between the world wars is the story of Prohibition and its effects, the judicial crime of which Sacco and Vanzetti were the victims, the clubbing of workers by the police, and the F.B.I. Only the most absurd comments by American public officials were included in the film; and they were described as stupid by the commentary, and greeted by loud laughter from the audience. Roosevelt's social reforms were mentioned, of course, but no one was allowed to understand how they came about, because nothing was mentioned about the leftist principles of Roosevelt's advisers. Nor was anything said about the state of public opinion which allowed Roosevelt easily to be re-elected three times. Indeed, it was im-

* The number of Jews who died in German concentration camps, plus those who were massacred elsewhere in Europe.

possible to believe that he could have been elected even once, since the country described in *Pourquoi l'Amérique?* was populated almost exclusively by lynch-crazed mobs of racists, brutal policemen, grotesque society ladies, and gangsters. In the sequence concerning the beginning of the war in 1939, the main emphasis was on one of Charles Lindbergh's pro-Hitler speeches, to the position of the extreme Right-wingers, and to the American Nazi Party. On the basis of history as presented by M. Rossif, it is hard to understand how the United States ended up arming and equipping the British and the Russians, as well as its own men, between 1942 and 1944. And it is impossible to understand how this crime-ridden and idiotic nation, after having intervened directly in Europe and assured the victory of the Allies, could have emerged from the war as the greatest economic, political, technological, and scientific power of the world. A strange destiny for a nation composed of brutes and fascists.

It may be that Europeans are right about America. If so, I am unable to explain why Europe, and not America, has been blessed with Hitler, Mussolini, the Moscow Trials, concentration camps, Pétainism, Franco-ism, racial persecution, the Gestapo, the G.P.U., and the political hatreds of Germany, Soviet Russia, Spain, France, and Italy. Why is it that the United States has always been able to preserve its democratic institutions and avoid fascism? And why is it that totalitarian regimes occupy the major part of European history in the twentieth century, and most of European territory today? In other words, we are being asked to believe that the causes of fascism have always existed in America, and that they are becoming more pronounced today; but, by some mysterious process, fascism itself always appears in Europe, and never in America. It is a paradox, of course; but we

have gotten too accustomed to it to realize it. Even the
political analysts do not seem puzzled by the fact that
the seed of fascism is always sown in America—and always
becomes a tree in Europe. Ever since I was old enough
to tell the difference between Europe and America on
the map, I have heard predictions of the growth of the
fascist Right in America, and of the socialist Left in
Europe. If those forecasts are correct, we are confronted
by one of the great mysteries of contemporary history.
We will never be able to understand why, in the last
fifty years, so many millions of Europeans have fled to
America to escape persecution, and so few Americans
have fled to Europe.*

Unfortunately, we tend to judge the United States and
the rest of the world by different standards. The lady who
spoke to me about anti-Semitism in New York answered
all my arguments by saying, "You can't use comparisons.
Comparisons are false in principle." Obviously, if we are
unaware of anti-Semitism elsewhere in the world, the anti-
Jewish snobbery of clubs and restaurants in New York
will seem the epitome of racism. My electric tea kettle,
if I have nothing to compare it with, appears to be the
principal source of heat in the universe. But there are
people who go further than that, and declare, once and
for all, that everything American is, by its nature, more
horrible than the most horrible thing that exists elsewhere. A film critic, for example, in speaking of a news-
clip of thirty years ago which showed a dance marathon

* There are, of course, considerable numbers of draft evaders, deserters,
and even of American emigrants to such countries as Australia. In addition, some Black Panthers and Weathermen live abroad. This is hardly
comparable, however, to the European phenomenon of mass emigration
(or mass flight), as exemplified in the exodus of Hungarian Jews, or of
Spanish Republicans. In the latter cases, it was not a question of emigrating to a more comfortable political climate, or even of finding a
better life elsewhere. It was often just a question of survival.

where the participants, after fox-trotting for forty-eight hours, were exhausted but still fighting sleep, commented: "I don't think I've ever seen anything more tragic, even in films on concentration camps."* The following example is less of a caricature: I remarked to a friend that I had been surprised at the number of ways in which Americans were able to defend their rights, and especially at the vigor with which the people made use of those means. In response to this thought, which he no doubt regarded as very unorthodox, he told me that once, in America, he had gone up to a policeman to ask directions, and that the policeman had threatened him with his nightstick. I suspect that there must have been something else going on, at the time, that my friend had not noticed. I have never observed that American policemen go around hitting people who ask for directions. Nonetheless, for my friend the policeman's nightstick told the story of the real America. And not only for him. Even though we Europeans have had more experience than anyone else with police regimes, I've noted that, in collections of photographs taken by Europeans in America, and in documentaries made by Europeans about America, there is always a picture or a clip of the cop-symbol—always with a bull neck, and always stroking the butt of his revolver.

When Europeans find themselves unable to criticize police repression in America, they turn their attention to sweets and other commodities which remind them of America. In a report on the French working-class, one reads: "Go into a supermarket . . . enormous stacks rise up, over six feet high—again a sales device imported from across the Atantic—containing cans of beer, jars of preserves, cardboard boxes . . . chocolate."** Apparently,

---

* Pierre Marcabru, in his debate with Jean-Louis Bory regarding the 1970 Cannes Film Festival. O.R.T.F., France-Inter, May 24, 1970.
** *Les Ouvriers,* a report by Philippe Gavi. Paris, 1970.

even beer and chocolate are evil when they are stacked American-style. Actually, even supermarkets in conservative societies display their merchandise in stacks, when they have merchandise to display. The symbol of commerce in an earlier, bourgeois society was the little grocery store, with its limited merchandise and even more limited variety, in which everything had its proper place on the shelves. And in which everything was proportionately more expensive. But that makes no difference. To be able to pick and choose in a store is wrong, because it is "American." And supermarkets are evil, too, because their prices are lower. "According to housewives," the report continues, "this is true [that prices are lower in supermarkets], but they end up buying more." I suppose we should advise the workers to pay more, but eat less.

Sometimes the purpose of anti-Americanism is to shore up our own sense of intellectual and moral superiority. And sometimes it indicates an unwillingness to take into account any fact that might disturb our prejudices. In the latter case, we are capable of extraordinary subtlety in coming up with unfavorable interpretations of any experience. Under this heading we can group our "proofs" of the inferiority of American culture. One day I told a friend of mine that, during a visit to the United States, I had met some very intelligent people and, above all, many different kinds of people. (That was the worst thing I could have said. Everyone knows that all Americans are imbeciles and conformists.) In rebuttal, my friend told me about an evening he had spent in California, during which he had not heard a single human voice. The only audible sounds were those of washing machines, vacuum cleaners, and lawn mowers. Even if my friend could prove to me that evenings in Castlenaudary or Pont-à-Mousson are spent discussing the *Par-*

menides, I would still not believe that his California example has a statistical value. For him, the memory of California has another value: it is a place of refuge, where he is protected from the humiliation of having to admit the possibility of a cultivated America.

A favorite target of anti-Americanism is the American politician, who is uniformly presented as a prodigy of bland self-conceit. Into this category are thrown both wheat and chaff, without distinction. There is Truman, "the haberdasher," belching out vulgarisms; and "smiling Ike," absorbed in his game of golf. In Rossif's film, *Pourquoi l'Amérique?*, one of the biggest laughs of the evening came when President Hoover was shown speaking his famous sentence: "We stand at the threshold of an era of prosperity without precedent in the history of the world"—words spoken only a few weeks before the crash of 1929. It was an unhappy choice of words, given what was immediately to follow—but neither inaccurate nor ridiculous, given what was to come ten or fifteen years later. Immediately after the Second World War the United States entered the age of mass consumption and attained a standard of living "without precedent in the history of the world." (Whether or not one likes the *kind* of life that that standard entails, is another question.) Political prophecies that are fulfilled are a great rarity; let alone political prophecies that are fulfilled in fifteen years. Therefore, Hoover's words, as disastrous as they seemed at the time, are much less so in retrospect.

Sometimes we have to depend on a twist in translation to make an American politician look appropriately vainglorious and narrow, and incidentally give a boost to the European ego. In February 1970 President Nixon submitted to Congress a 119-page report on United States foreign policy. For the first time, a detailed document on foreign affairs was used to complete the "State of the Union" address, which traditionally is devoted to domestic affairs. Having created a precedent, Nixon then announced that he intended to submit a similar report every year; and he went on to remark, at a press conference, that his report was "the most comprehensive statement that has been made in this century on the foreign policy of the United States." In Paris on February 20, *Le Monde* reported that Nixon had described this document as "the most pertinent public document published in this century . . ."* The substitution of the word "pertinent" for "comprehensive" changes the sense completely. It transforms Nixon's statement into a value judgment, and makes Nixon himself seem a man of extraordinary vanity. What readers of *Le Monde* were not told was that no other President of the United States had ever committed himself to making an annual report on foreign affairs. They were not told that the phrase "in this century" was intended as an acknowledgment that President James Monroe, in 1823, had made a similar comprehensive report. And so, a purely descriptive announcement was transformed, under the eyes of French readers, into a publicity stunt.

In the light of all this, one can understand why Jean-Jacques Servan-Schreiber's *American Challenge* aroused such fury in European "progressivist" circles. The book's thesis was that American successes were due more to intelligence than to force or to the abundance of natural resources. It was an intolerable opinion, but a strangely attractive one. And it stirred up a burning indignation—but indignation that was, at the same time, ambiguous and contradictory. That is in the nature of things; for we

* "*Le plus pértinent des documents publiés dans le siècle sur . . .*"

cannot deliberately ignore something real unless we are aware that it exists.

The most humiliating kind of defeat is a cultural defeat. It is the only defeat that one can never forget, because it cannot be blamed on bad luck, or on the barbarism of the enemy. It entails not only acknowledgment of one's own weakness, but also the humiliation of having to save oneself by taking lessons from the conqueror—whom one must simultaneously hate and imitate. It was for that reason that *The American Challenge* was virtuously denounced and, at the same time, avidly read. And this brings us to the second part of the anti-American phenomenon: a systematically unfavorable interpretation of everything American, to which is added the painful knowledge that this interpretation is worthless. When our backs are against the wall, we admit that American successes may not be pure luck, and that they may be due to the importance which both the government and private enterprise attach to basic research. But then we save face by poking fun at "American management," and by declaring that, since we reject American goals, we can hardly be jealous of American methods. In other words, the news that America has accomplished something is the signal for us to say that that accomplishment is worthless. When the American work week is shortened through automation, we say that Americans are technological slaves. When they reduce poverty, we sniff and talk about the "consumer society." And yet, the latter accomplishments are two of the secular goals of utopic or "scientific" socialism.

The intensity of the battle in America for the conservation of nature and for the restoration of the environment, for clean water and pure air, was the object of curious interpretations in Europe. In the United States, it is a popular cause in which everyone is interested. In Europe, however, and especially in France, the "battle" is limited to a few timid quarrels about such things as the preservation of natural parks. I commented on this once to a French professor visiting an American university. He said, "Yes, of course, but the American government really can't do anything, because it would have to fight the trusts." The trusts notwithstanding, in January 1970 President Nixon devoted a good part of his "State of the Union" message to ecology. Shortly afterward, a law was passed obliging the airlines, no later than 1972, to install devices which will reduce jet exhaust fumes by 75 percent. The French professor would no doubt say, "Yes, of course, but that is only to take the people's minds off the Vietnam war." We might reply that one safety valve is as good as another, and that if the national craze for sports has not made people forget the war, nothing will. And what happened, in fact, was that the peace demonstrations went on as before. And, what is even more striking, the Weathermen started their bombings. Finally, there came a tornado of protest, in the course of which people were wounded and killed, over the invasion of Cambodia by American troops. The explanation is that, to American youth, antiwar protests and antipollution protests are one and the same thing. The government cannot do away with one by listening to the other. The French professor mentioned above (with whom I still correspond) refuses to accept this. To his way of thinking, there *must not* be a revolutionary trend in America. And therefore by a curious logical twist not uncommon among leftists, he concludes that the battle for the well-being of the people, of which conservation is a part, is essentially nonpolitical. In the meantime, however, he has abandoned the theory that the conservation movement was a diversionary tactic of the government. He writes: "Public officials support the battle for the environment because elections for the Senate and for a large number of state governorships will take place at the end of the year, and not because they are concerned about the health of the people." I should have replied, "Then let's have more elections." Instead, I answered by return mail: "That is impossible. The elections are entirely rigged through the manipulation of public opinion by the mass media."

Nothing is easier than to interpret evidence so that it will answer to one's own needs. As another example, I offer the following dialogue (a synopsized version of an actual conversation):

FRIEND: Americans are both uncultivated and prudish.
REVEL: I beg your pardon. They read more than we do, and I have the sales figures to prove it.
FRIEND: That may be, but it's because most of the books they read are obscene.

Here is another:

FRIEND: Americans are not interested in the problems of the blacks. They don't even try to understand them.
REVEL: But Eldridge Cleaver's *Soul on Ice* sold more than a million copies.
FRIEND: If so, they were sold to blacks, and not to whites.
REVEL: A television network has just been set up, just for blacks.
FRIEND: Its purpose is to alienate the blacks even more. The blacks don't know how to read even now, because they've been kept illiterate.

In all fairness, I should point out that several minutes elapsed between each of these mutually contradictory statements, and I have given only the broad lines of the conversations. Nevertheless, it is not an exaggeration to say that this is precisely how the anti-American mentality functions.

I read the following headline in the March 15–16, 1970, issue of *Le Monde*: "Bombs kill four people in Maryland and New York." The story which followed was about the first Weathermen bombings—the Weathermen being an extremist fringe of the dissent movement who, along with the Black Panthers, believe that the time has come for illegal, and bloody, action. The first thing I noted about the article was that it should have given a few clarifications on the subject of "conformity," or of "passivity," or of indifference, or of "monolithism," all of which are qualities usually attributed to the "conditioned" public opinion of Americans. I mean that, if we are going to denounce the repression of Panthers or Weathermen, we have to begin by admitting that the Panthers or Weathermen were agitating. And how is agitation possible in a conformist, passive, indifferent, and monolithic society? But no such clarifications were included in the article. Instead of admitting the possibility that America was not entirely counterrevolutionary, the author, Alain Clément, emphasized the *reactionary* aspect of public opinion with respect to the Weathermen. And, understandably, public opinion at that moment was not very well disposed toward young revolutionaries. Clément concluded from this that the majority of the Senate would vote against lowering the voting age to eighteen.* On the subject of the bombings, he had this to say: "American police, on the whole, have never overcome the backwardness which resulted from

---

* Such a measure was passed in June 1970 and signed by Mr. Nixon. In December of the same year, the Supreme Court sustained its constitutionality as far as federal elections were concerned. This is another area in which Americans outstrip all Europeans except the British.

generations of amateurism and venality. The percentage of major crimes that remain unsolved is one of the highest among modern societies. The America citizen therefore has good reason to feel that he has no protection."

I must have missed something in all of this, because I was under the impression that the United States was a police state, where nothing could escape the attention of the F.B.I. However, when one is determined to find a scapegoat so as not to have to admit that a revolutionary climate exists in the United States, I suppose that police inefficiency serves the purpose as well as anything else.*

We might ask ourselves if anti-Americanism, while apparently directed against the Rightist aspects of American society, is not sometimes inspired instead by a fear of the upheavals in America—i.e., a fear that they may spread to the rest of the world. And that fear, in the final analysis, is really a fear of revolution. If that is not so, how can we explain the fact that a man in 1970 can persist in believing, all evidence to the contrary, that America is inhabited not only by conservatives, but, like all other countries, by opposing groups? How can he ignore the evidence that a battle is being fought in the United States, that its outcome is uncertain, but that the stakes are of the utmost importance for all mankind? Why would he breathe a sigh of relief every time he has the opportunity to strengthen his belief that reaction is triumphant in the United States?

If anti-Americanism is indeed founded on fear of revolu-

* I often quote from *Le Monde* in this chapter. It is certainly not because of any personal animus or feeling of hostility, but because *Le Monde* is an independent and neutralist newspaper. As such, it is a prime source of material illustrating anti-American sentiment in Europe, especially the aspects of that sentiment which are commonly accepted and have become an integral part of our political culture. Obviously, quotations taken from newspapers of the Communist Party or of the Right-wing nationalists would not carry the same weight.

tion, it may be that the anti-Americanism of the Left is
not very different from that of the Right. They are both
dictated by a fear of change, and by a feeling of resent-
ment at the thought that a civilization other than their
own has come to serve as a clearinghouse for the problems of the world. The anti-American of the Right re-
sents the United States, above all, for being powerful.
He does not find fault with the principle of world domination; but he would like to exercise that domination himself.
Moreover, he is afraid of the "corrupting" effect of the
American way of life on traditional societies, on societies
whose half-rural, half-industrial framework dates back to
the nineteenth century. The anti-American of the Left
also is upset at the idea of being disturbed. He, too,
longs for the nineteenth century—a century at the end
of which the "classic" transition from the first industrial
revolution to socialism was supposed to take place. It is
now evident to him that things have taken a different
course; and it is a course that he understands badly, and
had never foreseen. Above all, he hates to think that,
at the end of the road, a revolution may be waiting—a
revolution that is completely new, and that he cannot
understand. These two varieties of anti-Americanism, therefore, although they have different motives, share a single
function: to explain failure. For the anti-American of
the Right, the decline of his own country has been caused
by the inordinate increase of American power; that increase has been made possible by the decline of the
other great powers. For the anti-American of the Left,
the absence, or the failure, of socialist revolutions is what
must be explained, and the invention of a foreign scapegoat provides a much needed balm for the ego of the Left
which has been so bruised by so many defeats and be-
trayals. American "imperialism," therefore, is as good

an excuse for disappointed socialism as for frustrated nationalism.

One of the most harmful things about anti-Americanism is that it makes it difficult to arrive at factual data. It must therefore be the purpose of analysis to uncover such data concerning contemporary human problems as they are perceived and experienced in America. Whether we are talking about imperialism, freedom, economic struggle, racism, customs, culture, or information, we must try to penetrate to the situation as it really exists in America. And, once we have cleared away the rubble caused by sloth, fear, and absurdity, we most often find enough data to conclude that the situation involves both complexity and conflict.

Certainly, we cannot neutralize anti-Americanism by attempting to replace it with a pro-Americanism that is equally unsophisticated. There has been enough criticism of systematic *anti*-communism, for example, for us to have learned that the hardest thing to cure is systematic *pro*-communism. It is the very concept of any systematic "pro" or "con" position that is so harmful. In my opinion, it is not a matter of either approving or disapproving of American society, but of observing the antagonistic forces at work in that country. To approve or disapprove of a country as a whole is a very primitive way of looking at things. And a senseless one. All that we can try to do is to judge whether or not certain political, economic, and moral realities are leading toward a society which is regarded as a desirable objective. Therefore, it is not my intention to "defend America," because I do not regard America as a single unit. What I would like to do is precisely to show that it is *not* a single unit—so much as that its divisions have brought the country to the verge of civil war.

I maintain that there is a revolutionary America, and

an American revolution which is wholly new and which
has nothing to do with the revolutions of the nineteenth
century—or rather, with the revolutions dreamed of in the
nineteenth century. (It is because that revolution is entirely new that Europeans do not recognize it, or are
unwilling to recognize it. They feel that, if there is a new
revolution and a new civilization, they will have sur-
rendered their own dominant and creative role. Their
reaction is one of wounded leftist chauvinism.) If America
is indeed in the process of internal conflict, we can conclude that it is probably because there are some things
wrong with the system; but we can also conclude that
the most important thing, the ability to change, exists in
America to a greater extent than in any other country.
To say this is not to be "pro-American"—no more than
the Americans who are tearing down the old America
are pro-American. In fact, so far as I am concerned, pro-
Americanism does not exist. If we try to oppose pro-
Americanism to anti-Americanism, we are opposing two
equally irrational attitudes. What we must do is to oppose
an attitude of analysis to one of passion. And, since the
latter has no use for analysis, we can in turn afford to
ignore the "attitude of passion." Let me give an example.
A young writer, after reading an article of mine on the
subject of freedom of information in America, commented
that I was "praising America," and therefore praising the
war in Vietnam. How can one answer such a charge—
except by saying that to praise Beethoven is to praise
Germany, and to praise Germany is to praise Hitler.

If the conservative, conformist American citizen is
reacting today, it is because he has been vigorously
challenged over the last few years. His reaction, however,
is not very intense, as demonstrated by the fact that all
attempts to organize counterdemonstrations in favor of the

Vietnam war have failed dismally. Granted, however, that the American Right is strong, it is still unfair to speak only of it, and to omit all mention of the fact that the country is composed of two antagonistic camps of approximately equal size, and that the odds are in favor of the dissenters rather than of the conservatives.

Chapter 12

THE NEW DYNAMICS OF REVOLUTION

THE MOST COMMON error concerning the United States is to try to interpret that nation in terms of the revolutionary guidelines with which we are familiar, and which are usually purely theoretical. Then, when we see that those guidelines are not applicable to the American situation, we conclude that America is a reactionary country.

The revolutionary plans that we know, and that we usually try to apply, are all based on the existence of opposition, of antagonism: the peasants against the proprietors of the land; workers against factory owners; colonials against colonizers. The present American Revolution, however, resembles more a centrifugal gyration than a clash between opposing camps. It has certain characteristics in common with old-style revolution. There are the oppressed and the oppressors; the exploited and the exploiters; the poor and the rich. There are people who are morally dissatisfied with the present state of affairs—an essential condition of revolution—and there is a serious rift within the governing elite.

There are also traits which are entirely new, and peculiar to America. The "poor" are an unusual kind of poor; they earn between $1500 and $3000 a year, and, if their income falls below the latter figure, they are eligible for government aid. In Europe, such an income would place a family considerably above the poverty level—although, common opinion to the contrary, the cost of living in European urban centers is not much less than in America. In America, however, the phenomenon of prosperity makes everything relative, and, in consequence, some of the moral and psychological factors that are important in Europe do not play nearly so large a part in establishing revolutionary goals in America. The American revolution is, without doubt, the first revolution in history in which disagreement on values and goals is more pronounced than disagreement on the means of existence. American revolutionaries do not want merely to cut the cake into equal pieces; they want a whole new cake. This spirit of criticism of values, which is still more emotional than intellectual, is made possible by a freedom of information such as no civilization has ever tolerated before—not even within and for the benefit of the governing class, let alone at the level of the mass media. This accessibility of information has resulted in a widespread and strong feeling of guilt, and a passion for self-accusation which, on occasion, tends to go to extremes. And that result, in turn, has produced a phenomenon unprecedented in history: a domestic revolt against the imperialistic orientation of American foreign policy.

This revolt, however, is not the only indication of a

new revolutionary direction. There has never been a society* which faced a situation similar to that of the United States with respect to the blacks. In the face of this contagious domestic problem and of the demands of the Afro-American community, American society is being divided into factions and is entering upon the path of cultural polycentrism. And this process, of course, is playing havoc with our prejudices concerning the "conformity" and "uniformity" of American society. The truth of the matter is that American society is torn by too many tensions not to become more and more diversified.

Another unprecedented characteristic of the American revolution is the revolt of the young—the contagion of which, both at the national and international levels, was so virulent in the years between 1965 and 1970. This is, moreover, a new development within the context of upper-class divisions during revolutionary periods, since these young revolutionaries are mostly students; that is, members of the privileged class. It should be pointed out that this "privileged class" is less and less exceptional; it is a case, so to speak, of mass privilege. The current upheavals are due not only to the great number of young people in proportion to the rest of the population, but also to the great number of students in proportion of young people. Out of a population of two hundred million, there are presently seven million students**; and it is estimated that, by 1977, there will be eleven million.

It has been said that there are three nations in the United States: a black nation; a Woodstock nation; and a

* That is, a democratic society, whose traditions forbade cultural and physical genocide. France, under the Capetian kings, had no such restraints, and solved a similar problem by slaughtering the Albigensians in the thirteenth century.

** In France, for example, there are six hundred thousand students out of a population of fifty million people. If the proportion were the same as in the United States, there would be almost two million students.

Wallace nation.* The first one is self-explanatory. The second takes it name from the great political and musical convention held at Woodstock, New York, in 1969, which has been documented by the film *Woodstock*. It includes the hippies and the radicals. The third nation is embodied in Mr. George Wallace of Alabama, and is composed of "lower middle-class whites" whose symbol is the "hard hat" worn by construction workers. Each of these nations has its own language, its own art forms, and its own customs. And each has a combat arm: the Black Panthers for the blacks; the Weathermen for Woodstock; and the Ku Klux Klan, and various civil organizations, for Wallace. We could add other "nations"; e.g., the women of the Women's Liberation movement, who have declared war on sexism (a word copied from "racism") and who take their methods from those of the Black Power and Student Power movements. There is also a large group of citizens who are neither black, nor particularly young, nor especially intellectual. Far from being reactionary, they are sometimes militantly progressive, and are vaguely categorized as liberals. This group includes citizens with a wide range of opinion; from what, in Europe, we call the democrats, to the progressives. The liberals have often been able to contribute the appearance of a mass movement to demonstrations which, without them, would have been able to attract only the extremists. They demonstrated alongside the blacks throughout the great Southern revolt which began in 1952, and against the Vietnam war in the various moratoriums. They are on the side of the students, the Indians, and the Third World. On May 21, 1970, for instance, thousands of New York lawyers—what we might call the governors of the governing class—descended on

* See, for example, the editorial of Stewart Alsop in *Newsweek*, March 30, 1970.

Washington to protest American intervention in Cambodia. On the same day, the hard-hats demonstrated in New York in favor of this intervention. And, still on the same day, prices dropped sharply on the New York Stock Exchange, indicating, according to some American commentators, that the financiers, like the lawyers, were not in agreement with the Administration over the conduct of the war. No nineteenth-century class distinctions are sufficient to convey the nature of these new political classes— which are also sexual classes, racial classes, and esthetic classes; that is, they are based on the rejection of an unsatisfactory life style. Each of these categories has specific economic, racial, esthetic, moral, and religious or spiritual characteristics; each has its own customs, its own way of dressing and eating—even though, as a whole, they are referred to as a "community." In this instance, the image of a series of superimposed circles rather than of stratified social levels describes the nature of this community. There are common areas, nonetheless, where the circles intersect; e.g., the blacks—young radicals—feminists, who have some, but not all, cultural interests in common.

Chapter 13

THE INFORMATION REVOLUTION

In the preceding chapter, I used the word "cultural" in the sense of "that which relates to the form of a civilization." In the more restricted meaning of the term, however, it is used to designate activities related to education and information. In that sense, we may say that mass communications play the part of a revolutionary force in modern American culture, or at least act as a catalyst in renewing the internal dynamism of conflict. This is especially true of the most recent, and most important, of the mass media, television.

What can television really do? Is it, as Adorno and Marcuse have said, a means of irreversible conditioning? Can it actually engender passivity, hypnosis, conformity, and message docility in the people who have become "masses"? Even in a country as primitive in communications as France, political parties fight over the rue Cognacq-

Jay (in Paris, where our television stations are located) the way that ancient Greeks fought over their Acropolis. We hear politicians of the majority party saying, with the air of actors performing a great renunciation scene, "Since October I have only been on television three times." And politicians of the other parties keep their stopwatches in their hands: "In the past year and a half, I've been on for only seven minutes and forty-five seconds. What am I supposed to do with that kind of time?" Meanwhile, the television interviewer is glancing at the studio clock: only thirty seconds left to wrap it up . . . The Gaullist convention at Versailles, in June 1970 and the President's press conference which immediately followed it (July 2) confirmed the persistent unwillingness of the majority party to share the television screen with people of other opinions. "Television is the state" is what these gentlemen seem to be telling us.

In Europe our first awareness of the possibilities offered by broadcast communications came from a book that is now forgotten but whose title lives on: *Le Viol des foules* (The Rape of the Masses) by Sergei Chakhotin, published in 1940, concerning Hitler's use of media for political purposes. It is probable that Chakhotin's book had a good deal to do with our present attitudes toward media.

One of the most naïve of those preconceived ideas is the identification, constantly reiterated, of political propaganda with commercial publicity. The fact is that, today, political propaganda and commercial publicity resemble each other only to the extent that they are both methods of persuasion. They are completely different in the kind of appeal that they make to the viewer, and in the changes that they try to effect in his habits. Television viewers, after all, are not stupid. They may go out and buy a hundred tubes of a particular toothpaste; but no one will ever be able to convince them that toothpaste and political power are identical. Moreover, all sociological studies indicate that television commercials play a negligible part in the orientation of political trends.* It should be noted, however, that this holds true only when a viewer can distinguish a commercial from a political appeal. *Le Viol des foules* was concerned with a particular case, that of a political vacuum in which no voice but Hitler's could be heard, either on the radio or elsewhere; not even in private conversations, unless one were very careful. Under such conditions, it is obvious that the masses are completely at the mercy of their manipulators. But this situation is not due to radio or to television as such. It exists because an element is introduced which is alien to the nature of telecommunications, an element that can also be used in written or oral communications: the material elimination of contradiction. However, experience shows that opinions formed by monopolized means of communication are as easy to destroy as they are to create. The state, by controlling communications, can make the people believe whatever it wants them to believe; but counterpropaganda can destroy in one day what it took the state twenty years to build up. The implication of this is that television's impact is reduced in proportion to the diversification of information. In a pluralistic society, a television program cannot form public opinion unless it has something more to offer than the mere fact of being a television program.

There are several classic examples to prove this. During the Second World War, two groups of American soldiers were chosen as an experimental audience for a program on the subject of whether the war would be long or short. The first group heard a radio broadcast that gave only

---

* Jean Cazeneuve in *Les Pouvoirs de la télévision* (Paris, 1970) gives an excellent report on sociological research in this area.

the arguments in favor of a long war. The second group heard a debate which gave the arguments on both sides of the question. In the first group, only 36 percent of the men who had believed in a short war now believed that the war would be long; but in the second group, 48 percent now believed in a long war. The group that was subjected to "conditioning" proved less easy to influence than the other group; and, in the second group, the presentation of both the pros and cons had influenced the opinions not only of the men who were impressed by arguments in favor of a long war, but also of those who had been unimpressed by the arguments in favor of a short war. Next, both groups were made to listen to another broadcast, this one devoted wholly to the arguments for a short war. In the first group, which had not been exposed previously to both sides of the question, there was an almost complete reversal of opinion; but in the second group, which had already heard the pros and cons, there was very little shift.

Unilateral propaganda tends to reinforce existing opinions rather than to provoke change. It brings public support —but a public support which quickly evaporates at the first sound of a different drum. (The negative results of the 1965 presidential elections in France are often explained by this factor.) On the other hand, if the mass media present frequent discussions and opposing points of view, public opinion tends to stabilize. Thus, the famous television debate between Kennedy and Nixon, in 1960, greatly influenced the votes of those who, up till then, had not followed the campaign very closely. There were several other television debates subsequently, but the results were less dramatic. The first debate had had the greatest impact. The others allowed a margin for adjustment, and many people were thereby given the opportunity again to weigh opinions and candidates, and sometimes to revert to their original preference.

These considerations should put a damper on the talk about "American-style political campaigns." An American political campaign, first of all, does not consist of the candidate's physical attractiveness, or of airplanes, or of drum-majorettes, or of posters. To campaign American-style is, essentially, to create and to accept controversy. So far as the use of television is concerned, we might say that the more television there is, the more it will be used by different kinds of candidates; and the more it is used by different candidates, the less danger there is of abuse. It is not the exaggerated use of television that misleads people, but the control of information. Man is not brainwashed by the number and intensity of television messages, but by their scarcity and their mediocrity.

It is not possible for an American public official to refuse to reply to the demand of journalists for information and explanations. Just as it was not possible, in the golden age of parliamentary government, for a minister to refuse to reply to a demand for information from the opposition. The present decline of parliamentary government (a decline less pronounced in the United States than elsewhere) has been balanced and remedied by the control exercised by the media. The word "control" is not too strong; for it is obvious that a man in public life feels obliged, in moments of crisis, to appear before the cameras and explain a political action, or even an aspect of his private life. In 1952 Nixon explained the circumstance in which he had felt justified in accepting money from certain business interests. And Edward Kennedy, in 1969, felt obliged to clarify the circumstances of the death of a weekend companion. Some commentators explain these appearances by saying that they are attempts to "condition"

public opinion, to use the mass media to influence the
people—especially when it is a case of the speaker's buying
television time. They do not understand that, when a man
buys television time, it is because he is under considerable
pressure to justify his actions. They could just as well say
that a lawyer's courtroom pleadings are an attempt to
"condition" the jury—an attempt made even more scandalous by the fact that the defendant is paying the lawyer
a fee for his services. What they would not realize, in that
case, is that the defendant would much prefer not to
be where he is. Their attitude, if carried to its logical
conclusion, would lead to the writing of a bizarre kind of
parliamentary history of Europe. The books would have to
say that Lloyd George, for instance, put pressure on the
House of Commons by speaking from the podium, instead
of recording that Mr. George was required by the Commons
to make an accounting of his actions.

The practice of buying television time derives from a
particular necessity: that of defending a position that the
media do not necessarily find newsworthy. It is more or
less like vanity publishing, in which the author himself
pays for the publication of his book. Contrary to what is
thought in Europe, reactionaries are not the only ones who
buy television time (viz., the four antiwar senators who,
in June 1970, bought time to discuss the unconstitutional
nature of the Cambodian intervention); but that is not
the important point. The important point is that no
American in the public eye, whether he be a baseball
player accused of accepting money illegally, or the mayor
of a great city, or a union official, or a Hollywood star,
can refuse to appear on television to debate with his
adversaries or to answer the questions of an interviewer,
without almost wholly discrediting himself. The formula
reply, "No comment," is acceptable only in the case of

someone who does not have the authority to divulge the information requested—either because he is not sufficiently high in his particular organization, or because the information is "privileged." In America, however, even "state secrets" are only temporarily so. In April 1968, for instance, I saw Mayor Daley of Chicago give a lengthy and detailed reply to a reporter on the subject of the instructions he had issued to the police, regarding the action to be taken in the event of a disturbance among the blacks. Immediately afterward, Mayor Lindsay of New York publicly attacked Daley for issuing orders that Lindsay described as totally illegal. This kind of exchange is unimaginable in more sheltered societies, where the first of the two mayors would no doubt have been "regrettably detained by the burdens of his office, and unable to meet with the gentlemen from the networks"; and the second mayor would have prudently avoided going out on a limb, particularly on such a ticklish problem.

In France the extinction of parliamentary power has not been offset by any strengthening of the power of the media. In the United States, however, the latter has become so potent a force that it can force a justice of the Supreme Court, Abe Fortas, to resign for having accepted legal fees from private enterprises, in nebulous circumstances; it can require great industrial firms to withdraw products from the market; it can oblige F.B.I. agents to explain their methods and their goals, as it did during a series of programs broadcast in January 1970. It is significant that all of the European programs involving a confrontation of ideas have been patterned after such American prototypes as *Meet the Press*. Needless to say, the American model has been tidied up and scaled down to make it fit for the European consumption. I remember seeing M. Pompidou at his last television press conference in Amer-

ica, at the end of his official visit. Assailed on every side
by disagreeable questions, especially about Israel and the
delivery of French warplanes to Libya, he was obviously
surprised, upset, disconcerted, and indignant. Every time
a new question was asked, his expression seemed to say,
"This is really too much!" He was like a man who had
been shadowboxing all his life, and who had now been
punched in the mouth. What really outraged him was not
the questions themselves so much as the fact that the
reporters had the *right* to ask him such questions—and
that they were exercising that right.

When Pompidou returned to France, after his visit, he
was met at Orly airport by a flock of French reporters,
holding their microphones forward, respectfully, in order
not to miss a word of the inanities that were sure to
come. "Gentlemen," Pompidou said, "you will understand
that I must first make my report to the Council of
Ministers, which will meet tomorrow morning." Obviously,
it was good to be home. Such a statement would have been
inconceivable in America, because it would have been
interpreted (quite accurately) as evidence of a highhanded
contempt for public opinion; whereas, in America, a public
official is required to recognize that he is an emissary of
the people. Moreover, as an answer, it was absurd. Surely
M. Pompidou could have had the courtesy to say a few
words to his fellow citizens, sitting in front of their television sets, on certain aspects of his trip, without either
endangering the public order or depriving the august gentlemen of the Council of their fair share of his treasure chest
of opinions and observations.

There is a chasm between developed countries and underdeveloped countries; and there is another chasm between
informed countries and underinformed countries. Two
different kinds of men are being created. The first informa-

tion revolution was that which established freedom of the press and of written communication. Only a limited number of countries have, thus far, been affected by that revolution. The second information revolution established the freedom of the audiovisual media; and it has affected an even smaller number of countries. The power of the audiovisual media, which results from that freedom, is the only effective counterbalance to the quasi omnipotence of the Executive branch, the only source of energy which nourishes and buttresses the traditional means of parliamentary control. And that power must be complete or it cannot exist. Except for the necessity of protecting the rights of individuals to legal recourse against the media—rights which should be ample—and for insisting on the "equal-time" provisions of the law, which are imperative, any restriction, whether overt or secret, that is imposed upon the information media under the pretext of preventing abuses, is the equivalent of prescribing suicide as a cure for the common cold. Information must not be editorialized or moralized except to the extent that information itself is capable of having an editorial or moral impact. And the first prerequisite of freedom of information, like any other freedom, is abundance of information.

Frenchmen, when discussing television, often ask one another, "Did you see the program last night?" They do not ask, "What did you watch last night?" Most often, there is only *one* program; and sometimes there is not even that. In the United States, the chance of two viewers watching the same program is statistically small. In the larger cities, for example, there are eight or ten channels from which to choose. The term "American media" therefore signifies diversity. When, at eight o'clock in the evening, one can choose between a panel discussion on the pill, a detailed analysis of the Supreme Court and of the ways in which a citizen can appeal to it, a one-hour coverage of school desegregation in Mississippi, a course in dietetics, and, of course, old movies, game shows, situation comedies, and variety shows, then one is hardly a "slave to television." Indeed, it is more like being turned loose in a library.

In New York, there are programs for deaf-mutes, in which sign language is used. There is a preschool program, *Sesame Street,* on the so-called educational network, which gives some indication of what television could mean to elementary education. This educational network was begun during a strike at the commercial networks, and received immediate financial aid from the Ford Foundation and from private contributors. No commercial advertising is permitted. It is an outstanding illustration of what private initiative can do when a system is flexible and free from monopolies.

The flow of information in the United States is as free as possible, and there is no "news management." When Vice President Agnew (November 1969) launched a violent attack on American press and television news coverage, certain Europeans, as usual, immediately formulated a diagnosis of incipient fascism. That Mr. Agnew had the right to say what he did, is beyond discussion. The difference between Mr. Agnew's action, however, and that of M. Robert Poujade, secretary-general of the Gaullist Party, is that American press and television is not subject to Mr. Agnew's control (except to the extent that he is in a position to apply "pressure"). But Mr. Poujade, when he castigated the "lack of objectivity" of the O.R.T.F. (the French radio and television network), was attacking an organization that is under the direct control of Mr. Poujade's own political friends. Mr. Agnew's attack, therefore, was nothing more than an expression of opinion. But Mr. Poujade's was an open threat.

The fact that Spiro Agnew, the embodiment of American conservatism, was so unhappy about the news coverage of the two largest networks (C.B.S. and N.B.C.) demonstrates at least that their coverage is presenting a picture of America with which he does not agree. And that is hard to reconcile with our conviction, in Europe, that the American networks are the servants of high finance and conformism, and that they are obliged to present a "doctored" version of the news. What happens in fact is that all of America's problems are on public view on the television screen: the Vietnam war (exposés on atrocities and the My Lai massacre), the sufferings of racial minorities, juvenile delinquency, corruption, urban congestion, the destruction of the environment, and drugs. Even the drug problem in the army is reported and discussed, and it is no longer a secret that G.I.'s use marijuana; or that, when he is asked what he wants most, he is likely to answer, "pot and peace."

When something happens in America, the media cover every detail of the event: a Mafia scandal in New Jersey, with political implications; illegal betting on football games; the financial wheeling and dealing of a former secretary to the Senate Majority. There is never any "Mr. X." Names are given, and photographs, and details about the crime, and the amounts of money involved. On the series of programs about the F.B.I. that I mentioned earlier, for instance, former agents of that agency appeared in person to explain and criticize certain operations in which the rights of citizens had clearly been violated.

Though the television networks depend on commercial advertising as their source of revenue, they still retain a certain independence with respect to their sponsors. One indication of this is the fact that, even when cigarette commercials were allowed on television (they have been prohibited as of January 1, 1971), the networks also carried special programs that were designed to point out the dangers of smoking. (This is inconceivable in France, since the sale of tobacco is a state monopoly.) Another proof is the rise to prominence of Ralph Nader, the young lawyer who is known in Europe chiefly for his book *Unsafe at Any Speed*, and for his confrontation with General Motors. Since then, he has turned his attention to other subjects also, ranging from the intrigues of insurance companies to the ingredients of hot dogs, and his efforts have, on several occasions, resulted in congressional legislation. When Nader has something important to say about a particular product, or about an industry, he is accorded wide attention on the television networks, and most often appears on Walter Cronkite's celebrated newscast on C.B.S. When it happens that what Nader is going to say would offend a sponsor, the network informs the sponsor of the substance of Nader's report; then, if the sponsor wishes to withdraw, he is free to go in peace. Even so, there is a long waiting list of sponsors for Mr. Cronkite's half-hour program. In that sense, and contrary to what is generally believed, sponsors need C.B.S. more than C.B.S. needs sponsors.

In addition to product commercials, American television also carries various announcements and messages designed to inform viewers about their rights. One non-product commercial, for example, explains the existence of an antidiscrimination housing law, and gives a Washington telephone number that anyone can call for free legal advice on problems in that area.

Certainly, without television no one would ever have

suspected the amount of opposition to the Vietnam war that exists in America. Neither French nor British imperialism, in its heyday, was ever challenged from within to the degree that American imperialism is being contested by Americans.

We often hear people say that, even if the above description of the availability of information in America is correct, all that information serves little purpose. American public opinion is still dominated by emotion and self-interest. However, the recent history of the United States proves just the opposite. We tend too much to ignore the fact that, for the first time in the history of the world, a foreign war—especially a colonial expedition or a war that is supposed to be in the interests of national security—has been strongly opposed within the country waging that war. Usually, all struggles for freedom or justice take place at the domestic level, and are carried on for the benefit of the people in the country where they are happening. And, generally, even the lower classes share in the imperialistic ambitions of the governing class, especially when it is a matter of a colonial war. One of the most persistent lessons of history has been that the countries most on guard against abuses at home are the ones who most lack a critical or moral sense when it comes to abuses committed against other peoples. The transition from internal democracy to external democracy, or at least to a preoccupation with external democracy, represents a giant step—a step that the United States has been the first to take. That Americans were able to make that transition is due to the freedom of information in their country. It means that there has been real progress toward the abolition of the right to perpetrate crimes in the name of foreign policy. Neither Athenian imperialism nor the colonial adventures of the English, French, and

Dutch ever met with substantial opposition. Opposition, if it existed at all, was confined to a few intellectual circles among the privileged elite; that is, to those who were sufficiently well informed to be conscious of the atrocities committed for the sake of conquest. Popular sentiment was in no way engaged when it was a question of exploiting and exterminating foreigners. The French Communist Party, recognizing this fact, blinked at the French government's resumption of control over its colonial empire immediately after the Second World War. In the years following 1947—the year in which the communist ministers were forced to resign from the government—its opposition, however ineffective, to the wars in Indochina, Madagascar, and North Africa, centered around the more general conflict of the cold war. There was never any protest of sufficient breadth or weight to influence the course of events, or any internal protest against the injustices resulting from foreign policy.

There has never been, in any country, any dissent of sufficient breadth or weight to influence the course of events, or any internal protest against the injustices resulting from foreign policy. The moratoriums and other antiwar demonstrations in the United States are the first mass phenomena of this kind; and they are all the more significant since the participants are people of all ages and of all social classes. During the French war in Algeria, there were protests in France, but they came only from the extreme Left; or rather, they came from newspapers of the extreme Left and center-Left, and never succeeded in winning the support of the people—let alone of the middle class. Even young people, except for a number of students, did not rebel. Resistance to the draft was negligible, and public opinion strongly disapproved of draft evasion (of which there were not more than a few dozen cases). In the United States, however, there are tens of thousands of draft evaders; and, instead of being condemned, they are encouraged and aided. Any inquiry in Canada or Sweden will indicate the extent, and the degree of organization, of American draft evasion and army desertion since 1964. It has become a commonplace occurrence for a young man to return his draft card to his local draft board, or even for small stacks of the cards to be burned in the streets, as the owners of the cards look on.*

Never before has the "sacred ego" of a nation become a subject of political controversy; and especially not in a nation that stands at the apex of its power. The consequences of this development are incalculable, for the criticism of imperialism and nationalism is taking place, for the first time, at the very source of imperialism and nationalism, and it is being spoken by those who are in a position to do something about it. Other kinds of criticism are, for practical purposes, useless. One is always opposed to the imperialism of other people; and those other people could not care less. The hard thing is to be opposed to one's own imperialism. The whole world was against British imperialism during the Boer War, and against French imperialism during the Algerian war; and the only effect that opposition had was to exasperate

---

* Not all American youths receive draft cards. Curiously enough, in many parts of the United States it is not mandatory for parents to register the birth of a child, and the army has no way of tracking down a man whose birth was not officially recorded and who does not register for the draft at the age of eighteen. There is, therefore, a sort of "silent draft evasion" which is difficult to appraise in terms of numbers. It is just beginning to be noticed, since, according to the statute of limitations, draft evaders cannot be prosecuted after the lapse of five years. But draft evasion, whether it be overt or silent, has considerable political significance, particularly when one considers the rather broad interpretation given to the laws on conscientious objection, which allow a man to serve in the army without actually bearing arms.

the chauvinists of both countries, except in the case of a
few fringe groups without power or support.

We have not yet discussed the question of whether this
massive, internal, and non-elitist opposition to patriotic
imperialism is the result of the accessibility of information. The unprecedented power and style of opposition
in America seems to result both from the free flow of information and from the factors that made that free flow
possible. At the root of American democracy is the idea
that everyone has the right to improve his situation, but
that no one has the right to take unfair advantage in
doing so. This attitude has been incorporated into the
legal system, in the form of the antitrust laws—which
are far from being the joke that Europeans think they are.
It also involves the conviction that neither the state,
nor special-interest groups, nor institutions—however praise-
worthy their goals—nor industry, nor the army, nor anyone or anything else has the right to refuse to explain its
actions or to withhold information. This is particularly
true in the case of groups or individuals whose activities
are suspected of being detrimental, not only to the common good (a term which, of itself, means nothing),
but also to the well-being of this or that group of citizens.
Americans, in keeping with this principle, have never permitted newspapers to be closed down by the government,
or books to be censored either directly or indirectly. Today, not even films are censored, except in a single state;
and, in the latter case, the censorship is not political.

The federal structure of the United States, its legislative diversity, and the lack of uniformity in moral climate
in different parts of the country, all offer infinitely more
numerous means of fighting oppression and intolerance
than are available in countries with strongly centralized
governments. A legal argument to the effect that some-

thing is "harmful to the morale of the armed services" (an argument used in France even in peacetime, and most recently used to refer to journalists of the Left), is unheard of in the United States. A short time ago, following the success of the film *M.A.S.H.*, one legislator was inspired to introduce a bill forbidding the use of the American uniform in movies or plays that openly ridiculed the armed services. The bill was not taken seriously even at the congressional committee level.

This climate makes it possible for Americans to produce and distribute such films as *Dr. Strangelove*, *M.A.S.H.*, and *Catch-22*, in which war, militarism, chaplains, and the arbitrary and whimsical nature of decisions at the highest level are satirized with that same freedom from compromise that one finds in the tales of Voltaire. It would be impossible for such films to get beyond the script stage in almost any other country in the world, including more than half of the countries of Europe—and especially France. Eight years after the end of the Algerian war, G. Pontecorvo's *La Bataille d'Alger* (The Battle of Algiers), which won a Golden Lion at the 1965 Venice Film Festival, was ordered withdrawn from circulation within forty-eight hours; and the staff of the Premier himself contacted the French television network and forbade it to show a short clip that had been scheduled. It would also be impossible, in most of the world and especially in France, for anyone to make and distribute films on domestic policies, such as *Medium Cool* or *The Strawberry Statement*, which respectively depict, without understatement, the unleashing of police brutality, and recent instances of police brutality at the 1968 Democratic National Convention in Chicago and in handling students who had occupied a university campus. It is puzzling to see some French critics either treating these films with contempt, or else discussing them as though they were perfectly ordinary, everyday movies. Surely they must know it would be difficult, if not impossible, for a French producer to make a similar film, or even a watered-down version, on the events, say, of May 1968.

In France the state is not the only agency to censor what it does not like, but it is in a better position than anyone else to do so. Nonetheless, every citizens' group with the vaguest claim to power tries to imitate the state in this respect. *La Bataille d'Alger*, for example, was banned at the request of former French settlers in Algeria who had been repatriated to France. The alumni of the Military Academy at Saumur asked for, and obtained, the suppression of a television program about an episode in the history of their school. Farmers branded as "intolerable" a program on farming entitled *Adieu coquelicots* ("Goodbye, poppies"), and persecuted the author of it to such an extent that he was unable to find work as a journalist. Do-gooders succeeded in canceling a comedy program called *Tous en scène* (On Stage, Everybody) because it was mildly anticlerical, and in banning a film called *La Religieuse* (The Nun), which was a timid version of a story of Diderot's. The businessmen at beach resorts are complaining bitterly about the publication of a report on marine pollution, and are explaining that the report is entirely erroneous. Interestingly enough, the publication of the same sort of report in America led, in June 1970, to the institution of legal proceedings by the State of California against the army, and to the shutdown of underwater oil wells at Santa Barbara. In the same vein, there has been a tightening of controls on cigarette advertising, and on the sale of war toys for children. Contrary to what is often said, freedom of information in America often cuts into profits. Without that freedom, the activities of Ralph Nader would have been as impossible in America as they are in Europe. In some countries, the most important thing is to defend the interests of the consumer; in others, it is to defend the interests of the manufacturers and exploiters. We have even reached the stage, in France, where the hotel owners demand the cancellation of weather reports when it rains during the vacation season. How difficult it is for us to understand that the purpose of information is to serve the interests of the informed, and not the interests either of the newscaster or of the one whom the information concerns.

This simple distinction between the two kinds of information serves as a line of demarcation between two kinds of civilization. And, to me, it seems that only one of those civilizations has a future. The other seems destined to sink into a maelstrom of errors—errors that will never be recognized until it is too late, until the price of error has been paid and it is too late to do anything about it.

I saw an instance of this in December 1969, in a shantytown on the outskirts of Paris, where some black workers had been killed by carbon fumes. Apparently they had tried to heat their shacks by burning whatever combustible materials they had been able to find, since their gas and electricity had been cut off by a greedy landlord. On that occasion, I recalled a conversation I had had in 1968, with a prominent television reporter who was then working on a monthly magazine (*Cinq colonnes*), and who is now employed by a private agency. He told me that he had decided to give up trying to report on French domestic news. While working on a report on the situation of foreign workers in France, he had been censored—by a mere telephone call from a Gaullist deputy. This deputy's district included a fair number of foreign workers who, to be sure, were not even voters. This journal-ist's experience gives one an idea of the humanitarian ideals of some of the men in power. Is it possible that, if this reporter's findings on foreign workers in France had been published in 1968, the black workers who died during the winter of 1969 might still be alive? We had to have corpses before anything could be done about the ghouls who prey on foreign workers. That is the crux of the difference between the two kinds of information: in one case, free information allows a solution to be found *before* a catastrophe occurs; in the other, censorship makes it necessary for there to be a catastrophe before a solution is even considered. I do not mean to say that a free flow of information is always sufficient to prevent catastrophes; but it is obvious that it limits the number and extent of such events. After hearing of fatal accidents like the one mentioned above, politicians always feel that they must "do something." However, they might have had the same feeling if they had had the opportunity to see a television program on the way that those workers were forced to live. Such a program might have disturbed their peace of mind, but that seems a small price to pay for human lives.

Certainly, we French can console ourselves (and we do) with the thought that we are powerless to bring about freedom of information. And perhaps we can convince ourselves that we do not really need that kind of freedom by pointing to television's aggravation of the problem and of the blacks and Puerto Ricans in America. This tactic also enables us to forget about the three to four million aliens in our own country who do the dirty work in our economy and who are the target of the French workman's racism. The fact remains, however, that no people other than the Americans have ever fully accepted the feeling of guilt which followed the disclosure of horrors perpetrated by themselves or in their name. The Germans refused to admit the crimes of the Nazi; and the English, the French, and the Italians all refused to admit the atrocities committed during their colonial wars.

The education of the white man, from the time of the Greek city-states up to the present, has aimed at justifying crimes committted against humanity in the name of national honor. Reactions against such attempts to normalize atrocities are extremely rare; they have always been minimal, and they have never had the slightest effect either upon over-all policy or upon public opinion. To this rule, the United States is the first exception in the history of man.

It seems impossible that freedom of information is unable to change anything in a society that is exposed to front-page pictures in newspapers and magazines of atrocities committed by the American army in Vietnam, or to direct television coverage of the results of those atrocities, or to interviews with the soldiers, subordinate officers, and generals who have been indicted and handed over to courts-martial for war crimes. What is certain, however, is that never before has there been, in any country, either detailed information on crimes against humanity, or prosecution of those responsible for those crimes. It is not impossible that, somehow, the availability of information is what has made America the exception to that rule. Our own "silent majority" in France would never have permitted the publication of such incriminating news.* It seems that our silent majority is stronger than America's Silent Majority (if the latter is indeed a majority). In any case, the fact remains that America is the first country

* For example, a book by Marcel Ophuls (*Le Chagrin et la Pitié*) describing life in France during the German occupation, and containing the autobiography of a former "collaborator," has not been authorized for use on television.

in which, during a war, the opponents of war have been strong enough to effect a change in the long-standing principle according to which national expediency justifies any act.

When information has reached the stage at which it is capable of such achievements, it becomes an indication of senile decay for other nations to sputter clichés about "formal freedoms," or "alienation" by television, or "repressive toleration." American news-reporting is agonizing, guilt-ridden, humiliating—and, for those reasons, it is effective. It is probably because it is effective that, despite the crimes that it provokes and the hatred that it incites, it is supported by the conscience of the nation against those who deplore it. And, perhaps, it is unconsciously supported even by those who deplore it. The conservatives, on the one hand, realize that, in the age of mass media, information reaches everyone, and that it is no longer academic but has acquired an irreversible revolutionary impetus. They are therefore wary of it. On the other hand, they realize, or sense, that without a free flow of information, America's problems would turn into cataclysms. Their instinct of preservation therefore speaks louder than their conservative instinct. This situation obviates the necessity for theoretical arguments about whether information should be "limited" and about the abuses of information. Information, by its very nature, is unforeseeable, and therefore it cannot be controlled. That being the case, there is only one way of preventing the abuse of information by the news media, and that is to make available the greatest possible amount of information. So far as "objectivity" is concerned, France's most eminent authorities tell us that "no one knows exactly what it is." Let us therefore leave it to the pedants to philosophize about it.

Everyone knows what the opposite of objectivity is; and that should be enough.

The showing of insurrection on television incites to insurrection. The showing of dissent incites to dissent. The showing of Woodstock incites to Woodstock. The showing of the Silent Majority incites only to silence. The enemies of free information say that only crises, racism, poverty, and pollution make the news. And, of course, they are right. The subject of information is crisis. News, by definition, is concerned with "hot" information; and someone or something is sure to get burned. No news is really interesting unless it concerns a subject of some sensitivity, and unless the reporting of the news is disagreeable or irritating to someone in authority. The result is that there is always a great deal more "bad" news than "good" news; and the automatic function of this news is to serve as a disturbing influence. Moreover, it is not possible even to choose between this perpetual disturbance and censorship. Recently, a Hartford journalist suggested to Vice President Agnew, the chief of the anti-media party, that he establish a newspaper that would publish only good news, the name of which, appropriately, would be *Good News*. He also suggested that the Vice President himself put up the money for this undertaking. This, Mr. Agnew refused to do; he, like everyone else, knows very well that good information is composed of bad news.

When we say that the perception of truth by ever increasing numbers of people can have no beneficial effect on the course of history, what we are really saying is that revolution is impossible. Personally, I believe the opposite: that only the free flow of information, which has become politically so efficacious since the beginning of the age of mass media, can effect that synthesis of social revolution and democratic freedoms which has had so many false starts in the past century. By the same token, when I hear someone say that American television is a matter of commercial publicity, I always suspect that what they resent is not so much the commercials but the freedom that American television allows. This seems all the more true in view of the fact that no other television system, except the B.B.C., has ever allowed such freedom. (France, as usual, has gotten the worst of everything. We now have political control of television *and* commercials.)

The entry of mankind into the age of broadcast communications is interpreted and evaluated differently in Europe and America. In Europe, for the past thirty years, we have been absolutely unable to make sense out of the mass media, and we have contributed nothing original on the subject. Unlike the Europeans, whose commentaries have been almost entirely negative, American sociologists have made a real effort to come to grips with the electronic media. They have been able to recognize these media as the energy source of a revolution, as the constitutive elements of an informational *milieu* that is destined to produce a new kind of man, a new kind of education, new kinds of social relations, and a new human psychology. David Riesman (in *The Lonely Crowd*) was the first to try to describe this new kind of man. Marshall McLuhan, starting from Riesman's analyses, has gone on to argue that the "massification" of the media is not only in the process of accomplishing one of the most decisive revolutions the world has ever known, but that it alone constitutes and determines that revolution. A debatable thesis, no doubt; but that consideration should not keep us from acknowledging that McLuhan is above all an artist in explaining the mass media and their effect upon us.

The career of McLuhan's books in Europe is a curious example of self-contradiction. On the one hand, these books have not had the popular success in Europe that they enjoy in the United States. And, on the other hand, a large number of intellectuals cry alarm, and complain that the public is being contaminated by Mr. McLuhan's corrosive stupidity.

The first of these phenomena is easy enough to explain. It should come as no surprise that, in Europe, McLuhan is not regarded as a popular oracle to the extent that he is across the Atlantic. The central theme of his work is man as submerged in and changed by the electronic communications media—a subject that concerns us much less than it does the Americans. Despite the increase in television viewership in France (almost 13 million sets today, compared with 700,000 in 1958), and whatever the importance of the political problem presented by the state monopoly in television, no one can seriously maintain that Frenchmen live in an audiovisual civilization. Most French viewers can receive only one of the two networks, and neither network has more than three or four hours of programming per day. Could we say that we live in a "newspaper civilization" if we had only a four-page newspaper every day? Some of our neighbors in Europe have a greater choice of programs, and a longer television day. But they do not even approach the degree of impact represented by the eight or ten or twelve channels operating in America and Japan from eighteen to twenty-four hours every day.

Moreover, in Europe, our methods are archaic. In using television for teaching purposes, for example, we adopt the same methods that were used before television. We rely on words, on oral explanations, and we make no use of visual images. The same thing holds true for news coverage, in which the "viewer" listens to explanations much more than he "sees things." It should be clear, then, that the

European public has no great need for a philosophy of "electronic man." No more than a citizen of Bourges or Viterbo feels it necessary to plunge into the literature of megalopolis and urban gigantism.

The reactions of the intellectuals to Mr. McLuhan are somewhat more curious. Their cries of indignation, their violent rage, their shrieks of exasperation, their anathemas and interdicts, are so out of proportion to their alleged cause that one may look for a deeper motive than the mere reading of McLuhan's books. Surely one may discuss the question of whether McLuhan is original or banal, serious or a practical joker, or even partly interesting and partly grotesque, without being thrown into a frenzy, as though the author of *Understanding Media* were Hitler himself. The British and American authors of *McLuhan: Pro and Con** succeed, when necessary, in being categorically and sharply opposed to McLuhan, but without losing their calm or proclaiming that Armageddon is upon us.

Of what, exactly, do McLuhan's ideas consist? They can be divided into two parts. First, there is a small number of theses on the gradual replacement of printing by images, on the changes that the new media are causing in perception, thought, and sensitivity, on the new modes of communication and even of community that result from them, and in general on all the effects deriving from the fact that books are no longer the main vehicle of information. These constitute the valuable element in McLuhan's thought: a theory of audiovisual man. As a theory, it may be true or false, but it is at least an attempt to establish what audiovisual man has to offer that is new—and without bothering about whether the author is going to be applauded or jeered.

* New York, 1968.

A second group of ideas consists in rather cavalier views of history, in sometimes misleading generalizations, and in gross errors. These latter are certainly to be condemned. But are they sufficient reason for the hostility of the European intelligentia? It hardly seems likely. When comparable absurdities were discovered in the works of Nietzsche, Heidegger, Teilhard de Chardin, and Malraux, it was regarded as being in bad taste to mention them. The evaluation of a philosophical system according to the standards of exactitude generally accepted in history or science is usually regarded as evidence of a ridiculous scientism. Why then should McLuhan alone not have the right to make mistakes?

It happens occasionally that McLuhan says some very perceptive things more or less in the form of a joke; and then it is quite depressing to see European intellectuals take him literally and offer grave commentaries on what McLuhan himself calls his "rockets," the obvious intention of which is to provoke. McLuhan coldly states, for instance, that Americans will never understand mathematics until that science is taught over the telephone. He says that, visually, European cars are so ugly that their creators must have conceived of them not as things to be looked at, but as something either to pass through or to put on one's back, like a sweater. He defines a medium as a piece of meat, brought by a burglar to distract the watchdog of the mind; and he says that the effect of motion pictures as a medium has no relation to the content of the films. One must be totally deprived of that sixth sense, which is the sense of humor, to mistake McLuhan's intention.

With respect to McLuhan's ideas on the subject of the audiovisual culture of our time, it is hard to understand why certain intellectuals regard them as dangerous, or reactionary. In *Verbi-Voco-Visual Explorations*,* for example, there is a chapter on the future of education which was written before the world-wide student revolts, and which seems to me to be very "Leftist" in tone; the same is true for a "hippie" chapter on love. And McLuhan's views on war, democracy, the black problem, and international justice cannot honestly be called reactionary—although they are often pessimistic.

In the final analysis, there is no explanation for the horror with which European intellectuals view Mr. McLuhan's ideas, unless it is due to a sort of establishmentarian panic at the sight of an author who has concluded that, in a world where 60 percent of the people are illiterate, the primacy of the printed word has come to an end. In my opinion, their panic is not justified, either morally or practically. The fact that books may no longer be monarchs of all they survey does not mean that books, as such, will disappear; it means that the printed word will have a new, and probably a more precise, function in communication.

. The information revolution is both a political revolution and an intellectual revolution. It calls into question both power and culture. It challenges the distinction between governors and governed, between intelligentia and masses. No one can claim to be a revolutionary who wants to abolish the political revolution and support the intellectual revolution.

The mass media, above all, have proved to be a means not only of transmission, but also of causing people to act on an event, and no longer by propaganda, but through the information itself. This situation, commonplace as it is in the United States, was experienced by

* New York, 1967.

the French only for a few weeks in May 1968. On that occasion, the media were part of the events covered, and they affected those events. In the United States, television produces a constant rubbing-of-elbow among communities which, without television, might never meet, but which, through television, know one another with some intimacy. Direct coverage of a black riot or of police intervention on a campus not only allows the population as a whole to become better "informed" and to "reflect" on that information—which is the classic concept of information—but it also transforms the spectator into an actor; it makes him more than the product of his own personal experience; it incorporates him into the event.

It is this new, active function of the mass media that has struck fear into the hearts of the Spiro Agnews of the world, the men who almost everywhere exercise a monopolistic control over television. And they are right to be afraid.

Chapter 14

THE UNITED STATES: Detonator of Revolution

IF WE DRAW UP a list of all the things that ail mankind today, we will have formulated a program for the revolution that mankind needs: the abolition of war and of imperialist relations by abolishing both states and the notion of national sovereignty; the elimination of the possibility of internal dictatorship (a concomitant condition of the abolition of war); world-wide economic and educational equality; birth control on a planetary scale; complete ideological, cultural, and moral freedom, in order to assure both individual happiness through independence and a plurality of choice, and in order to make use of the totality of human creative resources.

Obviously this is a utopic program, and it has nothing in its favor, except that it is absolutely necessary if mankind is to survive. The exchange of one political civilization for another, which that program implies, seems to me to be going on right now in the United States. And, as in all the great revolutions of the past, this exchange can become world-wide only if it spreads, by a sort of political osmosis, from the prototype-nation to all the others.

The United States is the country most eligible for the role of prototype-nation for the following reasons: it enjoys continuing economic prosperity and rate of growth, without which no revolutionary project can succeed; it has technological competence and a high level of basic research; culturally it is oriented toward the future rather than toward the past, and it is undergoing a revolution in behavioral standards, and in the affirmation of individual freedom and equality; it rejects authoritarian control, and multiplies creative initiative in all domains—especially in art, life style, and sense experience—and allows the co-existence of a diversity of mutually complementary of alternative subcultures.

In Japan, we also find some of these conditions realized; a high rate of growth, and competence in technology and basic research. There is, however, a tendency to allow the authoritarian and feudal relationships of the old days to creep into business and government. Thus, Japan does not provide that aspect of change which would make it a model for other societies; i.e., the rejection of authoritarian controls, and the liberation of creativity in the form of new life styles, new experiences, and new behavioral patterns. For that reason, I do not believe that Japan, at least at present, has a revolutionary potential.

It is evident from the above that the various aspects of a revolution are interrelated; so much so that, if one aspect is missing, the others are incomplete. There are five revolutions that must take place either simultaneously or not at all: a political revolution; a social revolution; a technological and scientific revolution; a revolution in culture, values, and standards; and a revolution in international and interracial relations. The United States is the only country, so far as I can see, where these five revolutions are simultaneously in progress and are organically linked in such a way as to constitute a single revolution. In all other countries, either all five revolutions are missing, which settles the problem, or one or two or three of them are lacking, which relegates revolution to the level of wishful thinking.

The indispensable tool for the realization of these five revolutions and of the condition of economic growth and prosperity which is necessary for them to flourish, is political freedom. This is the same political freedom that resulted from the first world revolution, but within its present context of complete freedom of information at the level of the mass media. This freedom of information is the prerequisite for all political freedom as it exists today.

The liberty which resulted from the first revolution is therefore necessary. Without it, a modern authoritarian regime could crush any uprising or insurrection, except perhaps one resulting from defeat in a foreign war. (Nasser, however, survived even that—but only because of the state of intellectual backwardness in which he had kept the Egyptian people for twenty years.) Short of a military collapse, there is no possibility of a revolution in today's police states. The first reason is that, in practice, it is impossible to mobilize the means of protest. The second is that lack of information in those societies makes it impossible for revolutionaries to formulate accurate judgments; and therefore, as we know from experience, if they ever succeed in coming to power, they turn out to be as reactionary and as incompetent as the regimes they replaced.

Finally, I would say that the optimum conditions for the realization of revolution are those in which the forces of change exist in an atmosphere of constitutional benevolence, which allows them to make enormous progress without the necessity of provoking an actual civil war. In other words, the more that change is possible through legal means, the better the chances of revolution. The opposite is true of the authoritarian states, where violence and an open breach must necessarily occur at an early stage—a stage at which their chances for success are minimal. Despite all romantic revolutionary clichés to the contrary, it is a sign of weakness, and not of strength, to get rid of ants by burning down the house. Violence and resistance obtain the most substantial results when it is possible for them to present themselves as the exercise of constitutional rights. After all, the only important revolutionary results are those that endure. Even the most noble undertakings, such as the Paris Commune, lose all value for the future (except a certain sentimental value) the moment that they fail. The logical conclusion is that optimum revolutionary progress occurs when changes can be brought about within at least the letter of the existing legal framework, and when changes can be broadened within that same framework. Such changes are the only ones that endure. We may therefore say that revolutionary action is most profound, varied, fertile, and creative when it takes place within the classic liberal system.

This constitutional margin of revolutionary action—that is, freedom—is greater in the United States than in any other country. This aspect of America's revolutionary potential will be discussed in the following chapter. Then, we will examine some of the basic changes that are being allowed to happen in the United States; for revolutions are not measured by the things that are done, but by the things that are prevented and by those that are allowed to happen.

Chapter 15

THE RIGHTS AND THE MEANS

IN ORDER TO STUDY the reality of America, we must proceed by way of a double measurement. First, we must measure reality against the distortions of anti-Americanism; and then, we must measure it against the claims of the progressivist opposition in America itself. In the first case, we find that things are seldom as bad as they are made to appear. In the second, once we have been able to isolate the United States intellectually, and to put ourselves in the place of those who live in American society and with its problems, we find that our criteria have changed, and that criticism becomes justifiably more uncompromising.

The existence of these two factors obliges an observer to adopt a divided attitude. He finds that he must, on the one hand, protest against the habitually distorted view of America that is propagated abroad; and, in that case, he appears to be defending America from a conservative standpoint. On the other hand, he must constantly take into account the subversive forces that actually exist in America, and the reasons that explain and justify their existence. Every revolutionary critique, of course, is relative to the context of the revolution. The higher the level of civilization of the society affected by revolution, the higher the level of criticism. Thus, in May and June 1968, news of the revolt of the French student community was interpreted in eastern Europe at the eastern-European level rather than at that of France. The Czechs, for example, seemed unable to understand that it was not a revolt against France, but against de Gaulle; and, in Warsaw, many people refused to believe the news at all, and regarded it as just another propaganda exercise. Both both the Czechs and the Poles, whether or not they believed that the revolt was actually taking place, were perfectly willing to admit the relative nature of every revolutionary undertaking. In other words, they were aware that an Establishment may appear to be unbearably repressive in one country, and yet, to other countries, it may be the object of great longing and envy.

The people of Europe and the Third World, however, are unwilling to extend that awareness to the United States. The reason, no doubt, is that their self-esteem makes it impossible for them to admit Americans are more civilized and more democratic, and at the same time more revolutionary and innovative, than they are. When a Russian deplores the restrictions on freedom in France, he is perfectly justified—so long as he does so *within a French context*; that is, by taking into account French history and French culture, and by measuring those restrictions against a Frenchman's legitimate aspirations. But when a Russian, his voice quivering with pity, declares that, according to Soviet standards, the French government is dictatorial, he is being absurd.

The latter attitude is one that is so widespread with respect to the United States that even the most ardent partisan of the Left is tempted, if he is honest and has no need to blame someone else for his own failings, to rise to the defense of traditional America—if for no other reason than to emphasize the originality of the revolutionary movement that is attacking traditional America. Because of what this movement has already achieved, we must say, in any case, that it is operating at a higher level than revolutions taking place elsewhere. Most of these other revolutions are either concerned with catching up with the first world revolution or they are pseudo-socialist revolutions that have failed, and then turned their failure into totalitarianism; or they are more in the nature of a backlash than of a revolution—as in France, where it is directed against the established forces of conservative re-action, and where its purpose is to remind those forces, from time to time, that they had better not go too far.

In most of the countries that have had, at one time or another, a democratic regime, what is called "revolution" is not at all a transition from a society produced by the first world revolution to a second revolution that will introduce new elements. It is generally a guerrilla operation designed to recover the gains of the first revolution; that is, to prevent the dismantling of liberal democracy by a police-state regime and the substitution for it of a society that, in any case, would not be socialist. What European revolutionaries often forget is that this kind of guerrilla action is not necessary in America. Liberal democracy is essentially intact in the United States, and revolutionaries in that country do not have to spend their time trying to regain the freedom to sell leftist newspapers in the streets.

They can turn the whole of their attention to the problem of attaining the next revolutionary stage.

It seems to be indispensable to the peace of soul of most people to believe that the most powerful country in the world is almost the most reactionary. We must believe that, if we are to believe that the reactionary trends in our own countries are an offshoot of American imperialism. Sometimes this conviction leads us to the most incredible stupidities. On July 4, 1970, for example, a French radio station broadcast an item which said, substantially, that, in the United States, a newspaperman, as an experiment, had stopped a number of people on the street and read parts of the Declaration of Independence to them. Then he had asked them for their opinion of what they had just heard. The people all replied that the document was undoubtedly a communist manifesto, or an anarchist manifesto, or a radical manifesto, or a document of dissent, or at least something written by the Black Panthers—and that whoever wrote it should be sent to jail. Now, if we read the Declaration of Independence of July 4, 1776, we see that it begins by referring to America as a group of English colonies; then, it goes on to list the grievances of the colonies against George III, from the unjustifiable presence of British troops in the colonies to the imposition of exorbitant taxes. It ends by proclaiming the constitutive independence of "the United States of America." In other words, the Declaration of Independence is so easy to situate in history that it is hard to believe people could confuse it with a communist manifesto, or anything else. Certainly, the results of this poll, if the poll really took place, do not carry much sociological weight. But that is not the point. The point is that the story was picked up by the French newspapers, and made the rounds. By the end of July, it had been so widely repeated, and with so many variations, that I was not really surprised when a friend of mine, who is a cool-headed and generally well-informed man, began arguing that the vast majority of the American people had rejected the Declaration of Independence. Which meant, logically, that the American people were ready to swear allegiance to the British crown. Such nonsense is not without a purpose. It serves as a comfort and a consolation in a country where violations of constitutional rights are every-day occurrences—even though France is better off in that respect than many other countries.

Even when news is of a more serious nature, there is always a tendency to be partisan in reporting it. Commentaries, especially, usually emphasize the "fascist" aspects of a situation, and minimize the democratic aspects. In July 1970, for instance, Nixon signed an anticrime bill which, in certain circumstances, authorizes preventive detention and police search. Immediately, the press of Europe and Latin America began talking about "American fascism" and the drift toward a police-state regime. However, there are several things about the anticrime bill that were not mentioned in the foreign press. To begin with, until the passage of the anticrime bill, preventive detention was unknown in the United States; and this point certainly should be of some interest to the citizens of countries where preventive detention, despite laws to the contrary, is so commonly used that it has almost attained the stature of an established institution. Secondly, the preventive detention authorized by the anticrime bill is not preventive detention as we know it in France. It provides only for the detention of a prisoner on parole, who had already been convicted of murder or assault, and who now commits another crime. He may be detained only until his trial, and only if he is considered dangerous and likely to commit another crime unless he is locked up. One must admit that for a country in which crimes of violence are increasing at a high rate every year, this seems a fairly moderate form of detention, and one which affects only a limited number of cases. The situation is very different in France, for example, where about seventy thousand investigations are opened every year, which result in the preventive detention of some sixty thousand people. Moreover, this is in complete contravention of the very laws which French magistrates are supposed to apply. French law states that preventive detention may be used only when "there is good reason to believe that the accused may attempt to flee, to influence witnesses, to destroy evidence, to commit new infractions, or to disturb the public order." In other words, this law, which is not applied (and which, if it were, would result in the release of nine out of ten prisoners), but which exists on the books in France, is the same as the law that has been passed in the United States—and that has been branded as a fascist measure. Moreover, the anticrime law, which affects only two-time losers, or worse, is regarded in America as being extremely severe. This, of course, is all in the judicial domain; we have not even mentioned the police practice of detaining people for several days without any authorization whatsoever, which, common as it is elsewhere, is virtually unknown in America. So far as the police search "without knocking" that the new law allows, it has to do with special circumstances, and is designed to facilitate the battle against illegal use of drugs.

The Nixon anticrime law has naturally been attacked by the American opposition, since the threshold of alarm regarding the erosion of citizens' rights is much lower in America than elsewhere. For the moment, however, it is in force only in the District of Columbia, and before it can be applied on a nation-wide basis it must be approved by the state legislatures. Whatever the eventual outcome, the fact remains that this law, however unprecedented in America, is much more lenient than comparable legislation in almost all the other countries of the world, and much less liable to be used as a tool of repression than, say, the *loi anti-casseur*** that was enacted in France in 1970.

The most important political trials in recent American history are those of the Chicago Seven and of the Black Panthers; and even these, judicially, and juridically, have been handled as ordinary trials. It was enough for President Brewster of Yale University to say, "I doubt that the Black Panthers can get a fair trial in this country," for the Panthers' chances of getting a fair trial to become noticeably better. Police persecution of the Panthers, and the summary execution of several Panthers in 1969, has been brought to public attention by legal means. I know of very few countries where police machinations of this kind would be exposed so quickly. And it is even more remarkable when we recall that the Black Panthers are an extremist organization who make no secret of their intention of resorting to political assassination. From a revolutionary standpoint, one may or may not approve of this policy. From the legal standpoint, however, regardless of what society one is talking about, it is ridiculous to describe the prosecution of the Panthers as "fascistic." What society would not prosecute people who plant bombs in public buildings?

American revolutionaries, in effect, are in an ideal situa-

* According to the provisions of this law, any person who is present during a demonstration that causes material damage is subject to indictment, even if it is impossible to establish his personal responsibility for the damage. The *loi anti-casseur* therefore establishes the principle of collective responsibility—a principle which the whole evolution of modern jurisprudence has tended elsewhere to eliminate.

tion. They are the beneficiaries of the system whose failings they denounce. It is a situation that produces the maximum revolutionary return, especially at the propaganda level. And the results of this situation can easily be seen. The Panthers, for example, enjoy a great deal of sympathy from within the Establishment. Leonard Bernstein, one of the most celebrated conductors in the world, in January 1970, gave a reception in his New York apartment for their benefit and in their honor; and his guests were people famous in literature, the arts, and politics. An F.B.I. report of July 1970 points out that the Panthers receive large donations from the bearers of some of America's most illustrious names.

Regarding the trial of the Chicago Seven—seven men allegedly involved in the upheaval that accompanied the Democratic National Convention of 1968 in Chicago— what was most commented on in Europe was the torrent of sentences for contempt of court that poured down on the defendants and their lawyers during the hearings. What is usually not mentioned is that the Chicago Seven and their lawyers resorted to a deliberate tactic of provocation—addressing the presiding judge, Julius Hoffman, as "Julie," undressing in court, talking, yelling, and demanding that a picture of Washington be removed from the courtroom because he was "a slave trader." It is possible that those tactics were effective; but one really does not see what alternative Judge Hoffman had except to rule them in contempt—a lack of alternatives which did not prevent a large segment of the American press from branding the Judge's reaction as paranoid.

At that point, the problem was one of procedure, and jurists were at a loss. It was legally impossible to try the Chicago Seven if they were not allowed to be present in the courtroom. Someone suggested enclosing the defendants in a soundproof plexiglass cubicle, from which they could see and hear the proceedings, but not be heard; but that proved to be technically difficult. One of the defendants, in reaction to this suggestion, had himself photographed with a gag over his mouth and holding a sign that read: "From now on, this is how we'll be tried in the United States." And the picture, of course, appeared in the European press—and in one newspaper the photo was described as illustrating a measure authorized by the Justice Department.

Eventually, all seven defendants were acquitted, by a jury, of having "crossed a state line with the *intention* of inciting to riot," which was the basis on which the prosecution had proceeded. Five were convicted of assault and battery, and were released on bail (which was put up by "generous donors") pending an appeal. Judge Hoffman himself became the target of a movement to remove him from the bench for having exceeded his powers. And the law which the Chicago Seven were accused of violating, and which is regarded as unconstitutional by a large majority of experts in constitutional law, has been referred to the Supreme Court, where the constitutionality will be determined.

The follow-up to the trial of the Chicago Seven is a good illustration of the effective means at the disposal of American citizens to guard against the violation of their constitutional rights by the federal, state, or municipal governments. Every year, many such decisions are handed down, the purpose of which is to protect the rights of the American people. Some of these affect the course of history, as the 1954 ruling against racial discrimination. Others are intended to put a stop to the intrigues of various pressure groups, e.g., the ruling that reversed a decision of Nixon's to postpone school intergration in

Mississippi, and which fixed the final date for the achievement of integration as February 1, 1970. Another such decision, of April 7, 1969, declared unconstitutional "all laws intended to prohibit the private reading of obscene books or the private showing of erotic films."

The Congress itself has no power to legislate contrary to the Constitution. When it does, we are reminded that courts other than the Supreme Court have power to protect the rights of the people. Thus, in Boston, on April 1, 1969, a federal court declared unconstitutional a law which made religious beliefs the sole basis for conscientious objection. The ruling specified that Congress, in passing that law, had made use of "an unjustifiable and discriminatory principle, to the detriment of atheists and agnostics" whose moral beliefs would not permit them to bear arms. (To these achievements, let us compare the accomplishments of our Council of State in France, whose decisions are treated with such contempt when they find against the Executive branch; the nonexistent role of our Constitutional Council; and, finally, the astonishing flexibility of our Judicial branch in political trials.)

In the area of elections, citizens' activity is as effective as it is in the judicial domain. An excellent illustration of this is the American system of "primary elections." To us Europeans, the principles and the practical value of primaries is not very clear. In America, however, they have a very well-defined goal, which is to counterbalance the influence of party machines and professional politicians and prevent them from working to the detriment of the electoral body; that is, to allow the voter to make a real choice, rather than be presented with alternatives that have been decided beforehand by the bureaucrats. Primary elections, which go back only about fifty years, allow candidates to appeal directly to the voters without having to go through the party apparatus, and without having to obtain the party's *imprimatur*. This was the case in 1968, with Senator Eugene McCarthy, the advocate of immediate negotiation in Vietnam. Therefore, the myth of presidential candidates being handpicked by professional politicians at party conventions is precisely that: a myth. Primary elections are the most effective means of forcing the hands of the professional politicians. It is almost certain that Robert Kennedy, if he had lived, would have been nominated by the Democratic National Convention—despite the opposition of the official party machinery which was controlled by Johnson and committed to Humphrey. Moreover, Johnson's defeat in the New Hampshire primaries in March 1968 was an important factor in his decision (announced March 31) not to seek another term. (The refusal of a President of the United States to seek a second full term is generally regarded as an admission of failure.) In the period between Johnson's announcement and Robert Kennedy's assassination, the two declared (and rival) candidates for the Democratic nomination, Kennedy and McCarthy, were both unacceptable to the party machine; but this did not prevent them from scoring remarkable successes against party-backed candidates in the primaries. All this is even more surprising when we remember that, in Senator McCarthy's case, this success was achieved with virtually no financial support. Elections, obviously, are precisely what we allow them to be.

American primary elections have about the same function as the referendum in Switzerland. Referendums exist in France also, but they are not the equivalent of those of the Swiss. In France, the initiative for calling a referendum rests with the state alone. In Switzerland, however, the people share that initiative. Any Swiss citizen can draw up a petition calling for a referendum on any subject; and, if he can collect a sufficient number of signatures, the referendum must be held. Naturally, any system that allows the people to speak without permission, as it were, is profoundly distressing to professional politicians. There is nothing they hate more than to hear the people answering a question that they were never asked. Hence, the great scarcity of political systems that allow the people to speak for themselves.

Certainly, it would be wrong to think that citizens' rights in America are not constantly being threatened by the forces of reaction. The point is that, in the United States, those rights are defended more strenuously than elsewhere—especially more strenuously than in France, where citizens' rights are on the decline.* And the explanation is that the Left has been more alert and more powerful in America than in other countries. Therefore, when we hear Europeans say that civil rights are of no use to the revolutionary cause, we can be sure that it is a case of sour grapes. Civil rights are the result of earlier revolutions, and, as such, are important to subsequent revolutions. Moreover, a revolutionary movement can function much more effectively in a society where citizens' rights are respected—even if that society is partially repressive—than in a totalitarian society which is totally repressive and where those rights exist not at all. The more a revolutionary society can adopt elements of the society that preceded it, the higher the level at which it can operate. The very existence of such elements means that the previous society found solutions to problems of great complexity, and that it was therefore able to develop a countercivilization that was richer, from a human standpoint, than the civilization that it replaced. If

* On this subject, see Roger Errera's *Les Libertés à l'abandon*, Paris, 1968.

the best things in the Old Regime, for instance, had not survived the French Revolution, republican France would not have been worth much. If women had not been given the vote fifty years ago in the United States—that is, a quarter century before they got it in France and Italy— the women's liberation movement in America would certainly not be in a position to question, as it is actually doing, the validity of our whole male-oriented civilization.

To make a revolution is not to destroy everything that went before. It is to destroy what must be destroyed; and what must be destroyed is never that same thing at any given moment or in any given place. There has been only one coherent advocate of a contrary philosophy, and he defined the function of the revolutionary as follows:

> "We are barbarians, and we want to be barbarians. It is a title of honor. We are the ones who will rejuvenate the world. The world of today is dying. Our sole function is to finish the job."

ADOLF HITLER

Chapter 16

JESUS, MARX, AND AMERICA

THE "HOT" ISSUES in America's insurrection against itself, numerous as they are, form a cohesive and coherent whole within which no one issue can be separated from the others. These issues are as follows: a radically new approach to moral values; the black revolt; the feminist attack on masculine domination; the rejection by young people of exclusively economic and technical social goals; the general adoption of noncoercive methods in education; the acceptance of the guilt for poverty; the growing demand for equality; the rejection of an authoritarian culture in favor of a critical and diversified culture that is basically new, rather than adopted from the old cultural stockpile; the rejection both of the spread of American power abroad and of foreign policy; and a determination that the natural environment is more important than commercial profit. None of the groups concerned

with any one of these points, and none of the points
themselves, would have been able to gain as much strength
and attention as they have if they had been isolated
from other groups and other points. The blacks and
the feminists—one a racial group and the other a sexual
group, both of which comprise several socioeconomic
levels—are two categories of Americans which (along with
students, of course) have always been most strongly
opposed to the Vietnam war. The Chicago segment of
the women's liberation movement, for instance, wrote to
Playboy in July 1970, pointing out that the magazine,
by perpetuating the image of woman as man's sexual toy,
was indirectly responsible for the war. That accusation
may seem frivolous, or even unjust, particularly since
Playboy is aimed, at least in part, at an audience of
selfish hedonists. However, it also happens to be one of
the most progressive magazines in America, and its intellectual level is exceptionally high, given—or even abstracting from—its wide circulation (over five million). It
takes very advanced positions on political and racial questions, the Vietnam war, and individual freedom; and in
its interviews, which are at once comprehensive and detailed, well-known personalities are required to give their
opinions on explosive subjects. Certainly, it plays a paradox-
ical role as a liberating influence that no other "popular"
magazine has ever attained before. Even so, it is interesting to note that American feminists make a connection
here between a moral problem (the social inferiority of
women) and a political problem (the war). By the same
token, the defection of a part of America's youth from a
dogmatic and utilitarian culture is motivated by the fact
that they find that culture unsatisfying, that they want to
be happy and do not want to be "like their parents" or
members of the Establishment; but it is also due to the

fact that that culture results in a society where there is poverty, racism, slums, etc. The battle against an authoritarian society is expressed by the twin attitudes of political opposition and militant solidarity with minorities. The moral revolution, the new forms in music, art, and spectator-entertainment are all part of the battle. Sexual liberty, pop music, marijuana have become as much a part of politics as politics has become a part of morality. Pop-music festivals, of which Woodstock has become the prototype, are explosions of personal and sexual expression, of liberating behavior and music, in which all these elements take on political dimensions. That, no doubt, is the reason why the French municipalities were sufficiently frightened to ban pop-music festivals during the summer of 1970—even though the political content of such festivals in Europe is rather limited. Even in America, one of the most popular folk singers, Joan Baez, was jailed twice for her political activities. In an interview (in *Playboy*, by the way) Miss Baez said, "I have contempt for all flags, and not only the American flag. A flag is the symbol of a piece of territory that is considered to be more important than the men who live in it. We have to rid ourselves of even the concept of nations." Joan Baez's husband is currently serving a prison term for draft evasion.

The moral revolution, the cultural revolution, and the political revolution are but a single revolution. In San Francisco, a group composed of women and homosexuals (members of the Women's Liberation Front and the Gay Liberation Front), shouting "Cambodia is obscene! Sex is not obscene!" burst into a psychiatrists' convention which was discussing the "treatment" of homosexuality. The criticism of paternalistic and moralistic psychiatry, in this instance, not only takes on a political form, but also produces new courage in the affirmation of self.* The Homosexual Community and the League of Women Homosexuals publish several newspapers, and their demands and demonstrations receive television coverage. In Washington, D.C. on May 13, 1970, a representative of the underground press, with a few friends, forced his way into a meeting of the President's Commission on Pornography and bombarded the members of the commission with creampuffs, and then left—as the police stood quietly by.** A free-abortion law, and a law allowing divorce by mutual consent (or even on the basis of a unilateral decision), are both receiving increasing attention and support.

The interconnection between countercultural themes appeared again on June 10, 1970, at the Venice Biennale, when a group of American artists promoting an "artists' strike against racism, sexism, and war" withdrew their

* It was a rather stormy confrontation. The indignant psychiatrists began loudly counterattacking their putative patients. One of them shouted to a sign-carrying member of the Gay Liberation Front, "Please quiet down!" The other one answered, "We've been quiet for five thousand years!" And the psychiatrist shouted back, "In that case, a half hour more won't hurt."

** The commission itself, widely analyzed by the press, was not noticeably opposed to what the underground press stands for. In their report, which was submitted and published (all reports of presidential and Senate commissions are published) in August 1970, they concluded that there was no foundation for the belief that erotic magazines, books, or films give rise to sex crimes or constitute a threat to the morals of young people. President Nixon was then moved to "deplore" these findings—which shows how little the commission regarded itself as a presidential puppet. Moreover, the commission's conclusions were corroborated by the results of an investigation published in *Newsweek*, December 21, 1970, titled "Pornography Goes Public." Let me give the American reader an example of how such things are handled elsewhere. Michel Debré, when he was France's Minister of Finance, asked for a report on fiscal fraud. The report was compiled—but was kept secret because its conclusions were so shocking. This was not hard to bring about, since the commission members were not independent investigators, but employees of the Ministry of Finance. Compare this with the fact that the *Scranton Report*, on campus unrest, was not only published, but published just before the off-year elections of 1970, even though it was highly unfavorable to the Nixon administration.

works from the exposition as a protest against the policies of their government. This group comprised thirty-three of the forty-four persons selected to represent the United States at the festival, and included the cream of contemporary American artists, such as Josef Albert, Leonard Baskin, John Cage, Sam Francis, Jasper Johns, Roy Lichtenstein, Robert Morris, Claes Oldenburg, Robert Rauschenberg, and Andy Warhol. So far as I know, there was never a similar large-scale protest of first-rate French artists during the Indochina war or the Algerian war—I mean a protest involving a real sacrifice in terms of one's career. The same sort of phenomenon is taking place in all the visual arts: in the modern American theater, where drama has been recast and joined to an instinctual explosion; in such films as Andy Warhol's *Lonesome Cowboys*, which is a homosexual parody of cowboy Westerns, and which I saw in a commercial movie theater one afternoon in Chicago; in stage plays in which the sex act is performed on the stage; or in *Macbird*, a take-off on *Macbeth*, in which the President of the United States and his wife are openly accused of having had John Kennedy assassinated. Examples could be multiplied indefinitely to demonstrate the thesis that liberation must be complete, or it will not exist at all.

There have been political revolutions that failed because, among other reasons, they were limited to a single area, to politics or economics, and therefore were not able to generate the "new man" who could have given meaning to new political or economic institutions. In *Prolégomènes à un troisième manifeste du surréalisme*, André Bréton writes: "We must not only stop the exploitation of man by man, but we must also re-examine—from top to bottom, without hypocrisy and without dodging the issues—the problems involved in the relationship between men and women.". And Charles Fourier pointed out that the revolutionaries of 1789 had failed because "they bowed before the concept of the sanctity of marriage." If women had been allowed to become their own masters, he says, "it would have been a scandal, and a weapon capable of undermining the foundations of society."* It should be noted, however, that even the divorce law passed by the revolutionaries, and subsequently adopted by the Napoleonic Code, was so far ahead of its time that it was abolished during the Restoration. It was revived only at the time of the Third Republic, but in such a limited form as to be more restrictive than it had been at the beginning of the nineteenth century.

If ever a revolution was one-sided, it was the Russian Revolution of 1917. Its leaders would not permit the slightest degree of cultural or moral liberation. Thus, Lenin wrote to Clara Zetkin: "We have not reached the end of your list of sins, Clara. I have been told that, during an evening session of reading and discussion with the workers, you were concerned mostly with questions of sex and marriage. I could hardly believe my ears." And he adds: "Questions of sex and marriage are not regarded [by you] as part of the principal social question; but, on the contrary, the main social question itself appears as a part of, or an appendix to, the sex problem . . . This attitude can disguise itself in as many subversive and revolutionary forms as it wants; the fact remains that it is a purely bourgeois attitude . . . There is no place for such an attitude in the Party, among the militant proletariat which is conscious of its spirit of class distinctions."** And here is what the Great Revolutionary has to say about the educational liberation of young people: "I have also heard

* Quoted by Simone Déprou, in *Catalogue de l'Exposition internationale du surréalisme 1959–1960.*
** *Lénine tel qu'il fut.* Paris, 1934.

that sexual problems are one of the favorite subjects of your youth organizations . . . This is especially scandalous, and especially dangerous, for the youth movement. Such subjects can easily lead to overexcitement, to the sexual stimulation of certain individuals, and to a breakdown in the health and the strength of young people." And Lenin concludes: "I can never be certain of either the dependability or the tenacity in battle of women for whom personal romance and politics are all mixed together, or of men who chase every skirt in sight and who allow themselves to be bewitched by the first woman who comes along. No. These things have no part in our revolution . . . Sexual excess is a sign of bourgeois degeneracy. The proletariat is the rising class, and there is no need to get them drunk, or to make them deaf, or to stir them up."

It comes as no surprise to find the same sort of narrow-mindedness with regard to the scientific and moral revolution wrought by psychoanalysis. Lenin's position in that respect could have been lifted right out of the writings of France's super-Right-winger, Charles Maurras. Here is Lenin's opinion, as he expressed it to Clara Zetkin: "Today, Freud's theory is nothing more than a fashionable caprice. I have absolutely no confidence in the sexual theories which have been disseminated in articles, reports, pamphlets, etc.—in short, in the scientific literature that blooms with such exuberance in the dirt of bourgeois society. I am as wary of those who are constantly and stubbornly absorbed by sexual questions as I am of a Hindu fakir absorbed by the contemplation of the navel." It was perfectly logical, therefore, for the communists to be opposed to contraception, when the time came, even though that issue coincided with the beginning of real independence for women. The wife of Maurice Thorez declared that "birth control, or voluntary motherhood, is a trap for the masses; but it is also a weapon against social law in the hands of the bourgeoisie."* Also, one hardly need be reminded that divorce is nonexistent in a large part of Europe; or that, especially in Italy, the Left has often collaborated with the Church to prevent its introduction. I certainly do not mean to infer that the battle against sexual repression is the whole of the revolutionary struggle; but it is undoubtedly one of the surest signs of an *authentic* revolutionary struggle.

In practice, sexual repression indicates the existence of authoritarianism in a diversity of areas: in family life and religion; in relations between the sexes, between age groups and between races and social classes. Conversely, the appearance of sexual liberty is symptomatic of freedom from authoritarianism in those areas. When culture is "directed," we may be certain that it is involved in a relationship of authority; that is, it is subjected to force. One of the most striking characteristics of the revolutionary movement in America is that it is the first such movement in which all demands are part of a single front, and are advanced simultaneously on the same program. Demands belonging to the individualist-anarchist tradition, and those referring to the organized political struggle of the oppressed (or of the less nonoppressed, as the case may be), are, for once, all included in one demand.

This situation is what gives political value to the hippie movement, even though the hippies themselves do not want to "become involved" in politics. Their choice of a non-violent way of life, founded upon mutual consideration and help, is also a countersociety, a counterculture; and its influence is greatly increased by the fact that it affects not only young men and women of the middle class, but also such people as bartenders, gardeners, soldiers, com-

* Quoted by J. M. Brohn, in "La Lutte contre la répression sexuelle," in *Partisans*.

munications experts, and pilots. In New York, one can
buy short-hair wigs (for hippies who work in offices) and
hippie wigs (for short-hairs to use at night and on week-
ends).

Eroticism, drugs, long hair, street barricades, stone-
throwing, Molotov cocktails, street warfare—for parents,
these things mean that the devil has taken possession of
their children. And, for that matter, their sons do indeed
exhibit the full Satanic symptomatology: they are Priapean,
hirsute, and they have a fondness for burning things down.
And the hippie is the personification of all these vices.
This oversimplification is possible in Europe, where there
are too few representatives of the *genre* for an indifferent
witness, unaffected by sociological zeal, to make the proper
distinctions. For when dissenters cannot maintain contact
with one another, they break down into nonrepresentative
groups. In the United States, however, where hippies are
more numerous (not only in numbers, but also in proportion to the population), each individual group is sizable.
In 1967, for example, the hippie population of San
Francisco was about 300,000; and San Francisco's total
population at the time was less than 750,000. Given such
proportions, one can imagine that the hippie phenomenon
was easily discernible to all spectators, and even to those
who would have preferred to be blind to it.

The hippies are not identified completely either with
the radicals or with the various groups of the New Left,
such as the Free Speech Movement (F.S.M.), Students for
a Democratic Society (S.D.S.)—which is the model of
European dissent—the Weathermen (a terrorist group
responsible for the bombings of March and April 1970,
especially in New York), and the Y.S.A., or Young Socialist
Alliance, as well as the "yippies"—Youth International
Party—a group, very active in politics, that organized the

demonstrations at the National Democratic Convention in Chicago in 1968.*

There is, therefore, a basis common to all manifestations of the American revolt, and to its European extensions. That basis consists in the rejection of a society motivated by profit, dominated exclusively by economic considerations, ruled by the spirit of competition, and subjected to the mutual aggressiveness of its members. Indeed, beneath every revolutionary ideal we find a conviction that man has become the tool of his tools, and that he must once more become an end and a value in himself. The hippies are characterized by a particularly vivid awareness of that loss of self-identity and of the perversion of the meaning of life. A competitive society, for instance, or a spirit of rivalry, is a source of suffering to them. But they do not self-righteously condemn such societies, or attempt to refute them theoretically; they simply refuse to have any part in them. A hippie, therefore, is above all someone who has "dropped out"; a boy or girl who decided, one day, to stop being a cog in the social machine. Baudelaire suggested adding two additional rights to the Declaration of the Rights of Man: the right to contradict oneself, and the right to walk away. Hippies make much use of both those rights. This use, when it is so widespread as to no longer be marginal, is much more revolutionary than one is willing to admit if one insists on viewing everything dogmatically, in terms of classic political activity. When

---

* *Pourquoi n'êtes-vous pas hippie*, by Bernard Plossu (Paris, 1970), is made up of various interviews, and gives an accurate idea of the hippie movement, of what it has in common with, and what distinguishes it from, other groups of youth in revolt. Plossu is a Frenchman who became a hippie in America, and remained a hippie after returning to France. He is aware of—and his book takes into account—the fact that part of the art of the hippie life is unintelligible to the European public and cannot even be articulated in such a way as to convey its meaning to them. It would be like trying to explain the notion of "swing" to a maiden-lady piano teacher at Paimpol, in 1930.

societies decline seriously, it is because of this internal absenteeism, because its people have discovered new forms of commitment. And American society is painfully aware of this sudden disaffection and of this loss of love. The hippie is the well-known husband who went down to the corner to buy a pack of cigarettes, and never came back. Hippies are the two heroes of Peter Fonda's eclogue on walking away, *Easy Rider*—a film which was looked upon with condescension in Europe, and was barely recognized as a cinematic curiosity, possibly because the sensitivity that inspired it, and that is necessary to understand American counterculture, is less intense in Europe than in America.

Certainly, one can make a good case against the hippies for their political indifference and for their naïveté in rejecting every form of violence—for these are the attitudes that distinguish the hippies. One can even fault them for forgetting that the hippie way of life is possible only in an affluent society and because of a surplus in production (even though the hippie personally may be willing to live in comparative poverty). One can make fun of their nebulous ideology, which is a mixture of confused orientalism and adulterated primitivism (although they are likely to retort that they prefer pop music to ideology). One can jeer at their simplistic confidence in the strength of universal love as the key to all problems (a confidence which, nonetheless, has not prevented the misinformed from mistaking the Sharon Tate murderers for hippies). And one can be astonished at their belief that it is possible for an individual to have absolute freedom without infringing the rights of others. All these things are, no doubt, open to criticism from many standpoints; and they are all no doubt very limited concepts. The fact remains, however, that the hippies' refusal to accept regimentation in any form gives them a mysterious strength and a means of exerting pressure; the same sort of strength and pressure that is exerted by, say, a hunger strike. To those who try to persuade them to give their revolt a political or religious structure, the hippies offer a patient, but absolutely inflexible, resistance. The May uprisings in Paris, and the demonstrations at the Renault plant in France, all seem to the hippies to be too much the product of the harsh society that they are trying to escape. Plossu says of those who were involved in these events that "their ideas of revolt were, in the long run, chains," and their "attempt at liberation, only a form of slavery."

Such words as Plossu's are guaranteed to strike a sour note among lovers of the revolutionary praxis. Nonetheless, this rejection of solutions that are too immediate and too concrete originates in a basic intuition that one of the foundations of revolution that we most need today is the elimination of pathological aggression. Unless that elimination is achieved, no revolution can do anything but lead to a new form of oppression. We do not need a political revolution so much as an antipolitical revolution; otherwise, the only result will be the creation of new police states. Human aggression is a determining factor in human behavior; and it is accepted even more gratuitously, and is even more murderous, than all of the sacred causes by which it justifies itself and on which it bases itself. Unless this root-evil is extirpated, the hippies believe, then everything else will be corrupted. By reflecting that belief in their attitudes and behavior, the hippies at very least perform a useful function; they remind us constantly that a revolution is not simply a transfer of power, but also a change in the goals for the sake of which power is exercised, and a new choice in the objects of love, hate, and respect. Also, the hippies have the advantage of being able to point out, to those who still talk about "freedom at gun-point" in a world dripping with blood that has been shed in vain, that this slogan is nothing more than an outdated jingo.

It is not impossible that intimations of a new and even more thoroughgoing technological advance, and a radical extension of the applications of biological science, may have already decided the question of a "return to nature." The same sort of intimations, or presentiments, acted as a warning signal to man in the 1760s, before the first great technological revolution. And today, as in the time of Rousseau, the struggle for the preservation of the beauty and benefits of nature reveals our need to believe in the goodness of man, or of oneself, and the need to prove that goodness to ourselves. It is making us turn away from a single culture to several cultures. For that reason, it is absurd to regard the ecological battle as a mere skirmish or a spin-off from the main war. The ecological battle is one of the pieces of the revolutionary puzzle, and it is necessary to complete the picture. It gives us the emotional energy necessary, for example, to challenge the omnipotence of the great industrial empires; and such energy is not engendered by a political program, no matter how clear it may be. Not a week passes that we do not hear talk of a law forbidding the use of internal combustion engines by 1975, or of legal actions by New York State or other states to force the airlines to filter their jet-exhaust fumes.

We should have no illusions about the immediate efficacy of these steps, for it seems that the graver the problem the less money the nation-state can devote to its solution. The protection of the environment, in effect, presents problems the solutions to which it is difficult to envision; indeed, some experts see the situation as desperate. In any case, the alarm has been sounded more energetically

and more passionately in the United States than anywhere else. And, characteristically, it has taken two forms:
that of scientific and technical research, and that of a
collective emotion that is incomparably more intense and
widespread in the United States than anywhere else.
"Earth Day" in America was one huge pantheistic feast.
Some say it is because "America is more polluted than any
other country." Europeans always believe that nature is
nonexistent in the United States. They think of the whole
country as one vast Chicago. They forget that the populations of the United States and the nations of the Common
Market are approximately equal—but that the area of the
latter could fit comfortably into one-eighth the area of the
United States. It comes as a surprise to a European, when
he flies over America, to see that the country has more
open space than it does cities. And we see many American
cities surrounded by open countryside, and practically
hidden by greenery because of the practice (even in cities of
a million people) of building houses on wooded lots.

The young men and women, who, on a Saturday in
California, walk naked through the forests, singing and
playing their guitars and flutes, those who lie down in
front of bulldozers to prevent trees from being uprooted,
those who go to live in hippie communes—these people
rarely come from places as suffocated by bad air and
garbage as New York, or Paris, or London. There is a good
deal more to the ecological movement than the effect of a
practical determinism. After all, for thousands of years
mankind has lived (and, for the most part, still lives)
by drinking contaminated water, and he has survived the
resulting dysentery and typhoid epidemics. Suffering apparently is not enough to move one to fight for a better
environment. Malaria has never caused a revolution. In
order to fight, one must be able to see a clear relationship

between nature, technology, economic power, and political power. One must also be able to rise to the belief that nature belongs to every man, and to the realization that an oil slick on the ocean affects one's own good, or better, one's own happiness. The development of such a belief therefore implies the existence of a political awareness that calls for the reshaping of intrasocial relations, for co-proprietorship, for co-dependence, for co-responsibility. Those who still believe that the ecological movement is part of a plan to distract people, a sort of political smoke-screen, may not have seen a *New Yorker* cartoon in which one elderly and obviously wealthy golfer expresses his belief to another that the whole "ecology business" is "just another commie trick." Hardly. The communists, in fact, are as backward about ecology as they are about women and contraception. But, just as Europeans still believe that Americans are puritanical, they still picture Americans as slaves to "gadgets" and pollution-creating machines. The truth is that there is no country in the world where automobiles, for example, are treated more like ordinary tools—or where people drive less like maniacs. Moreover, it is in America that the moral revolution, and the ecological revolution that is part of it, has initiated an ear of caution, if not of outright mistrust, with respect to machines and "the techno-electronic society."

We can therefore conclude that a counterculture,* a countersociety, has already sprung up in the United States. And it is, as it must necessarily be, a countersociety that has nothing marginal about it. It is a revolutionary universe, characterized by the demand for equality of sexes, races, and age groups; by the rejection of the authoritarian relationship on which rest all societies that have been stratified by force and despotism; by the transformation

---

* The expression was coined by Theodore Roszak, in *The Making of a Counterculture*, New York, 1969.

of directed culture into productive culture; by the rejection of nationalism in foreign policy; by the realization of the outdated character of the "authority of the state," constituted without sufficient participation by the people, and exercised under conditions that allow an abuse of power to a degree that has become intolerable; by an insistence on economic and educational equality; by a radical reappraisal of the goals of technology and its consequences; by a demand for absolute individual and cultural freedom, without moral censorship*—which is a variant in the rejection of an authoritarian relationship. When all those demands have been met, it is highly probable that we will have a *homo novus*, a new man very different from other men.

These incentives for revolution, by their cohesiveness, by the great number of Americans who support them, and by the changes in depth that they have already achieved in the sensitivity, conduct, habits, thoughts, and acts of Americans, can be described as the first stage of a revolution. What usually happens is that a political revolution occurs at the top, and that no social revolution

* In order to answer the objections of opponents of "absolute freedom," according to which such freedom could be harmful to the individual himself or to others, I should point out that we are talking about the total abolition of all censorship affecting one's life on *moral* grounds. It frequently happens that a society, under the pretext of protecting the physical well-being of its citizens, exercises a repression that is actually based on moral—or even sadistic—considerations. In the nineteenth century, for instance, it was widely believed that too-frequent sexual relations caused tuberculosis and weakened one's intellectual energy—an obvious attempt to find a utilitarian justification for what was nothing more than a sexual taboo. We have already come a good distance when we are able to distinguish between moral and medical prohibitions. Regarding the drug problem, it is interesting to note that, in the United States, there is a growing opinion that, *if it has really been demonstrated that marijuana is not harmful*, then it would be wise to legalize its use and to concentrate one's attention on the drugs that are actually harmful. This is the first step toward an antidrug attitude that has no punitive or moral character; that is, there is no spirit of retribution on the part of aging drunks, directed against young people who smoke marijuana.

follows to make the political revolution durable. In the United States, however, the social revolution has been largely achieved. What remains to be seen is the possible political application of the reservoir of energy constituted by this mass countersociety.

A revolutionary force therefore exists. The results of its activity also exist: there are two societies, two humanities now confronting one another whose views on the future can hardly be reconciled. We can therefore say that a point of crisis has been reached. Not a halfway point. Not a crisis over this or that particular thing. But a crisis over society itself. What will be the outcome? The true revolutionary solution is to place oneself at the point at which the lines being drawn will converge, and to refrain from adopting any solution from the past.

The American "movement" has been compared to primitive Christianity, sometimes favorably in order to hail the dawning of a new era; and sometimes unfavorably, in order to analyze the narcissistic elements of dissent.* The Black Panthers, on the other hand, call themselves "Marxists-Leninists"; and the students of the Free Speech Movement, who play a dominant role in the New Left, call upon Marx, Lenin, Guevara, and Mao. (In one scene from *The Strawberry Statement*, a female student asks, "Did you know that Lenin liked large breasts?"—as she uncovers her own enormous pair.) The pro-Chinese Progressive Labor Party, whose student branch (W.S.A., or Workers-Students Alliance) set off the occupation of the Harvard campus in the spring of 1969, still clings to the dogma of the working class as the only revolutionary *avant-garde*—a position which, given the American situation, is rather quaint. The Weathermen, on the other hand, following in

* See André Stéphane, *L'Univers contestationnaire*. Paris, 1969.

the footsteps of Trotsky, Guevara, and Marcuse, believe that a world revolution can only come from the Third World and from the blacks.

The religious element of the American movement is undeniable. The *need for sacredness* is being satisfied by the confused adoption and the hit-or-miss practice of oriental religions, and by a return to the Indian cult of natural foods, to astrology (according to which we have now entered the Age of Aquarius, and the astral implications of that fact are being studied diligently), and to a rediscovery of Christianity. Above all, however, this need is being satisfied by the application of a traditional principle that has always been successful in America: the best religions are those that you find for yourself.

America has never had a state religion, either officially or otherwise. European wits who make fun of the endemic religiosity of America, as exemplified by the presence of Bibles in hotel rooms and the inscription "In God We Trust" on money, would do better to reflect on the consequences of a very important cultural fact: that no church of any kind has ever dominated, either by law or *de facto*, the moral, intellectual, artistic, or political life of that immense country. It is true that the President of the United States swears his oath of office on the Bible, and that the President of France does not. The President of France, however, is not the one who is more free of confessional influence. And the same can be said if we compare the two countries (not to speak of Italy or Spain) from the standpoint of freedom from religious influence in the classroom, in the newspaper office, and in the publishing house. *The Yearbook of American Churches* (1969 edition) lists seventy-nine established religions in the United States—and by "established" it means those which have no less than fifty thousand members. If we go below the fifty-thousand mark, the various churches may be numbered in the thousands. Just in Los Angeles, one could change one's religion every day of the year, if one wished to do so; for some of these religions last only a few months, or until their founders tire of the whole thing.

Standing in front of the Berkeley campus at noontime, one can see a group of "Buddhist monks" go dancing by in long yellow robes, their feet bare, their heads shaved—all natives of Oregon or Arizona. Meanwhile, a group of Christian hippies try to drown out the Buddhists' drums by shouting the name of Jesus, and a "naturist pantheist" sells fruits and vegetables grown without fertilizer. Jesus has always been an honored figure in hippie mythology, and there is a group that calls itself "Street Christians" or "Jesus Freaks." The name of Jesus Freaks was at first a term of derision, but the adherents of the cult took it over for themselves. They had no difficulty in finding rich, and generous, benefactors. One of them brought up the aspect of "primitive Christianity," of which some of the Woodstock people were already conscious. "I think you are being *very first century*," he told his friends. The Jesus Freaks have founded several hundred communes, both rural and urban; and they have their own underground newspaper, called *Right On*, in which they inveigh against sexual promiscuity, homosexuality, and drugs. They admit, however, that the drug culture possesses a spirituality that is lacking in the alcohol culture. (The religious connotation of drugs is important; as is the opposition between the two cultures: that of pot, and that of the dry martini.) Even though the Jesus Freaks are in favor of restrictions on personal liberty and call for a renunciation of "permissiveness" (a reversal which would be difficult to bring about), their movement may consolidate itself solely under its religious aspect and lead to a gigantic dropping out. Or millions of people may drop out and invent religious cults of their own. I once read this *graffiti* on a wall of the Santa Cruz campus: "When peace is outlawed, only outlaws can have peace." Thus, a massive countersociety continues to develop, one which lives on the fringes of technological society. For the moment, the latter is wealthy enough to afford a countersociety; but if the countersociety begins to grow excessively, it is obvious that the rate of economic growth in America will immediately begin to slow.

This effect upon economic growth is a possibility. It will not, however, resolve the crisis. One can conceive of a sort of suicide of technological society, an asphyxiation of American power from within, an immense boycott that would weaken and disorganize production. Then America, inhabited by vagrant mystics and ruined bankers, would crumble and sink into the Third World. At that point, international justice would be established and, with imperialism dead at its source, the world would once again move toward democratic socialism. But there is one catch: without scientific and technical progress backed by economic power—progress and power of which America is the main source—the world's problems are insoluble. Moreover, this fictive withdrawal of America into herself would aggravate the country's domestic problems, since it would destroy the very means of satisfying the demands of the blacks, the poor, women, students, and the cities. These groups would then rise up once more, and the result would be a process of decomposition without the possibility of a solution, instead of a revolution—which is a process of disintegration *with* a solution and a new integration of conflicting forces. America's economic and social downfall would make almost certain a drift to the Right among the middle classes, and an authoritarian political regime. It is nonetheless possible that a new religion of the future is being born in the world of the American underground. I do not know for certain. If that is the case, however, I doubt very much that it will be productive, from a revolutionary standpoint, in the immediate future.

These perspectives—or rather, this lack of perspectives—serve to show the limitations of dissent. These limitations have often been discussed—by psychiatrists, particularly, and with great perception—as childish efforts to skirt the "principle of reality." Regarding the ability of dissent to transform reality, Bruno Bettelheim,* in the United States, has much the same reservations as those expressed in Europe by André Stéphane in *L'Univers contestationnaire*. According to Stéphane, no revolution can be based on a rejection of reality. The middle-class youth (i.e., today's student and dissenter) is not so much in revolt against his father as he is unwilling to recognize his father's presence as it exists. Youth, Stéphane says, is dominated by narcissism, self-admiration, and intolerance—all of which are characteristic of the phases of sexual development anterior to the Oedipus complex. A true revolutionary spirit, however, leads one, not to run away from his father, but to take his father's place; not merely to do away with his father, but to *become* his own father. This doing away with the father (only in the youth's imagination, of course) brings us to the Oedipal universe; that is, a universe dominated by the mother, who is simultaneously good and evil, indulgent and frustrating—that is, the prototypical consumer society, from whom youth demands everything, and whom he wishes to destroy.

What characterizes the narcissistic stage is the child's desire to have everything at once. If he is not satisfied, then he takes refuge in the hallucinatory fulfillment of his desires. The need for omnipotence makes progressive action

* See Bettelheim's *The Children of the Dream.* New York, 1969.

impossible, for narcissism ignores the principle of reality and refuses to admit the incompatibility of contradictory solutions. To the narcissistic child, the idea of choice is unbearable.

We know how difficult it is for dissenters to describe the kind of society they long for. This lack of precise ideas, it is sometimes said, is justifiable; after all, it is up to adults to supply solutions. The role of the young is merely to express dissatisfaction, *modo grosso*. This explanation, however, ignores two facts. First, that the spirit of dissent is far from being the exclusive property of the young; and second, that the spirit of dissent excludes all concrete solutions, for solutions are always partial and always subject to expiration, either short-term or long-term.

Any technical discussion, any reservation concerning details—even on the part of those who approve of the dissenters' demands, but who emphasize the difficulties inherent in their practical realization—is regarded by the dissenter as an over-all rejection, and as an act of hostility. To begin a technical discussion is to call the dissenter back to reality; and that is something intolerable to someone for whom only total and instantaneous gratification exists, and who therefore cannot accept either the *quid pro quo* or the step-by-step progress of revolutionary action—let alone of reformism. Everything that contradicts the magical power of words is experienced as a repetition of the original narcissistic wound which was inflicted upon the infant when he first discovered his lack of independence with respect to his environment.

In this universe of all or nothing, of black and white, there is no question of action, but only of redemption. It is not by chance that dissent has been absorbed into some major branches of Christianity, and then refurbished and translated into religious terms. The redeemer may be the workman, the black, or the poor. All the dissenter needs is someone who is suffering, a victim that he can help. Since the Six Day War, he has found it difficult to forgive the Jews for no longer being downtrodden. Victorious Jews do not make good subjects for crucifixion. The rapidity with which some of Israel's friends have dropped that country, without bothering to analyze in detail the causes of the 1967 conflict, indicates that being pro-Israeli has lost its power to absolve from guilt. By the same token, we can easily see why it is necessary for workers to be miserable. "Are you hungry?" students asked the striking workers at the Renault plant—to the astonishment, and amusement, of the workers. If the workers are happy, they can no longer be the dissenter's means of redemption. This is the source of the Marcusian critique of the consumer society, which has as its purpose to reinstate the proletariat in its role as victim—this time by means of the subterfuge of "alienation." Therefore, we are not allowed to admit that the situation of the blacks in America has improved in the past twenty years. Thus to equate the well-being of the proletariat with a sort of counterrevolutionary terrorism presupposes serious distortion of the revolutionary ideal, and the existence of major conflicts within oneself.

No revolution can result from a pretension that one embodies absolute Good and opposes absolute Evil. For that reason, the ease with which purveyors of the irrational have taken over the movement of dissent is disturbing; as disturbing as the spirit of intolerance that has resulted. I am not the first one to notice the similarities between certain themes of dissent and certain themes of prewar fascism. We find the most rabid diatribes against the flabbiness of the French people as examplified by illustrated magazines, paid vacations, retirement benefits, be-

fore-dinner drinks, and the national lottery, in the works of
Brasillach, Rebatet, and Céline—all celebrated fascists.
And Mussolini himself pronounced high-sounding words
against those who longed for the "easy life"—words that
would have easily evoked applause in 1968 from certain
student audiences so long as one did not mention Mussolini's name. (In fact, some practical jokers did exactly
this in Berlin, with great success.)

Must we then conclude that dissent leads to counterrevolution? I do not think we can go that far; but it
seems certain that dissent, in itself, does not constitute a
revolution. In today's societies, dissent is a necessary
condition of revolution, but it is not a sufficient condition; it must be completed by something else.

By what? This brings us to a second hypothesis (the
religious hypothesis being the first). For the most enter-
prising among the adherents of the Free Speech Movement, the necessary "something else" is the classic Marxist
revolution; that is, the overthrow of capitalism and its
political system by the oppressed classes. And this is also
the view of all the partisans of the various "power"
movements: Black Power, Brown Power (the Mexican-
Americans), Red Power (the Indians), Sex Power
(women), Student Power—all of which are united under
the motto, "Power to the People." Marxist groups and
Christian groups easily find common ground in "Zen
Marxism" and "Pop Marxism"; and young people for
whom "Jesus is the best trip" and the Mao-Guevara group
arrive at an easy understanding with each other. The only
problem is that such understandings are more likely to lead
them to the comforts of religion than to the joys of power.

Revolution has been defined, quite accurately, as "a
movement of dissent that succeeds in attaining power."*

* Jean Baechler, in *Les Phénomènes révolutionnaires*. Paris, 1970.

Within that context, we may add that the crucial question of our time is this: How does one go from dissent to revolution? The answer, I think, depends on the meaning that we attach to the words "attaining power" in the above definition. In societies where government has a rudimentary and centralized form, the process of attaining power is relatively simple and quick. In a society as complex as the United States, however, power does not fall into the hands of anyone who succeeds in mounting an attack on the Capitol. And that is why the urban guerrilla warfare that we hear so much about is not actually a war of revolution, nor a transition from dissent to revolution, but only a form of armed dissent. It is merely the intensification of a form of action, and not the adoption of a new form. The anarchists who, at the end of the nineteenth century, made a practice of killing customers in Parisian cafés with bombs were belligerent dissenters, but they were not revolutionaries. Their chances of gaining power were zero. And the *sine qua non* of revolution is that power must change hands. Sometimes this transfer takes time, even though it is a revolutionary process; that is, it is brought about by means which go beyond, and violate, the normal rules of the political game. These means, however, must be relevant to the composition of a society, and proportionate to the forces involved.

In the case of the United States, one can hardly pretend that there really exists a Silent Majority and that, at the same time, the only possible course of action is civil war. For absolute insurrection to succeed, the army and the police must stand side by side with the insurgents; and that seems hardly likely in a country where the notion of a constitutional consensus is so deeply ingrained. The only thing that could bring about civil war would be a military disaster, accompanied by a state of acute physical want, such as occurred in Russia in 1917, or a war of national liberation, like that of China. And both those hypotheses are hopelessly unrealistic. Moreover, civil war presupposes the existence of certain sociological conditions that are not found in the United States. In America, class warfare is not a battle of "class against class." This psychological Manichaeism exists only in the minds of those who have fallen victim to it. America is not composed of a monolithic Silent Majority on one side (first of all, because it is not a majority at all; and secondly, because it is never silent), and, on the other side, a block of "victims of capitalism."

When Michael Harrington's book on poverty in America (*The Other America*) was published in March 1962, the news that poverty existed in the midst of abundance came as a great shock to certain optimistic economists. At that time, $3,000 was regarded as the minimum income necessary for an urban family of four; an income below that level represented poverty. In 1968 this minimum income was raised to $3553. By the end of 1970 it reached $3700. Below that level, a family of four is eligible for public assistance, in the form of additional income. The average annual income in the United States—not by family, but per capita—(in 1968) was $3412. In Portugal, it was $412. In Spain, $719. In Italy, $1300. In France, $1436. And in West Germany, $1753. In these circumstances, poverty (which is defined in terms other than that of income—by housing, for example, and educational opportunity) affects between one fifth and one sixth of the American people. This percentage allowed Michael Harrington to speak of "the first poverty minority known to history"—meaning not that the number of poor was small, but that, for the first time, the usual breakdown of society into a few wealthy families and a vast majority of poor families had been reversed. Politically speaking, this fact necessitates a revision of one's tactics. We can no longer say that the oppressed at least have numbers on their side, and that, at the first weakening of the repressive system, it will be enough for them to rise and the whole apparatus of government will crumble. Out of a population of approximately 205 million people (according to the 1970 census), there are approximately 25 million "poor" people in the United States. To that category belong about 29 percent of the black population, and about 8 percent of the white*; that is, some 8 million blacks (out of 25 million), and about 16 million whites (out of 168 million). The remaining "poor" are drawn partly from among the Puerto Ricans and partly from among the Mexican-Americans, who total respectively 1.5 million people and 500,000 people. It is obvious that the American poor do not constitute an actual "social class"; neither by reason of its size relative to the whole, nor by its composition, since the problem of poverty does not exactly coincide with the problem of racial minorities. One third of nonwhite families in America, for example, have an income of more than $8000 per year. In an article published in 1969,** Michael Harrington notes that the poor in no way constitute a "proletariat" in the socialist meaning of that term. And, in fact, the riots in the black ghettos of America might be called, like agitation on campus, a mixture of violence and pressure. If such riots and agitation were acts of pure violence resulting from an irreconcilable conflict of forces, and without an underlying "code," then the game would soon be over, both in the ghettos and on the campuses.

* "What the Census Will Show Us," in *The New York Times*, August 2, 1970.
** "The Other America Revisited," in *The Center Magazine*, Vol. II, No. 1, January 1969.

The progress, insufficient but undeniable, that has been made since the 1960 census in the fight against poverty, in the situation of the blacks and in desegregation, is due to a subtle mixture of violent revolt on the part of the countersociety with the utilization of opportunities offered by democratic participation and of the means offered by the American political structure. I have already given an example of this when discussing the strike of the California vineyard workers; a strike which ended, after five years, in July 1970 with a victory for the workers, when the grape growers made all the concessions required of them. After the strike began, Cesar Chavez, leader of the Chicanos (of whom many are not American citizens), organized a boycott of grapes which was remarkably successful in the large cities and especially on the campuses. The growers counterattacked by activating their lobby at the Pentagon, and arranging to have the army buy whatever grapes they could not sell. Whereupon, Chavez filed a suit in the Supreme Court, charging that the arrangement between the growers and the military constituted a violation of the antitrust laws; and the Court ruled in his favor. Thanks to the media, the Chicanos' cause became a nation-wide cause. On the eve of his assassination, Robert Kennedy took part, at Chavez's side, in a mass rally of Mexican-Americans. Even so, the strike went on for two more years, until July 25, 1970, when the grape growers' spokesman telephoned Chavez to say that the growers recognized his negotiations committee and that they accepted his demands.

I have referred to the grape workers' strike several times in this book, and the reason is that it reflects almost all the characteristics of an American conflict-situation. It included a racial and cultural minority; and racial minorities in the United States play the role of a revolutionary fermenting agent.* (Many whites, for instance, have had their political consciences awakened by working alongside blacks during marches and sit-ins.) The boycott was able to succeed because it received the support of liberal whites in the cities—personified by Kennedy—and of radical students; and this support was a manifestation of the division existing within the privileged classes and the governing elite. At a decisive moment, the law, by way of the Supreme Court, intervened to support Chavez's cause. Inter-union solidarity made it possible for the strikers to hold out for five years; and freedom of information allowed them to present their case on a basis of equality with the grape growers.

The tactics adopted in this particular case would have had to be quite different if the Judicial branch and the judges, as happens in some other countries, had been either too prejudiced or too servile to render their decision on the basis of law. Also, it would have been ridiculous to depend on "formal" democracy in the abstract. In each case, the only thing that can be considered is the level at which the existing legal system operates, both in social conflicts and in conflicts between the citizen and those in power. This level (which is nonexistent in some countries, average in others, and relatively high elsewhere) should be the determining factor in appraising the possibilities offered by a particular situation.

Thus, Huey Newton, chief of the Black Panthers, who had been sentenced to fifteen years for the murder of a policeman, was released on bail on August 15, 1970, as the result of a ruling by the Court of Appeals of the State

---

* It is interesting to note that linguistic minorities are also considered in the United States. In California, signs in public places, especially at the airports, are written in English, Spanish, and Chinese. And there are numerous Spanish-language television programs.

of California, upheld by the Supreme Court of that state, which set aside the verdict of the lower court and ordered a new trial on the grounds that the court had not taken into account the fact that Newton himself had been wounded, and that, at the moment when he shot the policeman, he was not in full possession of his faculties. As soon as he was free, Newton paraded triumphantly through the streets of Oakland, and then held a television news conference in his lawyer's office. He announced his intention of contacting the North Vietnamese delegation in Paris with the offer of an unspecified number of black volunteers who were willing to fight alongside the Viet Cong and help the Vietnamese people in their struggle against the American aggressors.* One wonders whether a French citizen who belonged to a terrorist organization during the Algerian war, and who was out on bail in the same circumstances (which would have been impossible in any case), could have brazenly announced his intention of forming a private army to fight the French in North Africa.

However violent America's civil struggles may be (and those struggles are essentially those on the campuses and those of the racial minorities), the fact remains that the best return on violence is achieved by its marriage to the legal resources offered by America's political system. And this is especially true since the country's federal structure, and the autonomy of its municipalities, allows one to act at several levels and provides numerous methods of recourse. For example, when a demonstration is forbidden in France, there is never any doubt about the source of the prohibition. If it is a question of a major political demonstration, it is the government; that is, the Minister of the Interior or one of the Prefects. In the United

* Reported in the *Los Angeles Times* of August 6, 1970.

States, however, when a demonstration is forbidden, the first question everyone asks is, "By whom?" It could be the president of a university, the municipality, the county, or the state (the Mayor of New York and the Governor of New York rarely see eye to eye). And the same holds true for the aftermath of a demonstration. After the death of four students at Kent State University, the federal government ordered an inquiry. The Department of Justice subsequently released the F.B.I.'s report, which concluded that it had not been necessary for the National Guard to open fire, and that no member of the Guard had been struck by stones. Moreover, the report recommended that six Guardsmen be indicted for second-degree murder, and it went on to list the name, rank, unit, and home address of each of the six.* In such circumstances, we can hardly pretend that armed insurrection is the only revolutionary activity possible in the United States; that there must be a complete break with the Establishment, without hope of negotiation; and that one must "conquer or die" in accordance with a script written in the nineteenth century for use against such autocratic empires as those of the Habsburgs or the Russian tsars. If such a regime existed in the United States, there would be no hope for the black people. The blacks constitute only 11 percent of the population; and only a small part of these (between 5 and 10 percent, maximum) favor the methods of the Black Panthers. By the same token, the terrorist policy of the Weathermen, the extremist faction of the S.D.S.

* The F.B.I. report was widely disseminated by the press. See, for example, *Newsweek*, August 3, 1970. The Guardsmen were subsequently tried, and acquitted, by an Ohio court. At the moment (January 1971) the case is being appealed to the federal courts. As in the case of the My Lai massacre, I know of no other country in which military personnel, or policemen, are indicted for their acts "in the performance of their duty"—even though these indictments may result in subsequent (and contested) acquittals.

(students of the Left) is acceptable to only 2 or 3 percent of the students. American Marxism-Leninism and Mao-ism, in fact, proceed on the basis of an error in analysis, since the white working class is, on the whole, conservative; since the business world favors reform; since the federal government, for the past twenty years, has been on the side of the blacks and against local racism; and since in 1969 and 1970, the Senate (with strong Republican backing) inflicted a humiliating defeat on the White House by refusing to confirm two Nixon nominees to the Supreme Court who were from the South.*

Paradoxically, the United States is one of the least racist countries in the world today. A large black minority has lived alongside the whites for many years, and the fight against racism, its extirpation and the analysis of its symptoms, a preoccupation with its rejection in others and with its domination in oneself—all these things are a reality with which America lives. Many other countries, however, are experiencing an upsurge in popular racism: a number of Swedes were furious because the United States, of all things, sent a black man as American ambassador to Stockholm (Ambassador Holland); the French, the Swiss, and the English, who, for the first time in their history, now find large North African, Portuguese, Jamaican, or Senegalese minorities in their midst. The problem is particularly serious because the social traditions of these countries contain no antibody against the disease of racism—no more than do the traditions of the

---

* Certainly, the reason for the negative vote of the Senate was not merely to block Nixon's "Southern strategy" (a strategy designed to weaken support for George Wallace). There were serious questions raised about Haynesworth's relationship with business interests, and there was much discussion of Carswell's "mediocrity" as a jurist. Even so—in Carswell's case, especially—the issue of racism was raised, and provided the basis for frequent allegations against Nixon's nominees. Carswell, for instance, was accused of having made racist speeches some twenty years earlier.

East African countries who oppress their millions of Indian immigrants. It would be impossible for the American government to sell arms to South Africa (as the French government is doing) without causing a great popular protest. And it would not be, as in France, a protest, promptly ignored, by a few intellectuals.

The demands of black Americans are, after all, more cultural demands than *class* demands. The blacks are divided into several social classes among themselves. Their two chief preoccupations are poverty in the ghettos, and cultural alienation. The latter is expressed uncompromisingly by the four to five hundred thousand black university students (out of a total student population of some 7 million), who do not want merely to enter the universities in large numbers—as they are actually doing, thanks to the lavish distribution of scholarships—but who also, within the universities, want to receive an education that has no connection with that given to the whites. They do not wish to know about white literature, white science, white history, or white theater; and they do not want white teachers—an attitude that will contribute greatly to an explosion in America in the years to come.

Black Marxism-Leninism does not seem able to become either politically operative or intellectually illuminating in American society. But then, neither does white Marxism-Leninism. It comes as no surprise that the "theoretical" works of the yippie leaders—Jerry Rubin's *Do It!* and Abbie Hoffman's *Revolution for the Hell of It*—are as puerile as they are incoherent. Nor should anyone be astonished by the fact that American "Marxists" are particularly fascinated by Mao, whose vague slogans save one the trouble of serious analysis. The tone of Maoism is that of a summary of Marxist-Leninism, embellished with folksy moral advice such as "We make progress when

we are modest" and "The hardest thing is to act properly
throughout one's whole life." Then there are truisms: "An
army without culture is an ignorant army," and "Unilateral examination consists in not knowing how to
see a question under all its aspects." Mao is not a
theoretician; or at least he is not an original theoretician.
His few theoretical works, such as *On Practice* and *On
Contradiction,* are limited to popularizing and simplifying
Lenin's *Materialism and Empirio-Criticism.* These writings, like all his texts, are products of circumstance and
of battle, intended to bring political pressure to bear on a
particular tendency either within or outside of the Chinese
Communist Party. The Leninist-Stalinist ideology, once
adopted by Mao, was never rethought by him. When he
appears to be creating an ideology, he is really pursuing
a tactic. However, like all communists he likes to dress
up the smallest details in abstract phraseology. In 1929,
when he wanted the Red Army, which was resting, to
remain in the country, where it would be on hand if
needed, and not go looking for diversion in the cities,
he wrote a resolution entitled, "The Elimination of Erroneous Concepts in the Party." Among those erroneous
concepts was "subjectivism," "vestiges of putschism,"
and "individualism"—of which the principal component
was a "taste for pleasure" which manifested itself chiefly
by the desire of "our troops to go into the large cities . . ."
Even the "theory" of the Hundred Flowers, as pleasantly
articulated as it may be, is not a true theory. It was
written in 1957 for the purpose of quieting those who
were demanding greater freedom of discussion within the
Party, and who were using the events in Hungary as a
basis for condemning authoritarianism. In this work, Mao
approved the suppression of the Budapest uprising. He
makes rhetorical concessions to unhappy Party members.

But, immediately afterward, he takes them back through the application of inflexible "right thinking."

In a discourse on the Hundred Flowers, delivered in 1957 and entitled *On the Correct Handling of Contradictions Among the People,* as in earlier works such as *On Popular Democratic Dictatorship* (1949) and *Against a Stereotyped Style in the Party* (1942), the reasoning is always the same: there is free discussion within the Party; but, in practice, objections against the Party come from two sources: enemies of the Revolution (and such people have no right to express themselves) and sincere believers in the Revolution (and these people should never be in disagreement with the Party). Thus, the authoritarian methods of democratic centralism are entirely legitimate, and, among the people, "liberty is proportionate to discipline." The same process is followed in matters philosophical: one may criticize the Party, because "Marxism does not fear criticism," and if Marxism "could be defeated by criticism, then it would be worth nothing." Therefore, since Marxism is invulnerable, all criticism of it is in vain. So, why bother? In art and literature also, the Hundred Flowers are allowed to bloom, but one is not to confuse "poisonous herbs" with "scented flowers," and Mao quickly adopts an attitude of cultural control identical with that of Zhdanov. The idea of a "cultural army" goes far back in Mao's works. There again, however, he is not innovating: culture is always the reflection of political and social reality. Once the economic revolution has been accomplished, therefore, one must look to the cultural revolution. This view is entirely in conformity with that of militant Leninism, without the slightest personal variation. I should make it clear that it is not my intention to formulate a political judgment with respect to China. I wish only to say that a study of Mao's texts leads me to conclude that, philosophically, the little Red writer does not exist; there is no "Chinese version" of Marxism; and there is no "thought of Mao."

The worst that could happen to the Free Speech Movement in America, therefore, would be for it to become involved with a nineteenth-century ideology and to see its creativity emasculated by a desire to make it conform to concepts forged in the prehistoric period of modern revolutions. The strength of the American movement is that, up to now, it has been able to discover modes of action that are suited to its circumstances and that work effectively at all levels of the society that it is fighting. If that revolutionary inspiration is allowed to be trapped in the theoretical dustbins of Europe, where one spends more time asking whether it is possible to make a non-Marxist revolution than in making revolutions, it will weaken and waste away. Let me repeat: revolution is not imitation. Revolution is not a settling of accounts with the past, but with the future. American revolutionaries sense this; and that is the reason for American originality in comparison to Europe—as unpleasant as that fact may be for European students, who consider themselves to be more Left than Americans, and especially more intelligently Left. It is also the reason why American youth is actually *creating* a revolution in place of, and prior to, visualizing a revolution. For, as Noam Chomsky observed, "The most stupid men learn how to talk, while even the most brilliant monkeys never learn."

I do not mean to imply that the classic forms of social struggle do not exist in America. White workers in America are very fond of combat, and union strikes are, as I have already mentioned, very complete and very long. There are, however, two things that frighten white workers:

the cultural revolution and Black Power. When Mayor Daley in Chicago issued an order fixing the percentage of black workers who must be hired for every construction job, the white workers had exactly the same reaction as the peasants in the south of France or on Corscia have *vis à vis* repatriated Algerian colonists, whom they regard as "privileged" because the latter have credit and compensations that they themselves do not have. And, in fact, the white worker in an industrial society is in a peculiar position. He does not play the role assigned by Marx in the nineteenth century to the working class; he is the twentieth-century American equivalent of the nineteenth-century French peasant. In *The 18th Brumaire of Louis-Napoleon Bonaparte*, Marx expresses his disgust with the peasant who, concerned only with protecting his little piece of farmland (which was his share of the revolutionary conquests of 1789, voted aganst the urban proletariat and for the man who promised law and order.* To be sure, the American blue-collar worker, although he may be highly paid on a basis of world-wide comparison, is not free of all material wants. But then, was the French peasant free of such wants? The fact that he was not, and that his living conditions were sometimes terribly difficult, did not prevent him from regularly throwing his weight behind the cause of conservatism. The workers in America's industrial society are much less submissive than were the French peasants, but they are as frightened by the extremists. And by *all* extremists. A Gallup poll, published on June 26, 1970, shows that they are equally opposed to the Black

---

* It should be remembered that the French Revolution, at least in the order of priorities, was not a revolution of the industrial bourgeoisie against the nobility (this was not to occur for another forty or fifty years), but an agrarian revolution, above all, that abolished the thousand-year-old ownership of the soil and distributed the land among those who worked the land.

Panthers and to the Ku Klux Klan: 75 percent of those polled were "highly unfavorable" to both groups.

So far as the so-called Silent Majority is concerned, it is difficult to evaluate it and its opinions. First of all, is it really a majority? According to a report in *Time** on the Middle American, this sociopsychological category comprises a little less than 100 million Americans, including 40 million workers and farmers, 20 million retired persons, and 36 million white-collar workers. What do the Middle Americans believe? Certain polls, such as that of C.B.S. in the spring of 1970, indicate the existence of a clearly defined hostility toward campus disturbances, and an overriding concern with law and order. Even so, this concern is less pronounced than in France. An IFOP poll** taken at the time when the *loi anti-casseur* (establishing the principle of collective responsibility, which would be inconceivable in America) was being voted on, 65 percent of French adults were favorable to the adoption of authoritarian measures against disorders among students in universities and high schools.*** In America, Amitai Etzioni, a sociologist at Columbia University, after a study undertaken during the summer of 1969, concluded that the belief that America was moving toward the Right was a serious exaggeration of fact. According to Professor Etzioni, "in operational terms, the country is 65 percent liberal, 21 percent middle-of-the-road, and 14 percent reactionary. (By "liberal" is meant "favorable to governmental intervention in matters of social progress.") This breakdown seems to be confirmed by the fact that, despite so much talk about "law and order," all the great liberal legislative ﹀

---

* Issue of January 5, 1970.
** Published in *France-Soir*, March 3, 1970.
*** The SOFRES poll published in *Figaro*, April 21, 1970, gave these figures: in favor first of discussion, but of repression if discussion fails: 52 percent; in favor of repression, and no discussion: 24 percent.

projects of the past few years have either come to a successful conclusion or are in the process of doing so: the
Bill of Rights of 1964, on the rights of black voters; laws
on school desegregation; the constitutional amendment on
equal rights for women (1970), the lowering of the voting
age to eighteen; more liberal laws on divorce, abortion,
erotic material, and so forth. Mayors of several large cities
—Washington, Cleveland, Newark—are black. And finally
it was noted that attempts of the Silent Majority to
organize anti-moratorium demonstrations on a national
scale regularly fall short of their goals.

Geographically, when we speak of the American Midwest
as representing the "real" America, we should add that
while that America may be real, it is also a desert. If we
look at a map showing density of population in the United
States, we see that the vast majority of the population is
concentrated on the eastern and western coasts, in the
southwest, and in four of the states on the Great Lakes:
Illinois, Indiana, Michigan, and Ohio. The "bastions of
reaction"—Iowa, Nebraska, Kansas, Oklahoma, and the
two Dakotas—are unmanned forts. It is hard to see how
Wyoming or Idaho, with a population density respectively
of two and six inhabitants per square mile, could lead a
crusade to reconquer the campuses of America. Barry Goldwater, the last presidential candidate who had a chance of
being elected and who ran on a Right-wing platform, was
defeated by the biggest electoral landslide in the history
of American presidential elections.

Of course, one can never exclude the possibility, in any
country, of a trend toward authoritarianism. We can say,
however, that the past decade gives no indication of a shift
in that direction, even though unrest, riots, great changes
in the style and principles of life, and a hardening of demands of all kinds are naturally resulting in fear, surprise,

misapprehension, and anger in those who are becoming the captives of a new America of which they have not had the imagination to become the creators.

Never, in any country or at any time, has public opinion, however well informed it may have been (which was hardly ever the case), reflected an element of dissent sufficiently strong to make known its condemnation of its government's abuses in foreign policy, and thereby to create a real political problem. Public opinion can, on occasion, turn against domestic injustices; but it has never before been known to rebel against external crimes. The American student uprisings are directly associated with the students' rejection of the war in Vietnam. And this rejection is not merely the position of minorities—as proved by the state of semi-insurrection that greeted the announcement of the Cambodian intervention, and by the Senate vote on a document recalling the constitutional obligation of a President to consult with the Congress before any commitment of American troops abroad. A Harris poll of May 29, 1970, showed that 50 percent of Americans were in favor of the Cambodian intervention, and 43 percent were opposed. Has there ever been such a large percentage of citizens (or subjects) to condemn a kind of action that patriotism traditionally presents as legitimate and honorable? One wonders what percentage of the French people would have expressed disapproval of the Suez expedition in 1956, or of the deposition of the Sultan of Morocco in 1953. Europe was highly indignant, and rightly so, over America's armed intervention in the Dominican Republic in 1965, in the course of a civil war that was already in full swing (and that the presence of American troops did nothing to stop). However, one would have liked to see similar indignation expressed in France four years earlier, when the French army started shooting down Tunisian soldiers and civilians in Bizerte, and killed and wounded six thousand people in just a few days. It is interesting to observe that American public opinion was more enraged over American actions in the Dominican Republic than over French actions in Bizerte. French media express indignation over the American army's disposal of toxic gases in the oceans; but neither the media nor public opinion in France seems to be bothered by the fact that, except for China, France is the only country that is still exploding atomic bombs in the earth's atmosphere.

Only rejection from within can cause the disappearance of imperialism. No imperialistic regime up to the present has ever been destroyed from without, by another imperialism. Therefore, the gain for humanity has been zero. The destruction of imperialism from within, and the application of the power on which it was based to other goals—that would be progress.

The interpretation of polls in this area is even more difficult than in domestic policy. The motives for condemning the war are of various kinds: some are moral, idealistic; others are founded upon a clear perception of the necessity for a revolution in foreign policy in the form of an abandonment of traditional sovereignty; and still others are purely selfish—which is to say, isolationist.* But the fact remains that, according to a recent poll (the end of June 1970), 56 percent of the American people think that America is wrong in the Vietnam war, and 36 percent think that America is right (8 percent had no opinion). In view of the fact that the war had already been the cause of Johnson's downfall, Nixon announced, on August 5, 1970, that all American troops will have been

* See "Silent Majorities and the Vietnam War" by P. Converse and H. Schuman, in *Scientific American* of June 1970.

withdrawn from Vietnam by the end of 1972, and that, as of May 1, 1971, American troops would be limited to defensive combat. Even then, certain cabinet members, followed by federal officials, protested against the President's plan as being too slow.

Even more important than the public-opinion polls is the fact that American youth has changed its mood with respect to America's role in the world in general. I realize that, for many people in Europe, Africa, Latin America, and Asia, it is difficult to tell the difference between the real activity of American imperialism and its imaginary role. "Imperialism" is too often a catch-all term that is useful in explaining both the failures of the Left in various countries and the economic failures or misfortunes of democracy. Was modern Greece, for example, really awaiting a sign from the C.I.A. to succumb to dictatorship? And can one be sure that Brazil and Argentina did not have a sufficiently strong Right to assure the success of fascism in those countries, even without the aid of foreign agents? Could it be that the C.I.A. was responsible for Porfirio Díaz, Mussolini, Salazar, Metaxas, and Pétain? Does the C.I.A. force us to show American cartoons and serials and variety shows on television, or have we been driven to it by our own mediocrity in that area? Is it because of C.I.A. pressure that the government of France has stopped subsidizing the Pasteur Institute and allowed the Ford Foundation to assume that responsibility? Does the C.I.A. force us to lock up our Leftists for trifles? I have no intention of trying to defend the C.I.A.; but I would suggest that, when we speak of reactionary politics and police regimes, we tend to overestimate the talents of that organization and to underestimate our own.

It is significant that protests against the C.I.A. and against imperialism originate among the American people, for this represents an important change in historical patterns—just as it would be an extraordinary sign of human evolution if there were even an abortive mass demonstration in Russia against the invasion of Czechoslovakia, anti-Semitism, and intervention in Egypt. Just as we seem able to ignore the fact that we Europeans exterminated the Indians; that we Europeans sold the blacks into slavery; that we Europeans started the process, and developed the methods, of subjecting the whole planet to the white race; so now, we want to forget the fact that the very existence of white America is a result of our invasion of the whole earth and, as it were, an extension and a continuation by proxy of Europe's onslaught against the rest of the world.

Today in America—the child of European imperialism—a new revolution is rising. It is *the* revolution of our time. It is the only revolution that involves radical, moral, and practical opposition to the spirit of nationalism. It is the only revolution that, to that opposition, joins culture, economic and technological power, and a total affirmation of liberty for all in place of archaic prohibitions. It therefore offers the only possible escape for mankind today: the acceptance of technological civilization as a means and not as an end, and—since we cannot be saved either by the destruction of the civilization or by its continuation—the development of the ability to reshape that civilization without annihilating it.

New York, January 8, 1970
Santa Barbara, August 11, 1970

AFTERWORD

LISTEN TO THE FIRST SENTENCE. "The revolution of the twentieth century will take place in the United States." *Pow!!!* The French reader is already seeing stars when the second sentence hits him. "It can take place nowhere else." Americans may feel bewildered, skeptical, glad or sorry to hear the news, curious to know more. But you have to be French to get the full impact, the "visceral reaction." Ever since you could count up to ten or spell *c-h-a-t*, you have been secure in the thought that the U.S. is the citadel of imperialism, racism, vulgarity, conformism, and now a *Frenchman* returns from a voyage of discovery to say it is a hotbed of revolution.

Blandly, with a straight face, the enormity emerges, buttressed by figures and arguments, precedents, citations. Is it a joke? No and yes. It may have started out as a hardy quip or demolishing retort, and somewhere behind these pages Jean-François Revel is still suppressing an inadvertent smile. We, his readers, not required to school our features, laugh out loud in delight. At what exactly? At the French, of course, and their starchy preconceptions, which are being shaken, jostled, disarrayed, like a matron in some old slapstick. But also at the author himself, that expressionless comedian, swinging from a precipice, teetering on a tightrope. We laugh at his imperturbability in the presence of his imminent danger, at his reckless aplomb in courting ridicule—the reverse of sympathetic chuckles. He is serious, he protests: "Why are you laughing?"

All Jean-François Revel's books are cliff-hangers. He is a pamphleteer, and his first necessity therefore is to boldly secure attention. Characteristically, in his opening pages he risks being removed from the scene in a straitjacket. His pamphlets are heresies and they generally result from prolonged exposure to piety. He is restive, like a schoolboy in a church, surrounded by hushed worshipers and prompted to commit a sacrilege—stand up and *prove* to them that the Bible cannot be true. His anticlerical nostrils are quick to detect the slightest smell of incense, and misfortune—or good luck—has placed him in a variety of churches, chapels, oratories, cenacles. He has passed most of his life among the devout.

Gaullist France itself is one huge basilica, consecrated to Glory. The Sorbonne is a monastery from which pilgrims set out for the wayside shrines of the national *lycée* system or go on foreign missions, spreading French culture. Revel was an *agrégé* in philosophy and taught, first abroad —at the University of Mexico and the University of Florence and at the local French Institutes—later in *lycées* at Lille and Paris: history of philosophy, history of art, French literature, geography. His first published blasphemy or tale-told-out-of-school was *Pourquoi les philosophes*, an attack on the then reigning gods of French philosophy. Next came *Pour l'Italie,* a tract *against* Italy—for Revel a natural by-product of four years as a lecturer in Florentine classrooms. A simple corrective, he would have said, of Italophilia, a healthy explosion of the whole bag of myths about Italian art, Italian culture, Italian virility, Italian gaiety, good looks, liveliness, all of which he found nonexistent and backed up the verdict with real-life anecdotes and observations, many true, many funny, some brutal, such as the one, which gave much offense to feminine readers of *Epoca,* that Italian women have hair on their legs.

Not a word, I am sure, was invented, and yet the book was biased to a point that someone who loved Italy could have considered almost insane. Or the result of some personal grievance—an idea that was aired in the Italian press at the time and that I rather subscribed to myself simply from reading the book, which has many complaints about the unavailability of Italian girls. Knowing Revel, as I now do, I no longer think that explanation can have been right. There is something wonderfully disinterested about Revel's biases, a joy in bias itself as an artistic form, embracing hyperbole and conducing, finally, to laughter. He has a Falstaffian side and only cares that his "slant" should run counter to respectable culture and received opinion. If he has a personal grievance, it is a long-standing, deeply nurtured one against the immovable forces of entrenched beliefs that insult his sense of the self-evident.

There followed one of his most charming and persuasive works, *Sur Proust.* It is not so much controversial as, again, heretical. Revel loves Proust, which means that he is against orthodox Proustians, including Proust himself at certain moments. He makes the convincing argument that what is good in *Á la recherche du temps perdu* is the worldly social side, the human comedy, whereas the "deeper" parts, the philosophy of time and memory, the *madeleine* and so on, are simply commonplaces of French philosophy already out of date at the time Proust wrote and often at variance with the book's real story—i.e., what is considered "superficial" in Proust is profound, and vice versa.

At this point in Revel's career, it might have been said that the man was simply an attention-seeker, moving lightly from field to field, in search of provocative positions to occupy and abandon, a journalistic *enfant terrible* or disgruntled academic whose formula was to assert the opposite of what "everybody" was saying. This would have been to ignore the solidity and breadth of his learning but, more than that, to mistake the impetus behind his contrariness, the irrepressible spirit of contradiction that guides him, like a dowser, in the hope of striking truth.

Self-dramatization, eagerness for the spotlight must count very low among Revel's motivations. He has some traits in common with Shaw (he was once meditating a book against Shakespeare) but he totally lacks Shaw's theatrical vanity and Irish flair for personal publicity. Unlike Shaw, Revel does not play the sage, ready for consultation by newsmen on all manner of subjects; no Isadora Duncans, so far as I know, have been asking to have babies by him. He is not a highly advertised "brain," in fact makes no pretensions to having anything more than common garden intelligence; if he is different from the majority, he would say, it is only because he is not ashamed to be caught using that very ordinary faculty—the natural light of reason.

Far from being a star or aspiring to prominence, Revel is very much the citizen, a bourgeois in the old Enlightenment sense of the term—a townsman, fond of domestic tranquillity and the arts of peace and commerce. His nature appears placid, benevolent, easygoing, sentimental, that of a private householder going about his business, reading his newspaper without the expectation of finding his own name in it, an urban Cincinnatus. He has a round, flat "Dutch" face (though he is of pure French blood) that looks as if it had seen service in the battles of William the Silent against the Spanish oppressor. It is a moon face; indeed there seem to be several moons perspicaciously turning in its dial, like in one of those grandfather clocks that keep track of astronomical time. He is a bettor and likes to go to the races, wears a gray suit and carries a briefcase.

Despite the stir of indignation excited by some of his broadsides, his person does not inspire fear nor cause a swift turning of heads in a restaurant. His picture, in *L'Express* every week over his column, has something bullish about it, the broad-browed, head-lowered promise of some intransigent charge into the arena, and yet it is a *good* bull, scarcely more than a rambunctious steer. He is occasionally seen on television and once ran for office (Cincinnatus called from the plow) on the Federated Left ticket in the suburban district of Neuilly—not his natural territory. He came in a bad third, behind the Gaullist and the Communist. Notwithstanding the weekly photo in a mass-circulation magazine, his "image" somehow, as if from modesty, retires from circulation; if polled, fewer Parisians could identify J.-F. Revel in the rogue's gallery of current celebrities than could identify Robbe-Grillet, Marguerite Duras, Roland Barthes, Michel Rocard, Alain Krivine, or the man, "La Reynière," who writes the restaurant column in the *Monde*. Not to mention J.-P. Sartre, J.-J. Servan-Schreiber, Simone de Beauvoir, Jean-Luc Godard, etc.

Yet in terms of meritorious service in the combat against

General de Gaulle and Gaullism, the outstanding antagonist was surely not any of the above-named opinion-leaders, left or center, nor François Mitterand, nor Lecanuet, but Jean-François Revel. His spirit of contrariety found in the General its absurd predestined windmill to tilt at indefatigably. Three brilliant pamphlets sprang from his pen: *Le style du Général, En France: la fin de l'opposition, Lettre ouverte à la droite.* He slew de Gaulle again and again, and if the General had more lives than a cat and more heads than a hydra, that did not really daunt Jean-François, though he publicly confessed to battle weariness. In fact, like the deathless General himself, he came back refreshed, reinvigorated, having found a new point of attack, new weapons, generally captured from the enemy camp.

He is still fighting, this time on the left flank. *Ni Marx, ni Jésus,* where the old Gaullist bugbear, the United States, is tenderly embraced as an ally, suddenly discovered, in the struggle, is another engagement with the adversary, resurgent in the form of Georges Pompidou, and that adversary's eternal cohorts, as Revel sees them, of the French Communist Party and the splinter grouplets of the left. If the emphasis here is more on the vacuities of the left, Old and New, than it was in some of the preceding pamphlets, it is only a *shift* of emphasis.

From start to finish, Revel has seen the so-called left as the right's accomplice, and vice versa, two sides of the same worn coin—an agreement to perpetuate the status quo. What he holds against both right and left is their joint blocking of the way to any real social advance. I am not sure whether Revel, like Shaw, believes in socialism in any accepted sense, but at least during his short electoral career he was running on a socialist ticket. Certainly he is a democrat and egalitarian. To him, plainly,

right-left in France is a symbiosis mutually advantageous
to both parties and deathly to human liberty. Or as de
Gaulle is supposed to have said of Jean-Paul Sartre: *"Sartre, c'est aussi la France."*

De Gaulle is France, Sartre is France, the C.G.T. and
the Communists are France. France, for Revel, is a suspended solution in which all these elements refuse either
to precipitate or to dissolve. What Revel is fighting, single-
handed, is "France," which has become to him the arch-
symbol of all those forces of inertia that the original
Adam in him felt bound to contradict when he still
thought their locus might be Shakespeare or the obscur-
antist jargon of the Sorbonne chapel of philosophy. He is
somewhat more indulgent toward the young Maoists,
Trotskyites, and Castroites because they are young and the
objects of a judicial campaign of terror, backed up by riot
squads. But for him they too are "France," in the un-
reality of their perspectives, doctrinaire slogans, and practical failure to get anything done.

Sometimes one feels that Revel, as an infant, was nurtured in a debating school where the training consisted of
being obliged to take the negative of such seemingly un-
assailable propositions as: The earth is round, Proust was
a snob, Fresh air is good for you, Travel broadens the
mind. And where daily exercise in the gymnasium meant
standing on their heads maxims like Klausewitz's "War is a
continuation of politics by other means" (*Without Marx
or Jesus*, "Foreign policy is an initiation of war by other
means"). This would not be such a bad school for educating not mere mental contortionists versed in paradox but
free minds. There is always the possibility that the exact
opposite of what you think (or think you think) may be
true. At least it is worth trying on for size, and experiment
will show that the converse of many dogmas, once stated,

appears just as plausible as the original. Moreover, anything repeated a sufficient number of times has a natural tendency to upend itself, as though obeying some physical law of balance, like a Cartesian devil or a Mexican jumping bean. E.g., if I hear often enough "Poverty is no crime," I feel an urge to reply "Poverty *is* a crime," meaning that it is against the laws of humanity or that to be poor is to be already two thirds of a criminal in the eyes of the police.

In reality few propositions are entirely true and many are lucky if they contain a grain of truth. Thus automatically to take the opposite of any received idea, say, that Proust was a snob or that the United States is the citadel of world reaction, is almost bound to disclose unexpected evidence to the contrary. The danger in such operations is to mistake those grains of truth newly brought to light for the whole truth and to fall into a reverse orthodoxy, which will not long have the merit of being your own private opinion or stubborn form of dissent but will soon be on "everybody's" lips. Far from being free to perceive what is there, outside, you are suddenly the captive of your own heresy and the adherents you have gained for it, many of whom have drawn near to listen not from an attachment to truth but from self-interested motives or simple love of novelty.

I do not think Revel has altogether escaped this danger in *Without Marx or Jesus*. Less than in his earlier polemics. The reason is that previously he stood virtually alone, his back to the wall, with not many more "voices" in his favor than he found to vote for him in Neuilly in 1967. But here the ally he has embraced in the shape of the United States is likely to smother him with warm moist grateful kisses. Even before U.S. publication, you can already hear those smacks resounding from the pages of *Time* and *Newsweek*. And in the French press, surprisingly, there have been quite a few huzzas. Only on the ultra-right and the ultra-left has the book been savaged. The Communist press, though naturally critical of his un-Marxist approach, has been remarkably unvituperative, no doubt because Revel's views, on some domestic issues, coincide with their own policy of parliamentary "opposition" and reprehension of extralegal and guerrilla tactics. The fact that Revel is offering a happily distant, transatlantic alternative to the awful specter of helmeted local revolutionaries armed with Molotov cocktails and preaching a Maoist or Castroite gospel must appeal to readers of *L'Humanité* as much as to readers of *Figaro* and *France-Soir*.

That is not Revel's fault, and if his thesis is true, it does not matter who takes comfort from it. Besides, if the French middle classes relax in the assurance that the revolution can only take place in America, they may get a surprise. More curious, and for Revel perhaps more disquieting, is that the French reviews paid almost exclusive attention to the "positive" sections of the book, those dealing with the United States, and virtually ignored the "negative" sections, those dealing with France. Yet to my mind these contain some of his most splendid tirades, his highest comedy, and most acute observations: e.g., Pompidou rebounding from rough American to deferential French newsmen is as good as a play.

Up to now, the complaint about Revel's pamphleteering has been that it is "negative," "Why does he have to tear down?" and so on. He answered the judgment at length in the final section of *La Cabale des Dévots*, where his defense rested on the common sense argument, How can you expect me to be positive about a negative?—in that case the calamitous and self-satisfied state of French philosophy. Of course his defense was right. The insistence on "constructive criticism" has no place in intellectual discussion. According to that notion, one could never "damn" a play, a picture, or a poem without putting in its place another play, picture, or poem, as though it were a question of an inventory and the withdrawal of one article from the common stock demanded immediate replenishment to maintain a constant level. A false equation is made with the necessities of practical life, where if I declare that the doctor treating a patient is a quack, I am under some slight obligation to try to find a more reliable man to speed to the bedside or the operating table. The idea that all doctors are quacks, true or not, is insupportable to a sick person, but quite supportable in argument.

Without Marx or Jesus, however, breaks with Revel's critical habit by offering a positive model, the United States, to offset the otherwise gloomy picture he draws of mankind's revolutionary perspectives. If it were not for the United States, he is at pains to show, they would be nil. No hope. But why, one might ask, is a revolution called for? Why not gradual evolution? It is true that to the emotions the world situation appears so grim that only a revolution seems capable of altering it for the better; we hope for a revolution as desperate peoples in the past hoped for a miracle to save them when all other resources had run out—battalions of angels flying in from the sky, manna flowering in the desert. A revolution *is* a sort of miracle, a widening crack in the social crust that is finally perceived to be an earthquake, and, like a miracle, it is outside the laws of prediction, except from the point of view of hindsight.

Given the common desperation, Revel can be excused for foreseeing a revolution in the U.S., since he cannot see one in the offing anywhere else. But to *argue* it is something different. At the risk of being destructive my-

self, I would say that his "revolution" is only a metaphor,
a play on words. If he means that the U.S. is different
from the stereotype of it in French thought and that
some changes are taking place there whose repercussions
are already being felt elsewhere (the Berkeley Free Speech
uprising anticipating "May" in Paris by nearly four years),
then he is not saying anything very revolutionary, except perhaps to French ears. I agree that draft refusal,
dropping out, Woodstock, the drug culture, the Panthers,
Women's Lib, the Yippies, concern about the environment, the back-to-Nature movement, open admissions to
universities show the U.S. "ahead" of all its partners in
the West, if that can be taken as a value-free term rather
than a blanket endorsement, for we are also "ahead" in
sophisticated weaponry. I agree too that all this diverse
effervescence may add up to some kind of transformation
already as alarming to most people over forty as a universal
bomb threat.

Very likely, as Revel says, American traditions embodied in the Bill of Rights and an old history of civil dis-
obedience going back to 1776 have favored these develop-
ments, although the very rootedness of those traditions
or folkways could suggest the opposite of his conclusion,
suggest, that is, that they are not very exportable. It seems
to be easier to transplant Coca-Cola than hominy grits or
habeas corpus. But in any case to propose that these
changes are a revolution is to detonate images of the taking of the Bastille, the Carmagnole, Trees of Liberty, the
storming of the Winter Palace, the shot-heard-round-the-
world. The reader sometimes feels that he is poring over a
rosy positive print of the negative that met Attorney General Mitchell's eyes—as reported by Martha Mitchell—
when he looked out his Washington office window and
saw a mob of "the very liberal Communists"—the Mo-

bilization marchers—and thought he was in St. Petersburg in October 1917.

Revel is of course careful to explain that he does not mean what everybody else means by a revolution, that most of what we call revolutions were really aborted revolts, e.g., the Paris Commune, the Russian Revolution, the Chinese Revolution, the Hungarian Revolution, which were either totally defeated or failed to achieve their end and bogged down in tyranny. He believes that up to now there has been only one revolution—that which took place in France, England, and the American colonies toward the end of the eighteenth century and which, despite many setbacks, eventually replaced the old order by new democratic institutions.

One wonders, though, whether by his own strict criteria that protracted spasm was not also an aborted revolt, since many of its objectives have failed to this day to be realized, not only on a world-wide basis but in the countries where the whole thing started: the Rights of Man remain in large part on paper, like the Soviet Constitution, and equality is still a dream. So far as I can see, if one accepts Revel's definitions, the only successful revolution, up to now, has been the Industrial Revolution . . .

If Revel does not mean what everybody else means by the word, why use it, unless to startle and amuse? Why not find another word, such as reform? Reform, in its root sense, is what Jean-François is actually talking about: a reshaping of society. He does not have in mind a violent overturn but a renovation brought about largely by legal means, such as strikes, marches, and boycotts, with little bloodshed and with a strong dose of voluntarism. Possibly this gradual evolution will take place in America. The trouble is, Revel does not say how in political terms, and that is what counts for us Americans. Perhaps he expects politics to wither away. If the young dropouts of the counterculture do not vote, then voting would become a mainly ceremonial activity (which it is now, in a sense), engaged in by oldsters until they die off, and the Nixons of the future would be something like constitutional monarchs, useful for meeting their opposite numbers at airports, signing bills, redecorating the White House, throwing the first baseball of the year into the Washington stadium . . . The Agnews would preside over the slumbrous Senate, another honorific body, like the House of Lords, and give employment to jokesters and makers of hate-dolls. Meanwhile the real majority life of revolutionized America would proceed undisturbed in communes and on campuses in a polyracial, polysexual ambience.

The drawback to this fantasy (my own improvisation on Revel's theme) is that the intervening steps are not clear. Who arranges the transfer of power? What do we do in '72? If there is nobody possible to vote for, which seems likely, what action do we take? While the occupant of the White House is gradually being defused, he still has his enfeebled hands on the levers of destruction. There still is such a thing as capitalism.

Revel bases much of his hope on the fact, indeed impressive, that the protest movement drove Johnson from office. Yes. But it did not end the war. The sad truth seems to be that whatever else the protest movement can accomplish—organizing marches and student strikes, draft-card burnings, moratoria, sending resisters to Canada and deserters to Sweden, blocking defense-research contracts in universities, promoting beards and long hair, the sale of love beads, pot consumption—what it cannot accomplish is the very purpose that brought it into being.

It looks as if *nothing* inside the country can do that, short of revolution (and not the gradual kind Jean-François means) or a massive economic depression. Or the second leading to the first. There, again, is the rub. One of the factors he considers essential for the renovation he postulates—a steady high growth-rate—is the obstacle to even such a small step in a forward direction as withdrawal from Vietnam. On the one hand, the certainty of American technical superiority rules out, for the presidential mind, the very thought of defeat or "surrender." On the other, American prosperity makes the country feel it can tolerate the war as it can put up with taxes, airport congestion, smog—the cost argument, repeatedly made by the war's critics, has never made the slightest impression, and as for morality, the scaling down of U.S. casualties, the changing of the color of the body count have allowed Nixon to do practically as he pleases. If, as Revel says, a large section of affluent youth is disgusted by the consumer society, the great majority of the country is not. Until something more than moral dissatisfaction with the ruling values is felt, the war will go on and expand.

Besides, Revel is too intelligent not to perceive and point out the flaw in his own argument which in logic amounts to this: If turned-off youth drops out in increasing numbers, the growth rate will fall to zero, and one of his necessary preconditions for successful revolution will no longer be present. If its numbers fail to increase, then drop-out youth will remain a marginal phenomenon, which present society can afford or else move to repress. Revel does not follow up on this reasoning, but the consequence, it seems to me, is to be driven back to one of the old Marxist models and trust that an upheaval leading to renovation will come out of a capitalist crisis and not as an accompaniment of steady capitalist growth.

Perhaps it will never come, by that route or any other. Yet I do not wish to be forced by Revel's ineluctable logic into agreeing that if the revolution—whatever that is—does not take place in the United States, it will not take place anywhere. For an American, that is too discouraging a vista.

And though Revel has proved to himself with dialectical relish that there can be no issue but that one, he is, again, too intelligent, too empirical, too in fact enamored of freedom not to be aware that any demonstration, no matter how rigorous, is only a demonstration.

If this little book is taken as a pamphlet, with all that connotes of provocation, surprise attack, deftness, rapidity, polemical sparkle, it will have done its work of disturbing —*agit prop*. But if American readers are led by it to believe that a Second Coming is materializing in the California desert, they will have misunderstood. They will be more right if they suspect that the America discovered by Columbus-Revel is an imagined and imaginary country, the antipodes of "France," though having many points of coincidence, naturally, with the homeland they know. Revel is a satirist in the tradition of Montesquieu's *Lettres persanes*, Voltaire's *Lettres philosophiques sur les anglais*, Swift's *Gulliver's Travels*. Like these fabulists, he contrasts the institutions of his native country with institutions affirmed to exist among some ideal race of beings thought by the vulgar to be savages—Persians, the English, or noble horses. There is also something of Molière in him (*Les précieuses ridicules*); the French sections of the book constitute a delicious comedy of manners. That was true too of *En France* and *Lettre ouverte à la droite*. For Americans, *Without Marx or Jesus* can be the occasion for a reciprocal discovery—of Jean-François Revel as a writer.

MARY McCARTHY

AUTHOR'S NOTE TO THE AMERICAN EDITION

In DECEMBER 1969, I arrived in the United States for a visit that was to last for about a month. Before leaving Paris, I had made an absolutely inflexible resolution: under no circumstances would I write a single word about the United States as the result of my visit. At the time, it seemed to me that, to do justice to the subject, an extraordinary amount of experience, and an unusual level of competence, was required. Moreover, there were already so many experts, and so much information available on America, that anything I might write would only have added to the flood of trivia and errors that were being published every day. I had already read too many *impressions de New-York*, too many glib articles on the South, and too many dull and pretentious "historical interpretations," to be willing to throw in my two cents' worth.

Even so, this particular visit was different from those that had preceded it. This time, I had come for the sole purpose of observing, studying, the United States. My previous visits—the first one in February 1950—had all been on business, either personal or professional. I had had the opportunity, of course, to make certain observations and to draw certain conclusions, rightly or wrongly; but they had always been more or less haphazard.

American society has been of special interest to me since the mid-sixties. The reason is that that society, for better or worse, is in the process of evolution, while Europe, despite its high living standard, is culturally stagnant. Europeans are making progress in the economic domain, but they are contributing nothing in that of civilization. In Europe, history is only repeating itself; or, more accurately, it has been reduced to quibbling. Once my interest was aroused, I began reading the American press more thoroughly and systematically; and the first thing I noted was that Europe was uninformed on the subject of the United States. Even worse, America was generally regarded in Europe as a sort of political Sodom and Gomorrah of the modern world. Certainly, the American war in Vietnam was, and is, useless abomination. On the Continent, however, it served a strange purpose: it provided Europeans with an occasion to project onto the United States the hate and shame they felt for themselves because of their own imperialistic past. Similarly, McCarthyism and America's racial problems allowed us to forget that we Europeans had been (and some of us were still) Fascists, Nazis, Franco-ists, Pétainists, and Stalinists. In these circumstances, I realized that, if I were ever to see things as they really were, I would have to spend some time in an exclusively American environment.

In April 1968, I was offered, quite unexpectedly, an opportunity to visit, not the United States, but Canada. There, two things struck me: the presence of deserters and draft evaders from the United States; and the presence of American television, since reception is quite good in the southern—that is, the inhabited—part of Canada. Regarding the deserters and draft evaders, I could hardly help comparing their numbers with those of the deserters and draft evaders in France during the Algerian War. And, with respect to television, I was astonished to see the kind of news coverage provided by the American networks. (I should point out that I was living under a Gaullist regime in France—a regime which, while it was not a dictatorship, nonetheless exercised dictatorial power over television.) My amazement was increased by the fact that, by a tragic coincidence, I was in Canada at the time of the assassination of Martin Luther King, and the civil and moral crisis resulting from that crime was constantly in view on the television screen. (The last time that I had been in America, in 1957, I had had no frame of reference, because European television, except in Great Britain, had not yet attained the level of a mass-communications medium.) I determined then and there to try to arrange my affairs so that I would be able to make an extended visit to America—a visit that would last until my curiosity about that country could be satisfied.

My return to France from Canada coincided with the beginning of the student uprising of May 1968. Like all French revolutions except the first one, the May revolution was a failure. Whatever it contained that was new and positive was imported from the United States, via the Free University of West Berlin and the universities of

Italy.* What had made it fail, however, was the French contribution: the conservatism of both the Left and the
Right in France.** This *dénouement,* the result of the
blindness of the militants on both sides, completed the
process of my disillusionment with French politics. And
I was brought to the same conclusion regarding similar
events in Germany and Italy, which I visited in January
and February 1969, in order to speak with the militant
students in those countries.

The conviction that the possibility of a new political
and cultural revolution in Europe was effectively blocked,
served to strengthen my curiosity concerning an American
revolution. And this was particularly true when I realized

* More recently—February 17, 18, and 19, 1971—the students at Paris'
state-supported high schools (the *lycées*) rediscovered the usefulness of
the sit-in as a means of protesting the conviction, on police testimony, of
a fellow student, and the conviction was reversed on appeal. The demonstrators avoided all obvious violence, and merely took over various streets—
notably, the Boulevard Saint-Michel in the Latin Quarter—by sitting down
on the pavement. This was the first time that this tactic (which originated
at Greensboro, North Carolina, in 1960) was used in France on so large
a scale, systematically, for a clear-cut purpose. The students' goal on this
occasion was the same as that of the Greensboro blacks: they wished to
apply pressure on the authorities, and they wished to do so without the
use of violence; for violence would have made police intervention inevitable. In this instance, as in others, America served as a testing ground for
revolutionary action, and as a laboratory for the development of revolutionary prototypes which are subsequently adopted by the rest of the
world. (As it happened, the students' sit-in was perfectly adapted to the
end in view, and the student's conviction was reversed at the request of
the prosecution—i.e., of the government—which was placed in the position
either of disavowing its police or of turning them loose on a bunch of
kids.)
** Even today, the government of M. Georges Pompidou has learned
nothing from the events of May. It still employs the same clumsy tactics
of repression as did the government of General de Gaulle; and it will
eventually reap the same fruit, in another form, as the latter did in May
1968. And then, once again, the Left will be incapable of taking advantage
of the government's situation to rejuvenate political life in France. This
peculiar hardening of the political arteries of France is described in detail
in my earlier work, *En France,* Paris, 1965 (published in the United
States as *The French,* New York, 1966).

that what was happening in the United States was actually modifying the *concept* of revolution, so that an American revolution, if it took place, would by no means follow the pattern set by revolutions of the past.

I made two visits to the United States in order to determine whether or not my conclusions and observations were correct; one during the winter of 1969–70, and the other in August 1970.* I traveled from New York to California, from the Establishment to the Underground. And the book that emerged from this trip is as much a book on the concept of revolution as it is a book on the United States. The two themes are treated in relation to one another. Indeed, I do not believe that it is possible today to understand one without the other. This conclusion, this identification between two hitherto independent realities, is what led me finally to break the promise I made to myself, and to write a book about America. For in order to write a book on revolution, I had necessarily to write about America.

America in 1971 is a mobile entity. It crosses all lines, not only financial, social, and familial lines, but also cultural and moral lines. And, containing as it does a diversity of cultures, and contradictory moral systems, it generates collective and individual crises with constantly increasing frequency. It is precisely these crises —which are numerous, permanent, and always new—that comprise a modern revolution; that is, a revolution as it is realized in societies that are too complex, and insufficiently hierarchical and centralized, to be changed overnight, by a single *coup* and in a single direction. Crisis has become America's second nature. But, in order to

---

* This second visit was made at the invitation of the Center for the Study of Democratic Institutions (Santa Barbara, California), an institution my debt to which I readily acknowledge. The theme of the Congress in which I was invited to participate, however, was not America or Revolution, but the philosophical trend known as Structuralism.

realize this fact, one must live it; and that is why the rest of the world perceives only dimly the true dynamism of present-day America.

I say "the rest of the world." So, obviously, I do not agree with Mary McCarthy's observation, at the conclusion of her afterword, to the effect that only the French could be surprised to read in my book that the events at Berkeley, in 1964, constituted a new kind of revolutionary action. My experience has been otherwise. In early March 1971 I attended at Austin, Texas, a conference set up by the Texas Union of the local university, a student group which had organized an *International Youth Movement*. In the course of that conference, I met student-delegates from Latin America, black Africa, and India. Everyone, I noted, was astonished to discover that American students were not sheep in the C.I.A. flock. Moreover, the avidity with which the visiting students sought out the "freak" or "head" bookstores, and bought stacks of publications from the underground press and the New Left, seemed to indicate that, in their own countries, there was either a dearth of new ideas, or else no freedom to express those ideas. When Mary McCarthy states that, in the United States and other liberal countries, "the Rights of Man remain in large part on paper," I can only reply that, for most of the students of the Third World, these rights do not exist even on paper.*

The off-year elections in America, in 1970, are a good example of how misinformed the rest of the world is about the United States. In France, Italy, and Germany, these elections were immediately presented by the press and other media as a triumph for Mr. Agnew. It was not until a full day had passed that the journalists and commentators rec-

* In passing, I might mention that, at this conference, I was able finally to see *La Bataille d'Alger*, Gillo Pontecorvo's 1965 film, which is not allowed to be shown in France; and also the uncut version of *Catch-22*—a movie which is shown in a censored version everywhere *except* in the United States.

ognized their mistake—and then, only very timidly and quietly.

With respect to Mary McCarthy's objection in principle (and in terminology) to my definition of revolution, I may answer that the whole purpose of my book is to re-examine the very concept of revolution. Mary's thesis re-flects the point of view of the American Left in the fifties, which was a projection of that of the classic European Left. This traditional concept, however, has been badly mauled by the events of the sixties, by new phenomena which surprised and upset the theories and organizations of this classic Left. The whole idea of opposition between reform and revolution, particularly, must be largely revised. What matters, in reality, is the ability *effectively to bring about change*—the fact that society itself changes, and not neces-sarily that political power changes hands immediately.* Political revolutions without social change are unfortu-nately more common than political revolutions with social change; and such revolutions quickly cease being revolu-tions.

Concerning the "suddenness" that is supposed to be an inherent characteristic of revolutions, I believe it to be secondary and circumstantial. The French Revolution, for example, did not really begin on July 14, 1789. It began at the death of Louis XIV, in 1715. At that time, men began to invent the society of the future.

In order to clarify this point in my book, I would like to quote several paragraphs from an article of mine which appeared in *The New York Times* of February 22, 1971:

* George Balandier—the French sociologist who originated the term "the Third World" and who has now been in the United States for sev-eral months—writes: "I am fascinated by the way in which American society is being questioned, not by rhetoric, but by social experimentation that is changing it from within." (A personal letter, dated February 27, 1971.)

The "Second American Revolution" causes some objection as soon as it is presented as a reality. In other words, this idea of revolution is accepted in its details but rejected as a whole; accepted in particular contexts— as in the issues of women, youth, race, peace, sex, the family—but rejected in any aggregate. So the question remains: do all these revolutions make a Revolution? We have been so sustained by a history of two centuries of short and spectacular uprisings that we only associate revolutions with civil war, an insurrection, a coup d'état, or a war of independence. We have licensed a sort of revolution of means while overlooking the fact that these means are only accessories. For example, we speak of the Revolution of 1848 in France, when, in fact, this revolution failed. We now say that there was no revolution in England in the nineteenth century, but if we consider England in 1800 and in 1900, we do not see the same society. Every year there are scores of coups d'état that are not revolutions. On the other hand there have been, for some ten years, revolutionary currents which have effected profound change in the structure of society . . . As for the methods by which this plan for civilization can be brought about— slowly or brutally, temporarily or permanently, by revolution or reform, with violence or passive acceptance— these methods will be determined by the particular historical context. Nor is it certain that the Second American Revolution, which, in my view, has actually begun, will continue. Historically, there are many more examples of revolutions that have fallen apart than there are of successful ones.

When Mary McCarthy therefore objects that the opposition has not been able to bring the Vietnam war to an immediate halt, I must reply that it was impossible for it to do so. Never, in any country, has internal pressure been able to have an immediate effect on foreign policy; and the reason is that, in the value system taught in the Nation-State, the notion of "patriotism" is paramount. Even so, never before, in any country, has there been so much internal pressure directed against foreign policy, and never before has that pressure accomplished so much, as in the United States in the sixties. This phenomenon must inevitably work a profound change in American society with respect to its foreign policy of the future.

It is true, as Mary says, that "capitalism still exists" in America. After all, revolution necessarily implies the existence of something against which one revolts. It seems to me that Mary begins by depriving Americans of the title of revolutionaries, and ends by depriving them of that of reactionaries. If there is to be a Left, there must obviously be a Right. But, if I understand Mary correctly, poor America is doomed to be neither Left nor Right.

I do not agree. On the contrary—in my opinion—in the United States the Left and the Right are in an oppositional relationship that is much more creative than anywhere else in the world.* To my mind, present-day America is a laboratory of revolution—in the sense that eighteenth-century England was to Voltaire. For the England described in Voltaire's *English Letters* (or *Philosophical Letters*) was not a Utopia. Until the end of the nineteenth century, she was the prototype for the whole of Europe. Before anyone else, she devised and adopted a representative government, separated the legislative, judicial, and executive branches, established freedom of the press, universal suffrage, and labor unions. Even today, the B.B.C. may well serve as the

* For instance, the elements of the far Right—men such as Joe McCarthy, Barry Goldwater, and Spiro Agnew—are periodically eliminated, and are replaced by elements at least partially acceptable to the Left. Nor is it accurate to say that President Johnson adopted the policies proposed by Goldwater; this may be true insofar as foreign policy was concerned, but it was certainly not true of his domestic policies.

model for the French Radio and Television Organization (O.R.T.F.); and, indeed, it is often put forward as such.

Before a revolution resulting in real equality can take place, a liberal political revolution must be effective in the *mores* of a nation.* This is confirmed by the failure of the present-day socialist regimes to keep their promises. This thesis, incidentally, as one might expect, is hardly acceptable to the Marxists; contrary to what Mary seems to think, I have been treated no more kindly by the communist press than by the Gaullist press.

Insofar as the European leftists are concerned (at least those of them who have not completely vanished), and French and Italian leftists in particular, it is their fate to resemble too closely the Stalinist Communist Party to which they are opposed and which is opposed to them. Their attacks against my book have been nothing more than a recital of the Marxist stereotypes of some twenty years ago. The French "Maoists" today suffer from precisely the same mental hardening of the arteries that afflicted the Stalinists of 1950. Or else, like Japanese students, the young French leftists are fragmented into twenty or thirty groups, according to their diverse Trotskyite tendencies, all of which work to destroy one another and therefore divide into even more numerous splinter groups. The thing they have in common seems to be an ability to multiply *ad infinitum*. This seems to explain the fact that, as Mary McCarthy herself told me, many of the American students who came to France because of the revolt of May 1968 re-

---

* For this reason, the "complete destruction of the system," that one hears so much about, could only result in the establishment of a dictatorship. We are back to the reform-revolution dichotomy, according to which anything less than "total destruction" may be classified as reform. This is a wholly abstract notion, akin to the need for a religious resurrection. To say, "I refuse to do anything within this terrible system," is the same as saying, "I refuse to do anything for this sick man because he is not in good health."

turned to their own country with a deep sense of disappoint-
ment at the sterility and lack of imagination of the French
leftists. I may be forgiven for repeating, once more, that
effective revolution consists in changing reality, and not in
working within the framework, and with the blessing, of
orthodoxy.

It is true that one can deny the existence of such changes
if they do not conform to one's idea of orthodoxy. In that
case, one must deny all progress, on the grounds that, since
capitalism has not been abolished, all progress is but "alienation." Nine times out of ten, what is called "alienation"
is nothing more than the satisfaction of a demand or a need.
If the worker has no money, he is being exploited. If he
has money, he is alienated. If he lives in a slum, he is the
victim of capitalism. And if his employer gives him a decent
place to live, free of charge, he has "sold out to the system."
According to this exercise in Marcusian logic, the history
of the labor movement is nothing more than the story of a
slow descent into hell. Every victory in the class struggle
is another link in the chains of slavery. Every amelioration
in the standard of living of the working class is a veritable
catastrophe, since such improvements help to make the
worker's life bearable.

People who reason thus are less concerned with knowing
what is happening than in knowing whether what happens
is in conformity with a Plan. But this mentality is not peculiar to our own time. In one of Molière's plays, a patient
is recovering his health by following an unorthodox method
of treatment. His outraged doctor tells him: "Sir, it would
be better to die according to the rules than to live in contradiction to the Faculty of Medicine."

Moreover, in every country it is necessary for the classical
Left to think it has the most reactionary government and
lives in the most reactionary country of the world. Radicals

everywhere and even liberals, especially the intellectuals, are outraged if you question that their country's Establishment is fascistic, and that the future of their own struggle is hopeless. Maybe this political despondency is necessary, as a psychological shield, in order not to compromise with the enemy. But by and by the habit of despondency can become so strong that you no longer are able to perceive the real changes when they take place, prefer not to hear about them, and feel deeply sad when you cannot avoid acknowledging an improvement. That attitude I would describe as characteristic of the "conservative Left," the Left that wants to maintain itself, its views and its future, unchanged in an unchanged world, less interested in destroying injustice than in proving triumphantly that every day brings further and greater injustice. The new phenomena we have been witnessing during the past ten years and the new concepts which are necessary to understand those phenomena are therefore almost as difficult for the classical Left to swallow as they are for the conservative Establishment—and perhaps more. That kind of "Continental" Left exists also in America (and Mary McCarthy is a good example of it) but with one important difference: in the United States if the classical Left does not believe the new revolution is serious, at least it does not try, as in Europe, to stop it in order to be right.

Paris, March 22, 1971   JEAN-FRANÇOIS REVEL